IT'S YOUR MONEY

Also by Gail Vaz-Oxlade

Money-Smart Kids
Never Too Late
Debt-Free Forever

It's Your Money

Becoming a Woman of Independent Means

GAIL VAZ-OXLADE

Collins

It's Your Money
Copyright © 1999, 2003, 2008, 2011 by Gail Vaz-Oxlade.
All rights reserved.

Published by Collins, an imprint of HarperCollins Publishers Ltd.

Originally published, in an earlier version, by Stoddart Publishing under the title *A Woman of Independent Means*: 1999 and 2003
Subsequently self-published, in an earlier version, by the author under the title *A Woman of Independent Means*: 2008
First published by Collins, an imprint of HarperCollins Publishers Ltd, in this revised and updated original trade paperback edition: 2011

Til Debt Do Us Part and *Princess* are copyrighted and used with permission from
Frantic Films Corporation.

HarperCollins books may be purchased for educational, business,
or sales promotional use through our Special Markets Department.

HarperCollins Publishers Ltd
2 Bloor Street East, 20th Floor
Toronto, Ontario
M4W 1A8

www.harpercollins.ca

Library and Archives Canada Cataloguing in Publication

Vaz-Oxlade, Gail E., 1959–
It's your money : becoming a woman of independent means / Gail
Vaz-Oxlade.

ISBN 978-1-55468-867-8

1. Women—Finance, Personal. I. Title.
HG179.V388 2011   332.0240082   C2011-905699-2

Printed in the United States
CWV 9 8 7 6 5 4 3 2

To my children, Alexandra and Malcolm. You helped me to
become who I am today. Your love is my air.

To all the women who demanded that I republish this book.
Thanks for the push.

And to Kate, who saw the potential.

CONTENTS

PART FOUR

INTRODUCTION

When I set out to write this book, one of my objectives was to help women put money in perspective. It seems money has become far more important than it should be. Our drive to amass wealth, the fear we feel when we think that we may not have enough, and the sleepless nights we endure as we wonder if the cheque will clear or bounce to the stratosphere are all unhealthy.

In 1997, *USA Today* published a graph that showed what people worry about when it comes to their money. Seventy percent of women feared not having enough money when they were old. According to the Statistics Canada publication *Growing Old in Canada,* an alarming 40% of women over the age of 75 who were living on their own had incomes below the poverty line. And since a woman 75 or older has a greater chance of being disabled than her male counterpart, this can paint a grey picture for our futures. But we can paint this picture with fresher, more vibrant colours. We have the ability to do what we must to take charge of our present and our future. But to do it, we have to understand how money works. And we have to be willing to take charge of our own financial lives.

Many women still believe that dealing with finances is a man's job. Time and again I speak with women who have given financial control completely to their husbands, fathers, or sons. I continue to be astounded. You might think that this is a characteristic of older women—women who haven't been educated in the finer points of feminism. You'd be dead wrong. Who's in a better position to have a handle on personal finances than an accountant or a financial planner? How about an accountant who is a financial planner? I have a story that clearly demonstrates how "knowing" and "doing" are two distinctly different things.

Marla had been married for several years when she and her husband separated. At that point, Marla was forced to take a long, hard look at her money situation. She was surprised to discover that despite the fact that both she and her husband had been saving and investing aggressively, their investment portfolio had not done much in the past few years. Marla had left all the investing up to her husband. He chose investments that performed badly and, in the end, Marla paid for it. After putting away a significant portion of her income each year, she had far less to show for it than she should have had.

What would motivate a well-educated, professional money manager to leave the decision-making to someone else? If money is so important in terms of keeping a roof over our heads and food in our children's tummies, then why are so many of us still willing to let our partners do the "dirty work"? The answer may be the same thing that motivated you to take this track. First, if money creates a conflict, and you want to avoid conflict, you choose the route of least resistance and let him do it all. If you have different investment strategies—and you've been convinced that doing it your way will take too long—you let him have his way. If you trust him implicitly, you let him make the decisions and live with the consequences, good or bad. No one is always right, after all. If you don't have the time, don't have the energy, or don't have the desire to do it for yourself, it's easy to give the responsibility to someone else.

We still have a long way to go in coming to terms with money and the role it plays in our lives. Money issues seem to pull us from one extreme to another: from complete denial to obsessive concern. Somewhere there is a middle ground—one that will be infinitely easier to walk—where we can put money into its correct context and deal with it in a logical, rational, and decent manner.

Most financial discussions fail to help people understand how they feel about money. While they may demonstrate how to budget, stress the importance of saving, and describe the various investments available, they seem incapable of motivating people to put into practice what many already know. What little has been written on the psychology of money often doesn't integrate the practical information. And despite the proliferation of books on all aspects of personal finance, the ability to convert that knowledge into practical, day-to-day good money management is elusive.

LIFE CYCLE FINANCIAL PLANNING

Part of how I want you to look at money differently is by thinking about your money in terms of where you are in your life. Different stages mean different needs. As your needs change, you must change what you're doing with your money.

Life cycle issues have been used for years to help manufacturers and retailers decide how to target their customers. If you're a single woman without children, you likely read different magazines, eat different foods, and wear different clothes than the woman who is mired in rug rats. When I was single, I ate out more often, I wore high-heeled shoes, and I hardly ever thought about spot removers for my carpet, my couch, or my clothes.

Just as where we are in our life cycle influences the goods we buy, so too must it be considered when we're thinking about which financial products we should use. As I've moved through my life cycle, I've gone from shopping for guaranteed investment certificates to shopping for mutual funds to buying the index. I've had to think about divorce, stepchildren, and satisfying financial commitments to ex-spouses. And I've been forced to face my own mortality and make a will.

Perhaps the one change in my life that most affected me was the birth of my children. I had no idea that having children would be this all-consuming, over-the-top, fantabulous experience. I've found in talking with women that I'm not the only one completely blown away by the experience. In fact, one of the questions I'm most often asked is, "How can I stay home with my baby and still help make ends meet?" This is just one example of how a change in life cycle can throw a spanner in the works of the best-laid plans.

Life cycle issues have become increasingly more complicated as our norms have changed. The traditional life sequence—school, job, marriage, child rearing, empty nesting, widowhood—has become jumbled. Many women complete their degrees well after the traditional school age. Many delay having children until their careers are well-established. And divorce has changed the family structure so that many women now must raise children on their own, or help raise stepchildren, without ever having considered what parenthood would hold for them. Just thinking about the various forms a family can take is enough to boggle the mind. And just as there are new structures within which we must live, so too are there new financial issues with which we must come to terms.

Since there is no such thing as a normal life cycle anymore, does that mean we have to throw out the concept of life cycle financial planning? I don't believe it does. After all, whether you are having your first child at 20 or 40, the issue of educational savings becomes important. And whether you are widowed at 55 or divorced at 30, you better have your own credit history established if you want to be able to function within the financial world.

Think about financial planning as a trip through the supermarket. First, there are the essentials you must have to keep body and soul together. What you put in your basket will be a direct reflection of your needs and the needs of those around you. If you are single, your essentials may be few and your fridge quite empty. If you're married with children, you'll need a larger larder.

Once you've done the core stuff, then you have to look at changes in the normal weekly routine that will affect what you're buying. If you're planning to have the folks over for a turkey dinner, you'll be adding cranberry jelly and stuffing to your basket. If you're throwing a birthday party, ooh, now we're getting to the good stuff: ice cream and cake.

Then there's the shopping you do, just in case . . . just in case friends drop in and you need pâté and crackers for a light nosh, or just in case you get a cold and need a steaming bowl of chicken soup.

The financial life cycle is very similar. First, there's the core stuff—the basics of your financial larder. Just about everyone needs a chequing account and a banking card. Everyone needs to establish a credit history. And everyone should begin investing as soon as they have an extra $25. (Yes, that's all it takes to get started, and the longer you wait the harder it is to convince yourself you can live without spending that 25 bucks.)

As you move through your life cycle—as your life changes—you'll need to add or subtract from your financial basket. Early on, you'll be adding. As soon as you have some assets, you'll need a will. When you have a partner, you might choose a joint account. And as you increase your income, you'll need to buy more and different types of investments to meet your long-term goals. Once you've established a good asset base and most of your dependants have gone their own ways, you may want to get rid of some of your life insurance.

As you move closer to retirement, you will consolidate your retirement savings for convenience and ease of conversion. You may even shift some of your assets into your children's hands, or into a trust, to reduce your estate and the taxes payable on death.

Finally, there are the financial precautions you take, just in case . . . just in case you lose your job, just in case you become disabled, or just in case you suddenly find yourself the primary breadwinner in your family.

In this book, I'm going to tell you what you need to think about. And I'll provide you with some tools, so that you can use your money to your advantage now and as you change throughout your life.

WHY A BOOK ABOUT WOMEN AND MONEY?

So you get the life cycle thing, but you're saying to yourself, Gail, why a finance book specifically for women? Money doesn't know x from y chromosomes. That's true, but apparently society, our work environment, our legal system—just about every social construct you can imagine—has yet to catch up. If you don't believe me, ask yourself:

- Why do women still make less than men for work of equal value? Yes, the gap is closing, but why are we still not equal?
- Why are elderly women and women with children the poorest members of our society?

- Why is it that when a couple divorces, a woman's income goes down and a man's goes up?
- Why did a vice-president at a mutual fund company with perfect vision once tell me that "women are not our market"?

This book isn't just about money. If it were, then the advice would be gender-neutral. This book is about women taking control of a part of their lives that, until now, they may have wished away or ignored. This book is about every woman having the power to make her life whatever she wants it to be.

Most financial planning books assume a person will continue to earn an income without snags for the majority of her life. They seem to abandon women who must deal with significant changes like motherhood, divorce, widowhood, disability, and caring for the elderly. Yet it is at these very moments that we need guidance, support, and information. When our life plans change, we must make adjustments to our financial plans, so we remain proactive in managing our money.

That's why we need a book for women specifically. And that's why I wrote this book. I hope that you will be able to take from it the information you need as you move through your life, adjusting your plan for significant changes and tweaking it for small ones.

The other reason I wrote this book is that I sometimes despair at women's unwillingness to be masters of their own fate. More often than not, the reason given for not taking control of the money is, "I just can't." Yes, you can. You are the author of your own life. If you choose not to take control, that's your choice. If you choose to write your own script and direct your own future, read on.

By the way, when I use the term "marriage," I mean it in the broadest sense: I mean your desire to have a continuing relationship with another person, regardless of your specific family structure. When I use the terms "spouse" and "partner," again, it's in the broadest sense. This is the person with whom you have, and want to continue to have, a relationship. Recognizing that families have changed—having lived in just about all kinds, I'm a first-hand witness—my definition of a family is EVERYONE you love, who loves you back (even if they also hate you periodically), and with whom you have to relate for the common good.

This book has been designed to deal with both the psychological and the practical. It will not solve your financial problems. I know that is the implicit promise of most books on money, but that promise is unrealistic. Just as money—or more money—is not the solution to most people's need for love, security, power, freedom, status, or comfort, this book cannot miraculously take you from where you are now to where you want to be. Only you can do that.

What this book will do, if you are a willing participant in the process, is help you uncover your personal feelings and attitudes towards money. It will provide you with information and proven techniques for positive money management. It will be a guide to what you must think about to stay on an even keel and keep money in its proper place in your life. It will ask you many questions that you must answer for yourself if you want to discover how to achieve financial health. By answering these questions, you will make some discoveries. You will find that money management is easy. You will learn new ways of dealing with money. You will achieve the results you want.

Sound good? Let's go!

PART ONE

UNDERSTAND
HOW YOU FEEL
ABOUT YOUR
MONEY

Everyone's seeking financial freedom. But ask 50 people what constitutes financial freedom, and you'll likely get 50 different answers. Often it's associated with having enough money to never worry again. But that raises the question, "How much is enough?" The fact is, *financial freedom has absolutely nothing to do with how much money you have.* Read that last sentence again. Financial freedom comes when you have control—when money anxieties and fears no longer creep into your thoughts as you lie in bed at night. We can all have financial freedom, regardless of how much we make, if we put money in perspective.

Money is a tool. That's all. It's a way of getting the things we need and the things we want. So why do some of us place such significance on its acquisition? Why do we compare ourselves with others and feel better or worse about ourselves based on how our family, friends, and acquaintances are doing? Why do some of us always seem to be running to catch up?

When I set out to write this book, someone asked me a question that significantly changed my approach: "Why do some women do absolutely nothing to take care of their futures despite the fact that they know better?" It's a good question, and I was stymied for several weeks as I rolled the idea around in my head. Why do some people save while others spend every cent they make—and then some? Why is it easier for some people to defer gratification, while others must immediately have it . . . whatever "it" is?

It isn't education or upbringing that makes the difference. Many people who know how to take control of their money, or know that they should, still don't. It is our values, intentions, and circumstances that together contrive to help or hinder us from achieving the outcomes we want.

Part of the problem is that what we think and say are often different from what we do. We think we'd like to own a home of our own, but we never save a cent for the down payment. We say we want to be secure, but we do little to take care of the "what-ifs." We know it's silly to pay loads of interest on a credit card balance, but we continue to carry that balance.

It also has to do with image. Some people seem to think that their worth is tied to the car they drive, the home they live in, or the clothes they wear. They use money to create the image they want others to see, and then they spend all their energy maintaining the image. Perhaps they want to be seen as generous, so they spend lavishly on children, lovers, family, and friends. Maybe it's the desire to be seen as successful that drives them to spend more than they make to keep up appearances. Even those with a negative image expend heaps of energy to maintain that image, sometimes without even realizing it. Rather than accepting control of their lives and their money, they continue to play the role of victim, battered by their circumstances. And some people feel guilty or ashamed about money. While they desperately wish they had more, they are resentful of their inability to get it and keep it.

Financial freedom doesn't begin with making more money. It doesn't start in a financial planner's office. And it doesn't have anything to do with investing to earn a return of 32%. *Financial freedom begins in your head.* It starts with how you think about yourself and your money. And it starts with understanding how you developed the feelings you have about money. That's what we'll talk about next.

1

IDENTIFY YOUR MONEY PERSONALITY

Your attitudes about money play a big part in how you deal with it. For all the savers I have met, there have been as many spenders. For each person who has worried about money, there is someone who avoids dealing with it completely. There are as many risk-takers as there are those who are terrified of losing money. For all the people who believe that money is the key to happiness, there are an equal number who think it leads to misery and corruption.

When I speak to people around the country, the "morality" of money inevitably comes up. People get all up in arms about what's right and wrong, about taking the moral high road, and about all sorts of perceptions and misconceptions.

When I tell parents they should be charging adult working children rent, they practically hiss and spit at me. They can't do that. It's wrong. Really? More wrong than teaching your child to live on a disposable income she will never again have?

More wrong than setting her up to fail when she finally sets out on her own?

When I tell parents to give an allowance tied to nothing, I can see the distrust on their faces as they reply, "I don't want my kids to learn that you can get money for doing nothing." No, it would be far better for them to learn that you have the money so you have the power—and if they don't do what you tell 'em, they won't get any, right? Sure, that's a much better lesson to teach than simply how to manage money.

When I tell parents to start talking about how much they make, how much they spend, and how they handle their money, they look at me as if I'm insane. They can't do that. Their kids will blab that stuff and other people will know their business. So the secrets of money management (or the lack thereof) persist, and we pass on to our children absolutely none of our experience, be it positive or negative.

Why are we convinced that any of these issues are "moral" issues or that money has "morality"? Does a car have morality, or is it the person behind the wheel who decides not to drive drunk? Can any inanimate object have morality, or is it the onus we put on that object that gives it such human characteristics?

Regardless of the impressions you grew up with, money does not have morality. Money is simply a tool. It is paper and coin, nothing more. To give it human characteristics is to place far more importance on this tool than it deserves.

It bears repeating: *money is a tool we use to pay for things we need and want.*

HOW DO YOU FEEL ABOUT MONEY?

The key to developing a healthy attitude towards money is to understand why you have the attitudes you do, and then find ways to build on your strengths and minimize your weaknesses. This usually involves taking an inventory and thinking some deep thoughts.

Ready to get started? Let's go . . .

Identify the following statements as true or false based on your first reaction to them:

True   False   I have a good relationship
                         with money.

True   False   If I had more money, I wouldn't
                         have to think about it as much.

True   False   When I feel low, I buy myself
                         something nice. Even if I have to
                         charge it, I feel much better.

True   False   Whoever has the most money has
                         the most power.

True   False   It's irresponsible not to have a
                         nest egg put aside in case of an
                         emergency.

True	False	I'd rather go shopping than save money.
True	False	My retirement is taken care of. I don't have to worry about it.
True	False	I'd bet $20 on a one-in-100,000 chance to win $1,000,000.

Done? Good. Now consider those statements again and then answer the questions in italics:

I have a good relationship with money.	*Can you have a relationship with an inanimate object?*
If I had more money, I wouldn't have to think about it as much.	*How much money is enough to eliminate your concerns?*
When I feel low I buy myself something nice. Even if I have to charge it, I feel much better.	*How do you feel when the bill comes?*
Whoever has the most money has the most power.	*In what areas of your life do you feel powerful?*

It's irresponsible not to have a nest egg put aside in case of an emergency.	*Saving is more important than . . . what? What are your priorities for spending?*
I'd rather go shopping than save money.	*Do you have a financial safety net? If not, how will you deal with an emergency?*
My retirement is taken care of. I don't have to worry about it.	*If your external programs (marriage, job, government support) changed, would you still be all right in retirement? What are you doing to take care of yourself?*
I'd bet $20 on a one-in-100,000 chance to win $1,000,000.	*What if the odds were 1 in 1,000,000? What if the odds were 1 in 10? Is it a matter of your chances of winning, or is it the potential downside to taking the bet that will influence your decision?*

Taking control of how you feel about money means asking yourself lots of questions. You need to work through where your attitudes about money came from and what influence your history has on your present. You have to look at your attitudes from all sides to make sure that you have a balanced and healthy perspective on your money. And you need to get real about it. It doesn't matter how much of it you have or don't have—if you don't get a grip on money's place in your life, you'll always feel like you're dangling from the end of a frayed string.

YOUR MONEY PERSONALITY IS WHAT INFLUENCES YOU

The next step in coming to terms with the role money plays in your life is to find out why you feel as you do about it. Some of what we have learned we absorbed by osmosis from those who influenced us as children. Some of our money personality is embedded in our genes. If we remain ignorant of our money styles, if we allow money to be a carrier for our emotions, we remain incapable of seeing it for what it is: a tool.

Read through the following categories and see how many you believe are true. Remember, styles may not be exclusive. And you may have shifted styles as you have moved through different stages in your life. What's your predominant style now? If you answer True to more than half of the questions in a category, then that money style is part of your personality.

Are You a Miser?

True   False   I enjoy holding on to my money.

True   False   I find it difficult to spend on myself.

True	False	I find it difficult to give to others.
True	False	I seldom give to charity.
True	False	I'm always on the lookout for the least expensive gift.
True	False	I'm afraid I won't have enough money.
True	False	I often put off buying something because I'm sure I can get it cheaper elsewhere.
True	False	My family often gets angry with me because I refuse to spend money.
True	False	I could never trust anyone else with my money.
True	False	I often say, "I can't afford it."

What drives the Miser? It's not really meanness, although it may appear that way to others. It's fear: fear of not having enough, fear of being poor, fear of catastrophe. To protect herself, a Miser makes sure she never runs out of money. The best way to have money is to not spend any. She has no confidence in her ability to make more money. She thinks the gravy train is about to end and she'll be left destitute.

If you're a Miser, money is a symbol of security. Stop playing out all those worst-case scenarios in your head that make you afraid. If you fear poverty so much that you create it in your daily life, you are living your worst nightmare. Instead of focusing so much on the future, live each day as if you have enough money. Remember, it's not money that makes you rich. Money is just coin and paper. It is what you choose to do with that money that will determine the richness of your life.

Help Yourself

Make a list of five things you would like to buy for yourself: flowers, books, music, a new blouse, candles. Ask a friend or family member to look at your list and add two things she or he has heard you say you want. For each of the next seven weeks, buy one item on your list.

Make a list of the people closest to you. Beside each name, write one item you know that person wants to buy, or that she or he would enjoy receiving. If you can't think of anything, write "a card and some flowers." Over the next few weeks, buy one of the items on the list each week and present it to your loved one.

Each time a catastrophic image comes into your mind, write it down on a piece of paper. Put it in a box created specifically for this purpose. At the end of each week, take those bits of paper and tear them up, burn them, or bury them in the garden. Destroy one piece of paper at a time, reminding yourself with each one that you will not give up control of your happiness to the Worry Demon.

Are You a Spender?

True	False	I love to shop.
True	False	I have a hard time saving.
True	False	I find it difficult to defer gratification.
True	False	I do not have any long-term financial goals towards which I am working.
True	False	I never seem to have enough to pay my bills.
True	False	My credit cards are maxed out.
True	False	I often pay for dinner and buy gifts for friends.
True	False	I cannot go into a store without buying something.
True	False	I can't resist a bargain.
True	False	I get angry if confronted about my spending.

Some Spenders are trying to create an image. For example, a spender may have an enormous desire to be noticed. She buys designer clothes, jewellery, expensive cars, and luxury items in her desperate attempt to impress and be validated. She may crave approval and preferential treatment, which leaves her vulnerable to any pitch that treats her as special. Or she may enjoy shocking people by being outrageous with her purchases.

Success is important to the "image Spender," and she is easily impressed by power and fame. She wants to be a part of the "in group," and she is prepared to spend her way in. She may want to be perceived as generous, so she competitively races for the bill and buys the most expensive presents. She'll go deeply into debt to maintain the façade.

Other Spenders are bargain seekers. They're in it for the hunt. When this type of spender finds a bargain, she feels victorious. While she can often afford to pay full price, the satisfaction comes from adding up how much she has saved. Paradoxically, she often buys things she doesn't need simply because the deal was too good to pass up.

Some Spenders are compulsive shoppers. Whether they have $5 or $500 in their wallet, they have to spend it as quickly as possible. After doing so, the bargain-seeking Spender may feel guilty or ashamed that she didn't handle her money better. She hits the shopper's low and feels anxious. Despite experiencing buyer's remorse, she shops again just as wildly. She shops to hide from her misery. She shops for the excitement. She shops to escape loneliness. She shops to enrich her life. She absolutely itches to shop. And because the buying is more important than the having, if you open up her closets, you'll find clothes with the tags still on them or household items still in their original boxes. She buys not because she needs the item, but to satisfy her urge to shop.

If you're a Spender, what you have to figure out is what's pushing your shopping buttons. You are more than the labels you're wearing, but if that's all you can think about, you've got a bad case of imposter syndrome and need to focus on your insides as much as you do on your outsides. If you're bargain hunting, then you should be saving your "savings" to make that bargain really count. And if you're shopping compulsively, you may need to seek help from a professional. At the very least, you need to stay out of the stores. Go in only when you must buy something that qualifies as a "need," and buy only the things on your list.

Help Yourself

Admit that your shopping is having a negative effect on your life. Don't beat yourself up; recognize that you have to take the problem seriously.

Keep a journal of your spending. Write down every item you buy, the amount you spent, and how you felt when you bought it. Don't "forget" your ledger and don't leave anything out. THIS IS A TOUGH JOB. Don't judge your spending; just note your purchases. At the end of each week, total up how much you've spent.

Go down your list of purchases and recall how you felt when you bought the item and how you feel about it now. What was the emotional payback for shopping? What was the emotional cost? Is buyer's remorse—that's the "What the hell did I do that for?" feeling you get after you've bought an item—making you uncomfortable? Is the debt you're carrying as a result of your shopping making you sick to your stomach?

Shift your source of enrichment from "getting" to "doing." Look for free or inexpensive activities you really enjoy and spend more time doing them: Potluck dinners with friends, long walks in the early evening with your partner, going to the park with your son. Make a list of 20 alternate activities you can do when you feel the urge to shop.

The next time you want to buy something, write it on your list and write the current date beside it. Agree to buy the item in two weeks if you still need or want it and have the money to pay for it.

Stay out of the mall. Turn off the shopping channel. Throw out the catalogues before you browse through them. Leave your credit cards at home. Carry only a small amount of cash with you.

Run your shopping like a purchasing department. Before a purchasing department will buy an item, it must be convinced that the purchase is of benefit to the company, that it is of good value, and that there is money available to pay for it. Before you buy anything, make sure the item meets these criteria.

Go through your closets, storage bins, and secret compartments and make a list of everything you own. Do you really need another little black skirt? Another purse? Another scarf, bracelet, or watch?

Switch from buying consumable items to investments. Buy some stock. Buy a Guaranteed Investment Certificate (GIC).

Buy a mutual fund. Shop around, compare rates, and bargain hunt. Get yourself an advisor to ensure you aren't just buying but are buying wisely. You'll be spending money to increase, instead of deplete, your net worth.

Are You an Avoider?

True	False	I don't reconcile my bank account and my Spending Journal.
True	False	I don't look at my bills when they arrive. I just stick them in a drawer for another time.
True	False	I don't know how much money I have in my wallet.
True	False	I don't know how much money I have in my bank account.
True	False	I don't pay my bills on time.
True	False	I don't have a will.
True	False	I don't read the financial press.
True	False	I don't feel very competent about handling my money.

| True | False | I don't know how much I owe on my credit cards. |
| True | False | I don't do my taxes until the very last minute, if at all. |

Women avoid handling their personal finances for all sorts of reasons. They feel overwhelmed by the prospect of managing their money. They may feel ashamed because of their lack of skill. But in almost all cases, the longer they avoid dealing with their money issues, the lower their self-respect. Married women who are Avoiders often leave all the money management to their spouse. They think he'll take care of everything. They are often unaware of the family's assets, and they're shocked to find out how well off or destitute they are when forced to face the realities of their financial life after a divorce or a death.

If you are an Avoider, one way of overcoming your sense of dread is to work with a financial planner. This doesn't mean giving over responsibility for your money; that can be a dangerous game. It's one thing to seek advice and another to give up all control.

Help Yourself

Once a week, do something to deal with your money, such as paying your bills. Set up a filing system for your financial statements and sort them out. Review your accounts online, and compare your transactions with those in your Spending Journal.

Stop procrastinating. Pay your bills as they come in. Sit down and do your taxes before the deadline.

If your spouse handles all the money issues, start communicating about what you both have (property, investments, savings accounts) and choose some responsibilities to assume (paying the utility bills, keeping track of the daily spending). Don't be surprised if your partner is hesitant about giving up control. You have empowered your pal by abdicating financial responsibility, and your partner may feel "challenged" by your desire to become involved. Be firm and persistent, but be gentle.

If you do not have your own financial identity, establish one. Open your own bank account. Establish credit in your name. Get yourself an advisor: a broker, financial planner, or accountant that is yours alone (as opposed to yours and your mate's).

Are You an Acquirer?

True	False	I love having lots of money at my disposal.
True	False	I'm very focused on increasing my net worth.
True	False	I often compare the amount of assets I have with others.
True	False	I feel in greater control when I have more money.

True	False	I often take a big risk to try to get ahead financially.
True	False	I think people who have less than I do are lazy or stupid.
True	False	I spend a great deal of my time working.
True	False	I believe money is power.
True	False	I believe time is money.
True	False	I ignore family and friends because I'm too busy working.

While a healthy attitude towards money means using it to experience life and enrich the lives of those around us, an Acquirer relates to money as if the acquisition is the ultimate goal. She believes it's not what you do with your money, it's how much you have. And since greed makes people vulnerable to get-rich-quick schemes, the desire to acquire doesn't always translate into wealth.

The desire for money does, however, translate into effort. Acquirers are notorious workaholics. Their motto is, "time is money." They ignore their spouses and children, and spend evenings and weekends on the phone or away from home doing deals or managing projects. And their perception of money becomes distorted: no amount is ever enough.

Acquirers will go to any lengths to increase their net worth. Some cheat. Some steal. Some involve themselves in shady schemes. The end always justifies the means. The goal is to get as much as possible, in any way possible. All that matters is money.

If you are an Acquirer, you need to accept that there is more to life than work, and there is more to your value than the money you earn and store up. And you need to do it before you end up sad and lonely like Ebenezer Scrooge.

Help Yourself

Look beyond your financial assets to the other assets in your life: spouse, children, friends, personal time, self-development, gratifying work, creative release, spirituality, relaxation, and community. Are you expending as much effort to increase your net worth in those areas? List the things that you consider to be assets in your life. How can you increase these assets?

Look realistically at the role money plays in your life. What are you doing to acquire money that is working against your personal well-being? Long commutes, long workdays, lost vacations, and few interactions with your loved ones are all costs associated with your drive to acquire. Today, decide to spend one hour with a child, mate, or friend, just shooting the breeze. Don't talk about money. Talk about life, dreams, loves, adventures, a good book, or a fine meal. Don't mention money.

What skills do you have that could benefit your community? Choose a community project and volunteer. Keep your commitments to the group.

Are You a Depriver?

True	False	I am always broke.
True	False	I feel unworthy if given a promotion or other form of recognition.
True	False	I have a low-paying job, but I often put in lots of unpaid overtime.
True	False	I often dream about ways to make more money.
True	False	I lose valuable items.
True	False	Each time I feel as if I'm getting ahead, something happens to put me back at square one.
True	False	If I enjoy what I do—like fixing cars or painting—I can't charge for it.
True	False	I don't feel capable of handling my money.
True	False	I'm not willing to buy into the system and give up my freedom.
True	False	I believe money just isn't important.

The Depriver constantly sabotages her own efforts to get ahead financially. She may feel undeserving. She may not want people to expect too much of her. She admits she doesn't know a lot about money, and she's unwilling to learn. To the Depriver, money is incomprehensible. Or perhaps it is dirty. She may even feel that having money will make her spiritually bankrupt or be politically incorrect. She thinks it is virtuous to be broke. Or perhaps she simply wants to stay within her (poor) peer group. After all, rich people are greedy, arrogant, power-mad, and selfish. To want money is to have all those other characteristics.

Some Deprivers seem to want to achieve financial security. This kind of Depriver is a dreamer, thinking of ways to get money and working out elaborate schemes to make her fortune. Unfortunately, she never quite gets the plane off the ground. She procrastinates or sabotages herself. Or perhaps she fails in order to reject her parents' obsession with money.

Some Deprivers are so afraid of failure they won't even try to succeed. Remaining poor feels safer. By not drawing attention to herself, the Depriver can avoid the pain of loss. She's sure that if she achieves success, others will envy her and want to hurt her.

If you're a Depriver, it's time to focus on just how valuable you are (say it out loud so your brain can hear it) and how you can use your money to make your life—and the lives of the people you love—better.

Help Yourself

Just for today, don't deprive yourself. Pat yourself on the back for a job well done. Treat yourself to a nice lunch.

Set some goals. What do you like to do? How can you use your skills to improve your financial picture?

Stop thinking and speaking about money as if it were evil or dirty. Money is paper and coin. What you decide it represents is a reflection of YOUR morals—not of the morals of money itself. After all, how can an inanimate object have morality?

Find a money mentor, someone knowledgeable and experienced who doesn't share your dread of money. Look for someone who will share your successes joyfully.

Are You a Debtor?

True	False	I get a thrill out of using my credit cards.
True	False	The more credit I have, the happier I am.
True	False	I believe you don't have to have money to spend money.
True	False	I pay only the minimum amounts on my credit card balances, and my cards are usually maxed out.
True	False	My creditors are always overreacting.

True	False	My account is usually in overdraft.
True	False	I don't pay bills on time even when I have the money.
True	False	I feel uneasy just walking into a bank.
True	False	When I divvy up the dinner bills with friends, I put the bill on my charge card and pocket the cash.
True	False	I've taken a consolidation loan and then run my cards right back up again.

Debtors dig themselves into a hole by borrowing excessively and misusing credit. Regardless of whether she can afford to or not, a Debtor borrows and borrows because she can't face the limitations of her budget. She finds it easy to delay paying bills, and she often blames others when the natural consequences occur: "How dare my bank bounce this payment!"

A Debtor believes she's living within her means because she has money left in her bank account at month-end, even though she's carrying a whopping balance on her credit cards. She thinks that a Buy Now Pay Later sale is just too good a deal to pass up—despite the fact that when repayment time comes, she's paying upwards of 35% interest on her purchase, back to the date she took it home.

If you're a Debtor, it's time to make a repayment plan. Skip the consolidation loan; it's not for you, because it frees up credit you'll immediately use up again. Don't fall into the trap of strapping your cash flow too tightly in your effort to get the debt paid off, or you'll be forced to use credit just to make ends meet.

Help Yourself

Admit to yourself, and to someone else, that you have a problem. Recognize that you cannot get out of debt by taking on more debt. More credit just exacerbates the problem. Become a critic of debt. Do you really want to pay interest on that dress, stereo, or dinner for the next three years? If you pay only the minimum amount each month, you could end up paying twice as much as the original cost for the item.

List all your debt—including student loans and car loans, Buy Now Pay Later plans, and overdraft protection—and note the interest rate you're paying on each. Using an online calculator, figure out how much interest you will be paying on each debt, and how much you'll be paying in total by the time you finish paying it all off.

Decide that you will not take on any new debt today. By going one day at a time, you'll move closer to freeing yourself from the Debtor's cycle.

Cut up your credit cards and close the accounts. Put the cut-up cards on the fridge or by the front door as a reminder. Paying cash ensures you won't take on new debt and makes you more conscious of what you are spending.

Don't spend more than you earn. Make a budget that shows

how you plan to spend your money. Include a few of the frills that make life more bearable: an occasional meal out, fresh flowers, a movie, a new book. If you don't enjoy the quality of your life, you won't stick to your spending plan.

Accept responsibility for your debt. This doesn't mean being harsh with yourself. What is done is done; get on with life. Call your creditors and work out a repayment schedule you can live with. Pay off the debt with the highest interest rate first, then apply more money to the next-most-expensive debt as it becomes available.

Okay, so now you're thinking about why you feel as you do about money and how you're going to try to rebalance those feelings. I know it's hard to admit our emotions—to face our demons—but it's the first step in really taking control. And it's what you have to do if you truly want to become a woman of independent means.

2

WORK WITH YOUR MONEY PERSONALITY

Want to minimize the uncertainties and pressures, the stress and anxiety, the fear and feeling like you're always juggling? Then you need to understand how, when, and why you developed your attitudes towards money. Who we are with money is a direct result of what we learned as children.

Answer the following questions to see what pictures emerge for you. It might be helpful to jot down some notes as you think about them.

- What are your impressions of how your mother dealt with money? How did she feel about her work inside and/or outside the home? What did she explicitly teach you about money? How did you feel about those money lessons?
- What are your impressions of how your father dealt with money? How did he feel about his work inside

and/or outside the home? What did he explicitly teach you about money? How did you feel about those money lessons?

- How did your parents relate to each other when it came to financial matters? How did they feel about each other's money habits? Did they fight about money?
- If you have siblings, did your parents treat you all similarly when it came to money? If not, what were the differences? How do your siblings deal with money now?
- Did anyone else—a teacher, religious leader, grandparent, or other relative—influence the way you think about money today? What messages did you get from them?
- Was your family rich or poor? Why do you feel you were either rich or poor?
- Did your friends have things you didn't? Did you get more or less allowance than your friends? Did you live in a nicer home? Did they have nicer clothes? What was cool to have back then, and did you have it?
- Did you feel ashamed of having more or less than your friends?
- Did you have to be good to receive special treats? Did you receive money as gifts? Were you rewarded financially for good grades or behaviour?
- Did you ever steal from the corner store, your mother's purse, your father's pocket, or your sister's piggy bank?
- How old were you when you got your first paid job? How did you feel when you deposited your first paycheque? When you spent your first earned money?

Most children feel powerless. Someone else decides when they'll eat, sleep, and play. Someone else decides what they'll wear and what they'll eat. Many people carry that sense of powerlessness into adulthood. Despite taking on jobs, raising families, meeting their commitments, and being responsible, they feel powerless in dealing with their money. For many people, there have been no money lessons and no opportunities to try and fail in a safe place. Every penny always counted. They remain scared to death of making a mistake. All the while, their childhood tapes are running, imbuing money with meanings they aren't even aware of. It's all in our heads.

So what does money mean?

MONEY MEANS POWER

"As long as you're under my roof, you'll do things my way." That's one of the most familiar power plays in a family. It means, "Since I have the money, I make the rules." But there are other things parents do that send the power message just as clearly. Allowances or support cheques that are promised but rarely delivered without a reminder; constant financial bailouts with verbal reminders of how lucky you are to have been saved; regular lectures on the respect, duty, or gratitude you owe for having been cared for. Is it any wonder Power Parents produce Spenders searching for validation and Avoiders who would rather the whole money thing just went away?

Of course, as with any myth, there's always a grain of truth that allows the myth to survive. The truth is that money does represent power for many people. After all, who of us has a boss who makes less than we do? Most supervisory power comes from the fact that the boss is the guy who can take your money away. Within families, the spouse who makes more money often has the right to decide how that money is handled.

Having more money often leads to more choices: a better education, the opportunity to start and support a new business, or the freedom to pursue creative outlets. Money can buy you better health care, a better table in a restaurant, and more acquaintances. Unless you're a Miser, in which case more money just means you're focusing on the catastrophic images of powerless poverty.

MONEY MEANS LOVE

Turn on your television and you'll be faced with myriad commercials trying to convince you that if you spend your money to buy something new and shiny you'll be better loved. If you're a Spender and you go shopping when you're lonely or unhappy, or if you're a Debtor and you buy things for others that you can ill afford, you've likely got the money-equals-love virus. Women who shower their mates with expensive presents are often using money as a symbol of love. People who lend money to friends may be trying to secure their friendships.

Listen to the words of anger often said when a love or friendship is betrayed—"you owe me," "I gave you everything," "you stole the best years of my life"—and you'll hear money words being used.

If you don't believe that people equate love with money, just look at what happens when love disappears from a relation-ship—especially when divorce isn't a joint decision—and all that's left to work out is the financial dissolution. The communication can get downright ugly. And look at the way we relate to our children: "If you're good, I'll buy you a toy." "If you get good grades, I'll give you money." Will those children then form the habit of rewarding themselves with material things when they feel down or stressed-out? Or will they choose to reject money because they see it as a means of control?

MONEY MEANS SECURITY

For many people, money represents security. Acquirers, for example, place a huge emphasis on preparing for the future, and their money-management style can be cautious and well-planned. However, when faced with a threat, money-means-security people may panic or become depressed or angry. While they seldom spend capriciously, money-means-security chicks seldom enjoy what they have. They are constantly squirreling away a little more, denying today's wants in favour of tomorrow's needs. For them, money offers no pleasure other than in its accumulation. Each dollar spent represents a dollar they will not have in the future.

Since women have traditionally been dependent on men—fathers, husbands, male bosses—for their security, they have learned to prize that security. They may anticipate desertion and disaster and try to prepare for it by hoarding their money. Or they may believe these "heroes" will provide them with security for the rest of their lives. All they have to do is be good little daughters, wives, and employees, and they can keep the income streams to which they have become accustomed. Witness the number of women who remain in abusive relationships—marital, familial, or work-related—because they believe they have no other way to support themselves.

MONEY MEANS HAPPINESS

When we equate money with happiness, we put too much stock in what money can do for us. When what you want (more money) is different from what you need (a sense of safety, a pat on the back, or a sense of personal accomplishment), you will never feel satisfied. Spenders who blow money to impress, Acquirers who pile up money to feel safe, and Debtors who substitute consumption for common sense are all searching for the elusive happiness. It's like trying to eat carrot sticks when all you really want is a big bowl of chocolate ice cream. No matter how much of the good orange stuff you eat, you can't fill the hole, and the hunger drives you to seek another substitute. In the end, you'll have your spoon in the ice cream container, exactly where you wanted it all along.

When you recognize that money is a tool—it is a means of acquiring the things you need and want—you'll have the right perspective. But if you substitute money for all the other things in your life you so desperately desire, if you see money as the source of happiness, you'll be casting this simple "medium of exchange" in the wrong role.

$ Gail's Tips: If managing money were only a skill, we could learn it and be done with it. But there's more to it than that. After all, some of the most skilful money managers in business are pathetic when it comes to managing their personal finances. Years ago, I worked with a woman who was a credit card maniac. Her wallet burst with more than forty cards. As an office manager, she was wonderful at keeping the books, keeping the spending in check, and keeping the bank at bay. At home, her personal finances were a disaster. I remember sitting at her kitchen table and watching her play what she called "credit card roulette." This was a game where she decided who would get their minimum monthly payment. Every card she had was run up to the limit. Her decisions about who to pay were based on which card she would need to use during the upcoming month. Whenever she was sent a new card—credit card companies are notorious for lending to people they shouldn't—she would sign the back and spend herself out of her blues.

She had new living room furniture, a new stereo, and heaps of other stuff. She also had headaches, backaches, and a short temper. This was a dreadful place to be. She ached physically from the stress. She couldn't see any way to clear her debts. So she resigned herself to living month to month, until the whole thing just caved in.

The cards were taken away, one by one. Sometimes, at the bank, the teller would simply keep a card with little explanation. Sometimes a card was repossessed in stores, where she was mortified to find the credit card company commanding the store clerk to cut up the card right in front of her. I was with her on one such occasion and she was a wreck.

Eventually, she took control of the situation and started using the skills she had all along. She dumped the remaining cards, got a consolidation loan, and paid off her debts. It took years, but she persevered.

This story may seem extreme or all too familiar. It illustrates the point that women often feel incompetent and inadequate in managing their own money, frequently in sharp contrast to their competence in other areas.

. . . .

MAKE PEACE
. . . .

The ancient Chinese book of wisdom has a wonderful saying: "He who knows he has enough is rich." Whether we make $20,000, $60,000, or $200,000 a year, few of us are happy with our financial lot. Witness all the people who never have time for a holiday, miss school pageants and dance recitals, or never take the day off in the middle of the week to walk on the beach or grab an ice cream cone with their best friend.

After my daughter was born, I started to pull back from corporate consulting. My accountant asked me how concerned I was about lower billings. He was trying to help me plan my income for the future. As I tried to explain to him that my life was changing, I suddenly realized that I was no longer prepared to do the things I had done in the past just for the money.

During my second pregnancy, these feelings grew even stronger. During one particularly tedious project where the client was being extremely petulant, my mind drifted to my children at home, and I realized my priorities had shifted. I was no longer prepared to put up with the corporate bull.

When I entered the world of TV production, I was very aware of how important my time was to me and to my children. I insisted on a shooting schedule that would not take me away from my family more than two days a week. And when I take on additional projects, I won't take just any job. I have to trust the client, and the client has to trust me. If not, I've found no amount of money compensates for the aggravation. I realize this is a luxury I've worked for and a choice I make to have less.

John Stuart Mill once said, "Men do not desire to be rich, only to be richer than other men." To free yourself of the self-doubt, the constant measuring against others, and the keeping up with the Joneses, accept your current situation and set a realistic goal for when enough is enough.

To cut through the Gordian knot of not knowing when enough is enough, you must quantify for yourself how much is enough, which brings us to the question of what a "need" is.

Everyone has things they want. I want a new dress. I want a new set of dishes. I want to be left alone. These are things that it would be great to have. But they aren't the things that hold body and soul together, and not getting them won't be the end of the world as we know it. The distinction between needs—things that do keep body and soul together—and wants are not always easy to see, particularly in world full of "new and improved." But there is a simple question you can ask yourself to help determine if something is a "need" or a "want": What will be the implication of not getting this whatever? If it is a life-threatening consequence, then it's a need.

There are people who prioritize wants over needs. Witness the number of people who drive very nice cars but have no disability insurance. Or people who enrol their children in myriad extracurricular activities but haven't saved a penny for their post-secondary education. Or life partners who put each other at risk by carrying gobs of debt and not thinking about the strain that debt is putting on their relationship.

Don't get me wrong. Sometimes it's perfectly fine to buy something just because you want it. I buy tons of books. I buy them because I want them. I have no goal in buying a book, except for the gratification it brings. I could go to the library. I could borrow books from friends. But I'd rather buy my books. I have quite the book collection, but if I see another one I like, I'll probably buy it just because I want it.

Understanding the motivation to buy goes a long way in determining the value of the purchase. Without an understanding of the motivation for buying, people will inappropriately place the same value on one purchase as on another, hindering their ability to judge the appropriateness of the buying decision.

Here are three questions to ask yourself as you shop:

1. How will this purchase make me feel more fulfilled?
2. How will this purchase move me closer to my purpose? (Your goals, your image of your life, and what you want to accomplish.)
3. How will this purchase affect those around me? (Will it affect my ability to meet my commitments or fill important needs other members of my family may have?)

Once you can distinguish between needs and wants, you can focus on what's really important. And if you have the money to satisfy a want or six along the way, you can do so knowing that you've taken care of the needs. If all you can satisfy are your needs, you can either make peace with the idea of living a simple life, or you can get your butt in gear to earn the money it'll take to have all the stuff you want. Ultimately, you're in charge of your life. Live it consciously, and you can realize the independence you want to have. Make peace with what you can afford, and regardless of how much you make, you will be happy.

FIND YOUR MONEY SET-POINT AND MAKE IT WORK FOR YOU

Dietitians know that people who use only a diet to change their weight usually return to the same weight, because we each have an internal metabolic rate that is set. The only way to truly change our weight is to reset our internal thermostat by increasing that metabolic rate. Consider the possibility that we may also each have an internal thermostat that measures our comfort level with our savings and net worth. When we seem to be moving above this point, we do whatever is necessary to return the equilibrium: go shopping, change jobs, leave the work force, or acquire some debt.

I have a girlfriend who can't get her savings account above $1,800. It's a marker she has set for herself based on absolutely nothing. No matter how much we've talked about the importance of setting up an emergency fund, each time the account rises above her marker, off she goes on a holiday, buys a new painting, or gets a new outfit.

By allowing your set-point to be prescribed by some internal gremlin, with no rhyme or reason for the specific number chosen, you are not in charge. To take control, you must either evict the gremlin by resetting your set-point or trick the bugger. Evicting the naughty tenant won't be easy. To begin, sit down and determine what your set-point is. Next, figure out if it works for you. Is your savings or net worth set-point livable? If not, what should it be?

If you can't evict the gremlin, then you'll have to trick it. I know one woman who has multiple savings accounts. Each time she gets to her set-point, she walks away from one bank account and opens another. It's not a very convenient or efficient system, but it works for her. A friend of mine reset her set-point by convincing her gremlin that it was appropriate to have a different set-point for each of her objectives. The more objectives she has, the higher her overall set-point. At last count, she was saving for retirement, a return to school, a down payment for a second home, her three children's education (separately), and a fund to care for her parents should the need arise later in life.

FACE THE FEAR

We're all very busy. We're running to work, our next appointment, or daycare to pick up the kids; we're running the kids to hockey, swimming, or dance class; we're running to the grocery store, the mall, or our parents' place to make sure they're fine. No matter what job you have—whether you are selling real estate or coffee, working as a vice-president or a secretary, focusing on your career or on your family—you manage to make time for the things that are important to you. As a wise man once said to me, "If I spent as much time taking care of my money as I do others', I'd be rich." Time, or a lack of it, doesn't prevent you from dealing with your money. Fear does.

As a young adult, I remember reading a book entitled *Feel the Fear and Do It Anyway.* Its premise was that we all have fears we carry around, and it is those fears that stop us from doing. As children, we are constantly taught to be afraid: "Be careful!" "Don't run into the street, you'll be squashed like a bug!" "Watch out!" These messages stay with us, heightening our anxiety and creating barriers to our achievement. The only way around them is to face them head on and get over them. If we do not, those fears continue to grow like tentacles, strangling our ability to achieve peace.

What are your fears? Do you worry that you won't have enough when you grow old and you'll end up a bag lady? Do you worry about whether your children will be okay should something happen to you? Are you afraid of how you would manage to keep a roof over your head and food in your children's stomachs if something happened to your spouse? Do you worry that you just can't keep up, or that there's no other job you could ever do?

We all have fears that creep into our minds and steal away our serenity. But if you don't know what you're afraid of, you can't come to terms with it. Voice your fears if you want to get over them. Begin by asking yourself, "What am I afraid of?" If nothing comes to mind immediately, give it time. Make sure you write down your fears. Looking back at the questions about where your money attitudes came from, can you see a connection between your fears and the messages you received as a child? If you don't immediately see a connection, that's not unusual, since many of our earliest memories are deeply buried. Just keep thinking about it, and I'm sure the picture will become clear for you. Then banish the fear associated with that picture. You're a strong, independent woman now, not a needy child. You're in charge. Act like it.

GET BACK IN TOUCH WITH MONEY

Go into your wallet and take out a 20-dollar bill. Now tear it up. Could you do it? Most people couldn't. Yet every day we toss money in the garbage: the book we bought that we've never read, the leftovers we scraped into the garbage can, the dress that was on sale that we've never worn, or the interest we're paying to credit card companies and banks.

We can fool ourselves in dozens of ways when it comes to "stuff," but it's a lot harder when it comes to the actual money. That's why it's important to start touching the real stuff again.

If you feel a little divorced from money, it's not really surprising. Each technological advance has distanced us from our money. Each has made it more convenient for us to spend. Cheques, for example, are a representation of money: a promise to pay. But if you've ever written a cheque you knew would bounce (or written one that bounced unexpectedly), you know that a cheque and money are two separate animals. Then there's the debit card—a brilliant invention that puts a layer between our cash and us. Another technological advance is the credit card, which gives us the ability to spend money we haven't yet earned. Sometimes we don't even call it a credit card. Instead, we refer to it as plastic, distancing ourselves even further from what it actually represents: potential debt.

Automatic withdrawals, direct payments, quick passes, telephone banking, online banking—these conveniences all stand between you and the actual paper and coin that is money. But just because there are dozens of new ways to spend money— and money you have yet to earn—doesn't mean you have to be a willing participant in this game. To get back in touch with your money, for the next month or so, spend nothing except cash. At the end of the month, compare your expenditures with your previous month's. Is there a difference? How inconvenient was it for you? How did you feel about spending each time you took cash from your wallet? How much money do you have in your wallet now?

BE RESPONSIBLE

"I am responsible," you say vehemently. Right. So you have a will and a power of attorney. And you have enough insurance so your family will manage if your income is suddenly gone. You've taken precautions in case you become disabled. And you have a retirement plan so your children won't have to support you. You have six months' savings put aside, so if the unexpected occurs, your kids can sleep peacefully in their own beds. You also have a pay-yourself-first plan, because you know the importance of investing.

A big part of financial freedom is having all the *i*'s dotted and *t*'s crossed, so you can free yourself from worrying about the "what-ifs" of life. Saying you'll get to it isn't enough. Saying you love your spouse and your children is not enough. You must prove it by doing the responsible thing. The mere knowledge that you've taken care of yourself and your loved ones will move you a long way down the path of financial freedom. When you put your affairs in order, you are putting money in its right place: people first, then money. After all, if you fail to be financially responsible, how much joy, love, and laughter will the money truly bring?

DO IT!

To be financially free, you can't just think about it. You've got to act. And while people are more important than money, the money won't take care of itself. That's your job. Not your accountant's, broker's, banker's, lawyer's, husband's, son's, financial planner's, or mother's. It's your job. If you don't respect money, you'll find little money available when you need it. And if you don't take active control of your money, you will never find the financial freedom you're seeking.

WHERE TO GO FROM HERE

So, what have you learned so far? Do you have more of a sense of why you feel as you do about money? Do you have the skills, but not the emotional competence? If you don't have the skills, the rest of this book will help you. If you don't have the emotional competence, you're going to have to do some soul-searching to come to peace with how you feel about money. You may want to see a psychologist who deals with money issues. You may want to talk more about it with friends and family. The very fact that you are reading this book means you want something to change. But you're the only person who can make that change.

Next, we'll look at the things we have to do to achieve that sense of financial well-being and put a plan in place.

PART TWO

BUILD YOUR
FINANCIAL
FOUNDATION

It's been 50-odd years since women reportedly burned their bras, and I think it's high time we also embraced our independence financially. We've made progress, but not enough, since many goils are still a long way from being in control of their money. We have to stop thinking that there's some magic to becoming financially healthy. There isn't. Most of what women need to do is plain ol' common sense.

One thing that has always bugged me about most articles and books on financial planning is that financial health is so often equated with investing. Some websites even put "personal finance" under their "investing" section. Talk about putting the cart before the horse! Being financially healthy goes far beyond understanding the ins and outs of the stock market. It is more than retirement planning. And it is more than finding new ways to beat the Tax Man. To be financially healthy, you need to look at your money as a whole, not in pieces.

Taking a holistic view of your true financial picture means weighing what you own against what you owe. It means mitigating your risks with the appropriate tools, such as insurance and a will. And it means weighing what your debt is costing you against what you're earning on those investments you're so proud of.

If you have a $5,000 investment earning 5% interest, this year you'll earn $250. But that interest is taxable, so at a marginal tax rate of 30%, you'll end up with just $175 in your pocket. If you also have a $5,000 balance on your credit card on which you are paying 18% in interest, this year the loan will cost you $900. And that's in after-tax dollars. That's gobs more than what you're earning on your investment. By holding on to your investment and paying the interest on your debt, you will fall behind this year by $725 in after-tax income. Your investment isn't making you richer. Your investment combined with your debt is, in fact, making you poorer.

Now, let's put all the money back into one pot. If you took your $5,000 investment and used it to pay off your $5,000 debt, you'd be even, right? Nope. You'd be ahead. Remember, before you were $725 in the hole (the difference between the interest you earned and the interest you paid). By eliminating the debt, you eliminate the negative cash flow. This year you'll be up $725, which you can then use to start an investment plan.

Gail's Tips: I'm sometimes criticized for encouraging people to save when they are still paying down debt. I want to be clear on this: If you are not a saver, the only way to become a saver is to start saving. And the only time to do it is right now, even if you are paying down debt. This may seem in conflict with what I've just said, but it isn't. When I talk about becoming a saver, I'm not talking about setting aside huge gobs of money for investing to the detriment of your debt-repayment plan. I'm talking about setting aside $50 a month, or even just $1 a day, to move from being "not a saver" to being a "saver."

When I talk about selling investments to pay down debt, I'm speaking to the people who are deluding themselves, thinking of themselves as "smart investors" when, in fact, they also have debt. If you have $2,500 in savings bonds and you're carrying $2,500 on your credit card or on your overdraft, you have NOTHING. Stop pretending.

As with everything else in life, there is an exception: your emergency fund. If you have money in an emergency fund, do not cash out to pay off debt unless you're dead sure you can rebuild that emergency fund in no time flat.

Oh, BTW, when I talk about selling investments to pay off debt, I'm never talking about registered investments (like your retirement savings). The tax bill would defeat your efforts!

This is an example of how I'm going to have you examine each brick in your financial foundation, with the goal of being truly independent. If you think of your financial plan as a house, each part of the plan is a foundation stone that makes that house stand strong. Leaving out an element leaves the whole plan vulnerable. You must cover all your bases, from setting goals to planning how you want your estate to be handled. Only then will you be able to adapt your plan as your life changes for better or worse. That's what it'll take to truly be a woman of independent means.

3

SET GOALS

Whether we want to buy a home, provide for our children's education, or retire to a small island in the South Pacific, money is one of the means we will need to achieve our ends.

Life is full of choices. We make them every day. Monday we had the choice of going to work or staying home. Most of us went to work. Tuesday we chose to see a movie. And Friday, we'll either go dancing or catch up on that John Grisham novel.

Every decision we make is based on a choice. We choose to live in the city or in the country. We choose to contribute to a retirement plan or buy another handbag. We choose to charge that fabulous little black dress to our credit card or to pay cash. Once we recognize that it is we who are choosing, it becomes easier to see how much control we have over our money, as opposed to it being the other way around.

How we choose to use our money depends on what we envision for ourselves. However, if you feel it's the money that's giving the orders, you may not be able to see beyond your immediate circumstances to the dreams you want to achieve.

A DREAM IS A GIFT
WE GIVE OURSELVES

Had any good dreams lately? What's stopping you? Maybe you can't remember how. Ask yourself, "If I could have anything I wanted—no holds barred—what would it be?" Grab a pencil and paper and write down your ideas. Don't limit yourself to financial goals. Remember, no holds barred. Keep going. Think! Absolutely anything you want. How's your list coming? You should have 10, 27, 53 things by now.

Now it's time to prioritize your dreams. Start by creating a short list of the dreams that are most important to you. Choose six items from your list. Even within your short list you will have priorities. To decide which goals are most important, weigh them against each other. Is having a home more important than taking that trip to the other end of the country to see your ailing grandmother? Is buying a car more important than paying off your credit card debt? Is taking a trip to see your grandmother more important than paying off your credit card? What's your priority? Reorder and number your dreams one through six in order of priority.

Goals Are Dreams with a Deadline

Now it's time to set a date for achieving your dreams. This doesn't mean that the date can't change. But without a date, there is no sense of urgency and no commitment to moving forward. Go ahead. Set your dates.

Now you know where you want to go and you have an ETA. That's the hard part. The rest is easy. It just takes a plan, a commitment, and, perhaps, a guide to help you through the maze of alternatives and information. Use all the resources at your disposal: books, seminars, friends. Talk to your banker, your broker, and your financial planner—whomever you trust to act as a guide. And remember, you won't get there just by dreaming about it. You need *telesis* to get there.

TELESIS

Telesis is defined as the "deliberate, purposeful utilization of the process of nature and society to obtain particular goals." It is progress that is intelligently planned and directed. It is the attainment of desired ends by the application of intelligent human effort to the means. It is what you must *do* to get to where you want to be.

Instead of planning to save, you save. Instead of planning to invest, you invest. And instead of planning to pay off those debts, you start paying them off. It doesn't mean you will achieve all ends immediately. What it does mean is that you will no longer put off starting. You won't wait until your next raise to open up your pay-myself-first investment plan. You'll do it immediately. You won't wait until you have a "decent" contribution to begin using a retirement plan. You'll start with the first $50 you manage to squirrel away. And you won't wait to get out of debt. You'll throw those cards behind the fridge and begin the process of getting back into the black.

Now, don't get me wrong. I don't expect you to immediately rush out and fix your financial life this afternoon. Remember, we're into balance and realism this time around. However, I am presenting a relatively novel idea when it comes to financial planning. Think of it as just-in-time financial planning. Instead of being thrown for a loop when you're faced with a major change in your life, you'll simply adapt your strategy as the need arises. You'll retool on the fly. You'll be responsive to changes in your circumstances. You'll constantly re-evaluate your goals to ensure you're still in tune with what you want your outcomes to be. Most importantly, you'll move from *intending* to ***doing***.

One of the few things you can count on is that whatever plan you lay for yourself, it will need to change because your life changes. If you're so focused on the end, you may be side-swiped, or you may find yourself unable to adapt to take advantage of new challenges and opportunities. Instead, take a lesson from a sales theory of productivity: focus on the activities, and the results will take care of themselves. Build the habits and let the outcomes flow.

BUILDING MOMENTUM

Just as you won't be a saver until you actually start to save, you won't be financially healthy until you take the steps to make yourself so. Once you're moving, it'll take a 10-foot-wide brick wall to stop you. Having established your pay-yourself-first investment plan, you will keep saving and investing every month for the rest of your life. A good friend of mine, Victoria, refers to this as "painless portfolio building." She says, "You only miss the money in the first month. By the second month, the pain is gone." She's right. That's the beauty of momentum. Once you are on a roll, you'll continue to roll unless some remarkable force gets in your way. The same is true for getting to debt-free forever. While the initial pain and horror of fessing up to the mess may feel like torture, once you've figured out what you have to do, made a plan, and committed to making those payments consistently, you'll move closer and closer to being debt-free with every payment you make. *Telesis* at work!

The first step is to put in place your financial basics: the strategies and habits you'll need to keep your financial body and soul together. Where to start? First you need a plan . . . a spending plan.

4

MAKE A SPENDING PLAN

One of the biggest challenges that women face is how often they must revamp their spending plans. Whether it is to accommodate a maternity leave, to adjust for staying home with the kids for a while, or because an elder relative needs care, women see their best-laid plans fall to pieces as their need to nurture climbs into the driver's seat. But just because you know the plan is going to change, it doesn't mean you can just avoid the plan altogether. That's a cop-out. If you want to use your money—as little or as much as it may be—to your advantage, you have to have a plan for how you'll put that money to work. You have to make a spending plan.

I remember a time when I thought that if I could just make $30,000 a year, I'd be set. Since I was only making $10,000 at the time, I couldn't imagine what I'd do with all that money. The reality was that by the time I was earning $30,000, I had higher expenses. I had to pay more tax, buy a car, and dress in more expensive business attire.

It's easy to spend money once you get used to having it. And it doesn't take long to get used to it. I use the analogy of expenses being like water: they flow up and down based on the size of the container (your spending plan), and they can overflow if you let them. The more money you have, the more you'll spend. But people who let the spending just happen inevitably end up drowning in a sea of debt. They become exhausted from bailing out the creditor boat, and finally give up and sink.

A spending plan is a way of keeping track of the money you get and the money you spend.

$ **Gail's Tips:** I'm using the term "spending plan" here instead of "budget" because it is more descriptive of what we're trying to do: create a plan for how you'll spend your money to achieve the independence you're seeking. But a budget and a spending plan are exactly the same thing.

The best thing about a spending plan is that it gives you a very clear picture of your financial reality. Many people cringe when I talk about the need for a spending plan. They relate being proactive about what they're spending with having to give up things they enjoy. In reality, a spending plan gives you the freedom to enjoy yourself because you don't have to worry about how you'll pay the bill when it comes in. You'll know right from the start whether you can afford the purchase or not.

The trick with any spending plan is to not let it be the tail that wags the dog. Without a keen sense of where you're going and what you want to achieve, it's very easy to fall into the trap of spending more and more. As Mr. Micawber says in Charles Dickens' *David Copperfield,* "Annual income twenty pounds, annual expenditure nineteen six, result happiness. Annual income twenty pounds, annual expenditure twenty pounds ought and six, result misery."

Most people don't keep track of where their money is going. It's too much work. It's anal. It's a pain in the ass. Hey, if you don't take the time to track your spending, you'll never be in control of your money. Where did the last $100 you took out of the bank go? Stop for a minute and write it down. Chances are you can account for most of it, but there may be $5, $10, or $20 missing from your list.

If you lost track of even $5 of that $100, I'll bet you don't have a solid handle on where your money is going. Do you know exactly what it costs you to live each month? Most people underestimate their expenses because they forget the things that don't occur consistently. Did you think about your gym costs even though you pay them once a year? How about your house or car insurance? Did you think about the cost of your haircuts, your contact lenses, or your vacation? Do you pay someone to shovel your snow, clean your windows, or do your taxes? Did you buy one or two cords of wood last winter? Did your kids go to camp? What about your vet bills, the flowers for your garden or patio, or your co-worker's going-away present? Or how about those magazines you picked up at the supermarket checkout, the batteries for Tickle Me Elmo, or the charcoal for the barbecue? And what about the bottle of wine you took to your friends' place when you went for dinner, or the $5 here and $10 there your son or daughter hit you up for?

When you do all your money management in your head, it's very easy to forget things—sometimes important things—that will have an impact on your overall financial life. If you write cheques without recording what you've paid for, it's easy to forget how much you've spent. You're always guessing how much you have left. And you shouldn't really be surprised when your account is overdrawn. After all, if you don't know how much you have, how can you know how much you can spend?

Think of a spending plan as an architectural drawing. Without one, you may build too big a bathroom and end up not having enough space for all the bedrooms you need. Or you might put the staircase in the wrong place. Maybe you won't remember to put in enough windows. Your rooms will be dark and you'll have to spend more money on lighting. With a spending plan, as with an architectural drawing, the first thing you do is take care of the must-haves. Then you build in the want-to-haves. You'll know your rent is covered each month, so you won't be evicted and have to spend extra money moving. You'll know just how much you can afford for food, so you won't eat steak for the first three days of the month and then live on macaroni and tuna for the remainder. You'll know just how much you can afford to spend on transportation, so you can decide whether you can afford to indulge in a cab ride without having to walk to work for the next four days. Once you make a spending plan, you will be in control of exactly where your money goes.

WHAT'S THAT_____ REALLY WORTH?

Before you get to work creating your spending plan, I want you to consider the idea of "relative value." Relative value refers to the relationship between what an item costs and what you have to do to pay for it. It's not a new concept. Adam Smith talked about it in *The Wealth of Nations* in 1776, when he wrote, "The real price of everything, what everything really costs to the man who wants to acquire it, is the toil and trouble of acquiring it."

What does it cost to buy that new coat? The relative value relates to how long you have to work to come up with the cash. That's calculated using something called your "disposable hourly income"—the amount you make hourly that's above and beyond what you need to cover your butt. That can put a whole new perspective on the real cost of the coat.

The idea of a disposable hourly income is not one most people are familiar with. It is your net income less your total fixed expenses and your must-have variable expenses, like food and medical costs, divided by the number of hours you work. Let's say you net $24,500 a year. Let's also say you have two weeks of vacation, so you work 50 weeks a year, and you work a 45-hour week. That's 2,250 hours per year. Your monthly expenses (things like rent or mortgage, loan payments, food, utilities, phone, drugs, transportation, and savings) total $1,775 a month, or $21,300 a year.

If you deduct your yearly expenses ($21,300) from your net income ($24,500), you'll see that you have $3,200 of disposable income each year. That's $3,200 to spend on whatever your little heart desires. Sounds like a lot, doesn't it? You can absolutely afford that beautiful $260 coat.

Hang on. We're not done yet. Now take that $3,200 and divide it by the 2,250 hours you worked. It turns out your disposable hourly income would be $1.42:

$$\$24,500 \text{ (net income)} - \$21,300 \text{ (yearly expenses)} = \$3,200$$
$$= \$1.42 \text{ / hour}$$

$$45 \text{ (hours)} \times 50 \text{ (weeks)} = 2,250 \text{ hours / year}$$

If you want to buy a coat that costs $260 and your disposable hourly income is $1.42, you'll have to work for about 183 hours to earn enough money. Yikes!

You probably don't even want to do this exercise. It looks pretty depressing. But if you don't do it, you're putting on blinders, because you're not really thinking about how hard you have to work to pay for the item you're thinking about buying.

Not being aware of their disposable hourly income and its impact on the relative value of the stuff they buy is how many people who make what seems to be an extremely good living get themselves into holes. Let's take the case of Margaret and her husband Frank. Frank is an executive who makes $150,000 a year. That's a lot of money, right? So Margaret could never figure out why they never had any money. After taxes, Frank's income dropped to $96,000 a year. But as Margaret saw it, that was still $8,000 a month, so what was the problem? When they did their spending plan, they discovered that their monthly expenses were very high: a $2,000 a month mortgage, a huge food bill to feed themselves and four kids, clothing, school fees—it all added up to about $6,000 a month. Then, of course, there was Frank's habit of buying whatever took his fancy. And Margaret, who considered herself a smart shopper, found that she would use any excuse to buy: new drapes, new clothes for the kids, and fresh flowers for the house. It all added up. After keeping track of their spending for three months, they became far more aware of where their money was going. Then Margaret calculated Frank's disposable hourly income. She tracked his hours for three months, and since he travelled quite a bit and worked hard, she came up with a weekly average of 57 hours. It turned out that Frank's disposable hourly income was just $8.42.

You might find it useful to go through the exercise yourself. It would be good to know exactly how hard you have to work to buy whatever just caught your fancy. Only then can you decide if those new designer sunglasses are really worth it.

COMING OUT EVEN

A spending plan is made up of two parts: income and expenses. Income is the money that comes in. It's your net (after-tax) salary or commission, dividend or interest income, alimony, child support, pension, or disability income. It is all the money you receive, whether it comes in monthly, quarterly, or in some other time frame. It does not include money you think you might get. So, if your bonus is not guaranteed, don't include it in your spending plan. After all, if it doesn't flow in when you expect, and you've already planned to spend it, you'll be up the creek. Better not to include it in the plan and then use it to boost your savings or cover a long-wished-for treat if it does materialize.

Expenses cover the money going out: your monthly costs in after-tax dollars. When you pay amounts annually—insurance, camp fees, tuition—divide these amounts by 12 to come up with a monthly amount that you can work into your spending plan.

The best way to figure out your expenses is to gather all your bank statements, credit card bills, and whatever other records you have of how you spent your money for the past six months. Make a category for each bill: telephone, hydro, food, vet bills, gym fees, child care, health, gifts—everything. Total each category and divide by six; that's your monthly average. Now add all the category averages together. This is the average amount that you spend each month.

$ **Gail's Tips:** People who barely make it from one paycheque to the next are often surprised when they take the time to figure out where all their cash is going. They may not have realized just how much they spend on impulse purchases, lunches or drinks with friends, parking tickets, candy bars, or lottery tickets.

One of the best ways to gain a perspective on cash spending is to track every transaction. Now, don't go all cross-eyed on me. The idea is to figure out where you're spending all those five-, 10-, and 20-dollar bills that seem to go missing each month. It's also about learning more about yourself and your priorities. This isn't about shame, blame, or deprivation. You don't have to change anything you don't want to change. But you should at least know.

. . . .

Are you surprised by how much you're spending? Is it more or less than you thought? Now let's see if you're living within your means. Take the amount you're spending and subtract it from your monthly net income. Are you spending more than you are bringing in? If you have a negative gap, there are two things you can do about it: make more or spend less.

Look back over your categories and think about how much you want to spend for each. Notice that I used the word "want." You're in charge of this. You say how much you will or will not spend. You can keep right on digging a hole, or you can decide to take control.

The thing about a spending plan is that it isn't carved in stone. It would be nice if life were predictable, but it isn't. A smart spending plan makes allowances for things that you think "just won't happen." Spending plans should have a repairs and maintenance, or supplies and services, category that accounts for these kinds of expenses. On my spending plan, the Holy Crap category is labelled "unusual expenses."

Now that you have done all the work to come up with the numbers for your spending plan, here comes the really tough part: the discipline of using it. A spending plan has three columns for each month:

The Planned column will show the money you expect to spend on each of these areas. You may plan to spend $25 a month on prescription drugs, $150 on food, and $10 on books and magazines.

The Actual column will show the amount you laid out. While you may put aside $200 a month for children's clothes, it's unlikely you'll spend $200 every month. However, in September, as you ready the kids for school, you may find you spend considerably more than $200. If you spend $375, this is the figure that would go in the Actual column.

The Difference column is the planned minus the actual amount spent. If you intended to spend $5 a day on lunch, but you brown bagged it three days each week because your horrendous workload meant you were chained to your desk, your planned amount would be $100, your actual would be $40 (for the two days each week that you escaped from the office), and the difference would be $60 followed by a plus (+) sign to show you've still got that money. On the other hand, if you planned to spend $25 on a gift for a friend, but you actually spent $40, the difference would be $15 followed by a minus (−) sign to show you overspent in that category. At the end of the month, all the plusses and minuses in the Actual column have to come out to a positive number (indicating you have money left) or zero for your budget to have balanced. If you have a negative number, you're likely carrying a balance on credit or you're into your overdraft. Stop that! Now!

If you go off track in a particular category one month, don't panic and think you've blown the whole deal. Look at other categories and see where you can adjust to make up the difference. If you planned to spend $3,000 a year on clothes, but blew your budget by September, you could either stop buying clothes, or you could steal the money from your vacation category. It's your choice.

If you're saying to yourself, "Get real. There's no way I can keep up this record-keeping stuff," or "I'd rather be poor than be a slave to this stupid form," grow up! You drag your sorry butt out of bed each day, regardless of the weather, how crappy you're feeling, or how tired you are, to earn money. You should be willing to put a little effort into managing that money. It only takes a couple of minutes every day to update your spending plan so you can see on paper where your money is coming from and where it is going. The point is to get it out of the nebulous grey zone of "I think I spend . . ." to the black-and-white facts.

If you don't believe a spending plan can make a significant difference in your life, I challenge you to use one for just three months and prove me wrong. Then write me and tell me how little use it was. I believe that once you do the plan and use it for three months, you'll find real value in having gone through the exercise.

If you don't believe you can find the time to do this for even three months—I've heard this before too—here's a sad statistic: on average, Canadians spend 10 hours a year taking care of their money and 1,000+ hours a year watching TV. You'll have to decide where your priorities lie.

TRIMMING EXPENSES

Many categories of your spending plan will have fixed amounts, but many others can be fiddled. If you buy lunch at work every day, you could decide to skip the lunch out twice a week and save. If you get a haircut every six weeks, schedule it for every eight weeks and save some money. If you buy magazines off the rack, subscribe and save 50% or more. Or go to your local library and binge in the periodical section. Or share a subscription with your sister. Decide to trim—a little here and a little there—until what you spend matches what you want to spend.

Here are 9,999,999,999 ways to save. Just kidding!

- If you smoke, quit. If you smoke a pack of cigarettes a day at $11 a pack, you'll save over $4,000 a year. If you put that $4,000 in a retirement plan for the next 20 years and earn an average return of just 5%, you'll end up with over $137,000. Another reason to quit: if you don't smoke, you'll pay 10% to 15% less in premiums on most life insurance and disability insurance policies, your house insurance costs will go down, and you won't spend the last 15 years of your life gasping for breath.
- Take your lunch to work, at least some of the time. If you save $35 a week on lunch, in a year you'll save $1,820. Invest half of that in a retirement plan and earn 5% on it, and in 25 years you'll have over $41,000.

- Share newspapers with co-workers. If you buy a paper twice a week, instead of six times, you'll save $200 a year.
- Subscribe to magazines. If you buy a monthly magazine that costs $3.50 at the newsstand, it'll cost you $42 a year. Buy a subscription, and you might pay only $21. Even better: share subscriptions with friends.
- Use the library. Check out books, magazines, CDs, and DVDs instead of buying them.
- Use a long-distance package. Do the research and choose the package that saves you the most. If your phone habits change (when your daughter goes off to university in another city), check to make sure your plan still works for you.
- Pay your life insurance premiums a year in advance if the company offers a one-month discount.
- When it comes time to renew your mortgage, negotiate. If you can shave just half of a percent off your mortgage, you'll save $500 a year on a $100,000 mortgage.
- Accelerate your mortgage payments. Paying your mortgage on an accelerated basis means an extra payment every year that goes directly to your principal. On a $100,000 mortgage at 5%, amortized over 25 years, you'll save just over $12,000 in interest over the life of the mortgage.
- Check the blue-book value of your car to determine if you should still be insuring for comprehensive and collision.
- Are you insuring heirlooms that you could never replace even if they were lost or stolen? Weed out the things you don't need covered anymore.

- Ask your insurance agent for the various discounts available: claims-free policyholders, those who insure both home and car in the same place, and people with security systems get a break on their rates.

- Increasing the deductibles on your home and car insurance can save you big bucks. You have to be sure you'll have the money to pay the deductible yourself. Sticking it on your credit card and carrying it for months defeats the purpose. But if you don't intend to make a claim for under $500 or $1,000 because you're concerned about how it'll affect your premiums, then you might as well raise your deductible and save.

- Don't buy extended warranties on household appliances. Instead, use a credit card that automatically extends the warranty.

- Set up a co-op babysitting service with other parents in your neighbourhood. You take care of three kids once a week, and you'll have two days off.

- Grocery shop with a list and stick to it. If you run out, wait until your next planned shop. Buy in bulk, if you'll use the items, and buy generic (at least try the generic alternative). Buy in bulk with friends and split the savings.

- Buy off-season. Your son's next winter wardrobe will be considerably cheaper at the end of this winter, providing you can reasonably estimate your child's next size.

- Don't even go into convenience stores. Almost everything is more expensive.

- Buy gifts when they are on sale and put them away for birthdays, anniversaries, and other special holidays.

- If you're carrying a balance on a credit card, switch to a card that charges lower interest. On a $3,600 balance, switching from a 17% card to a 9.9% card will save you over $250 a year in interest. Cut up the cards you've transferred the balance from so you aren't tempted to use them. If you give into temptation and run those balances up again, you'll be in even worse shape.

- Review your bank statements to see how much you pay per month in service charges. Would you be better off with an all-inclusive monthly fee? Do you have the option of free transactions if you maintain a minimum monthly balance? Shop around for the right account.

- Don't bounce cheques. A friend of mine regularly bounces cheques, and each time she does it costs her $30 in service fees—never mind what she's doing to her credit rating. And it's not that she doesn't make enough money. She's just a bad money manager.

- At the grocery store, comparison shop and buy on sale. Buy seasonal items in season; what is plentiful will be cheaper.

- Check unit prices to see what things actually cost. Those little calculators on the grocery store shelves serve a purpose. I've often been surprised to find that the bulk items are sometimes more expensive than the regular items on sale. When stuff goes on sale, buy enough to last until the next sale.

- Buy second-hand. It's amazing what you can get in a garage sale or thrift shop: good quality at a great price. My stepdaughter once outfitted herself for an entire season at the Goodwill store for $35. And I've scored big at garage sales and second-hand shops: beautiful baby clothes for a fraction of their original cost, a mountain of Lego for $30, and lovely books that my children and I still enjoy together.

- Leave your credit cards at home except when you plan to spend. Taking them with you leaves you open to impulse purchases.

- Use public transportation. Figure out what it's costing for the convenience of having a car and decide if it's worth it. Here's a case in point: Julie owns a car. Her loan payment is $236 a month and her insurance payment is $416 a month, for a total of $652, which is exactly one-third of her take-home pay. She doesn't live in the car. She doesn't use the car for work. She has the car in case she needs it. Wow!

- Go to the movies on Cheap Tuesdays or when matinees are less costly. Or wait for the movie to get to a second-run house and see it there for half the price.

- Write letters, texts, or e-mails instead of making long-distance telephone calls. Or try Skype.

GIVE YOURSELF AN ANNUAL CHECKUP

Since women face all kinds of challenges in terms of keeping their income steady and dealing with competing priorities, don't just assume the spending plan you make this year will continue to serve you well. Give it an annual checkup. Even if your income hasn't changed, look to see if lifestyle inflation is pushing you to spend more. Are you eating out more often? Seeing more movies? Spending more on clothes? Would it make sense to return to your previous standard, or is your new standard of spending right for the time? And if you must spend more on one category because things are more expensive, where will you cut back to make the spending plan come out even?

The whole idea is to make sure your needs, wants, and desires are in the right proportions and that you're fully aware of where your money is going. If you feel it is your right to go to that concert, lease a new car, or eat out a couple of nights a week because you work hard, just remember that—because you work hard—you also have the right to be debt-free, well-balanced in terms of saving and spending, and on your way to achieving your financial and life goals. It's your money. Make it work for you.

5

ESTABLISH AN EMERGENCY FUND

An emergency fund is used to fill the gap if your income is suddenly reduced or disappears altogether. Think sickness. Think unemployment. Think time off work to deal with a family emergency. Without an emergency fund, you'll likely turn to credit to deal with the shortfall in your income, creating problems down the road. With an emergency fund, you have money, so you have options. (If you're in debt now, this may sound unrealistic to you—but read on to see why you need an emergency fund and how to get one.)

The size of your emergency fund will depend on your financial commitments. My general rule of thumb is to have the equivalent of six months of essential expenses set aside for emergencies.

Gail's Tips: There are some financial gurus who encourage people to set their emergency fund at $1,000. How people come up with these arbitrary numbers is beyond me. Maybe $1,000 is enough of an emergency fund if you live under a rock. Yes, you'll need less of a buffer if your home is paid for, you have no debt, you walk everywhere you go, and you're happy eating ketchup soup three nights a week. If you want a realistic emergency fund—one that actually gets you though the rough—figure out your monthly essential expenses and multiply by six. That's how much you need.

FIGURE OUT HOW MUCH IS ENOUGH

Grab your spending plan and highlight all the expenses you would have to pay even if your income evaporated. That may include rent or mortgage payments, food, medical costs, insurance, child care, car payments, gas, and whatever else is a need. Keep debt repayment on your list of needs or your credit history will go into the crapper, your credit score will plummet, and your interest costs will skyrocket.

Be brutal about cutting back, particularly if you have high monthly fixed costs. Go over your spending plan again and cut out anything you've kept that's not a real need. If you've just lost your job, cable is not a need no matter who in your family thinks it is. Neither is entertainment or anything else you wouldn't die without. You still need to eat, but it'll be far less expensive food for a while. Cut your essential expenses back to the bare bones (don't underestimate though), and add them all up. If your essential expenses add up to $1,650 a month, then you will have to set aside $1,650 x 6 = $9,900 to have a good emergency fund.

Impossible! No, it's not. Time to get busy saving.

Some people find it easy to save, others don't. Think about how much you have saved right now. Do you think it is enough? Does saving seem like an impossible dream because of your current financial circumstances?

The reason most people don't bother with an emergency fund is that they figure nothing terrible is ever going to happen to them. Optimism is fine to a point, but not when it puts you and your family in jeopardy. Here's a scary story:

Madelaine found herself unable to work. She was experiencing a variety of weird physical symptoms and was severely depressed. She had a disability plan at work and, under the instructions of her psychiatrist, decided the pressure and stress of the job were too much and stayed home. She claimed her disability benefits only to find that she was declined because the insurance company felt she could work—if not at her present job, then somewhere else. She had no diagnosis to support her physical complaints. Madelaine went through hell. With no emergency fund, she found herself even more stressed out. It took almost 10 months for the doctors to locate the problem. And it was a serious one too. In the meantime, Madelaine had no recourse. Luckily, her husband was able to fill the gap. But the strain on the relationship was obvious. And the strain on Madelaine only made her physical condition worse. (Imagine if Madelaine had been a single woman supporting herself and kids. What a mess!)

If you don't think bad things can happen to you, wake up. If you're 25, there's a one-in-four chance you'll become disabled before you turn 65. If you're 35 to 45, your chances fall to one in five. You'll probably experience a cash-flow crunch: either you'll receive less money than you normally are used to living on, or you'll have to live through the wait period before your benefits kick in.

Disability isn't the only potential problem we face. There's the job that disappears, the kid that gets sick so you have to stay home from work, or the emergency trip you must take to deal with a family crisis. If you don't have an emergency fund, you may get through the crunch, but you'll probably use credit to do so. And you'll end up paying for not having been prepared.

Once you have your emergency fund set up, keep it in conservative, highly liquid investments. While it can be a really sad thing to watch thousands of dollars languishing in a savings account, return isn't the priority with an emergency fund. Access is. Stick that money into the market, and it may not be there just when you need it most. Stick it in a high-interest savings account, and while you may be irked by the pittance you're earning in interest, the emergency fund will be at the ready when you hit the wall. Remember, the point is to have a safety net when the unexpected happens.

$ Gail's Tips: A line of credit is NOT an emergency fund . . . it is debt waiting to happen. The people telling you to get a line of credit as an emergency fund are the same people who offered you ways to satisfy all your whims while spending money you hadn't yet earned. They're the same people who continually raised your limits until many of you had enough debt to bury an elephant. If you hit a wall and end up racking up tens of thousands of dollars in debt on a line of credit, how is that diverting disaster?

WAYS TO BUILD YOUR EMERGENCY FUND

Set up an automatic deduction from your regular account to a high-interest savings account or Tax Free Savings Account. If you don't have much to save, it doesn't matter; the important thing is just to start . . . to convert your intent into action. As long as you haven't started, you're not creating the means for dealing with what life may throw at you. Commit $25 per pay to your emergency fund. Once you've begun, you've put momentum on your side. Then it becomes only a matter of how to boost the amount you're setting aside to grow your stash of cash.

Gail's Tips: Saving is the act of accumulating money by setting aside a portion of your income. Let's say you have an automatic savings plan that deducts $50 from your chequing account and puts it into an investment for you. Let's also say you go out and charge $50 on your credit card that you can't afford to pay off this month. YOU HAVEN'T SAVED A THING! Since you didn't take the money out of your cash flow (you used your credit card to put it back into your cash flow once it was deducted from your chequing account), you're not saving. Don't fool yourself. If you have "savings" and "debt," you've got less than you think.

Investing is what you do to earn a return on the money you've saved. So if you have $500 in a savings account earning 0.25%, it's invested—not particularly well, but it's invested. As long as it's earning a return, it's invested.

Do you buy coffee every day on the way to work? Calculate how much you're spending, cut it in half, and send the difference to your emergency fund. Do you smoke? Quit! Always pick up the latest magazine at the checkout counter? Subscribe to premium cable? Go out for a drink with your friends after work? Buy your lunch at work? How quickly could you build your emergency fund by focusing on being safe as opposed to being satiated?

Here are some more ideas that may help:

- Purchase savings bonds through a payroll deduction plan.

- Invest part or all of any windfall, such as tax refunds or gifts you receive.
- Practise being thrifty. When you save money on an item, immediately put the savings in a jar at home. Once you have $25, put it in your emergency savings account. If you save on an item and immediately spend that money on something else, you haven't saved a thing.
- When a regular expense, such as a loan payment or tax instalment, is eliminated from your spending plan, contribute half to your emergency fund.
- When you get a raise, save half your increased earnings.
- Contribute to a retirement savings plan, and use your tax refund to boost your emergency fund.
- Cut $25 a week out of your grocery budget—do some meal planning, shop with a list—and watch your emergency fund grow instead of your thighs.
- Swap eating out for a potluck with friends and save the difference.
- Combine your errands, carpool with a co-worker, or hop on your bike and bank what you save for an emergency.

If you're not turned on by watching your money grow in a savings account, you'll have to find some other motivation for accumulating your emergency fund. How about this: *you're supposed to do it.* And if you don't do it, you'll have no one but yourself to blame when you find yourself up to your armpits in alligators. Plan like a pessimist so you can live like an optimist. Yes, you could lose your job, get sick, smash up your car, or have a tree fall on your house. Those are good reasons to have some money set aside. A more important reason is that taking care of yourself and those you care for is your responsibility. Saving is part of a healthy financial plan. You must have some cash at the ready if you want to be able to deal with whatever life throws at you.

6

MANAGE YOUR MONEY

Most people have a chequing account and a savings account. When they buy a house, they get a mortgage. When they apply for a credit card, it's often their bank's version of a MasterCard or Visa. And when they begin investing, they often start with the term deposits, mutual funds, and other investments offered at their local branch. It doesn't matter whether you deal with a bank, trust company, credit union, or caisse populaire—for the purposes of this section, when I say bank, I'm talking about the place where you deposit your pay and through which you pay your bills.

PICK THE SMARTEST CHEQUING ACCOUNT FOR YOUR NEEDS

Choosing the right chequing account can be a real test in today's complicated world. And banks haven't made it any easier for us. With the introduction of new-and-improved-this and better-than-ever-that, we now have an overwhelming variety of account features from which to choose.

Once upon a time, the main consideration in choosing an account was convenience. We chose a branch that was close to home or work. But you don't have to buy from the bank on the corner any more. Online banking, telephone banking, and ATMs make it easier to choose a bank based on the products offered and the service you get for the money you pay.

Despite all the options available, people still end up with accounts that cost them $40, $75, or even hundreds of dollars in fees. Sometimes it's because they're awful at planning, so they use the ATM like a wallet, and they use their bank account like a squash court, bouncing cheques off all the walls. Sometimes it's because having chosen a bank account, they just stick with it. Never mind all that's available today—resistance to change keeps them using the old, very expensive bank account.

Want to be smart about choosing a bank account? Figure out how much money you plan to park in the account. The higher your average balance, the more likely you are to get services bundled in for free. Minimum balance requirements vary; you'll likely need to keep $1,000 or more as your minimum to have fees waived. What better use for your first $1,000 in emergency savings? Now that money is doing double duty. Can't scrounge up the minimum? Stick with a no-frills, flat-fee basic account.

Estimate how many cheques you'll write each month. While

cheques have been made almost obsolete by the combination of automatic pay, debit, and smart credit card use, some things are still more conveniently paid by cheque. Figure out how many cheques you typically write, and get an account that gives you the best deal.

How will you use your bank account? The overall number of transactions you make will affect your costs. Some banks give you your account for free as long as you're prepared to go the do-it-yourself route. But some people like or need to deal with a body, and for this they sometimes pay dearly if they don't choose wisely.

If you have to use special services like certified cheques or money orders, you'll pay. If you want to put a stop-payment on a cheque, you'll pay. And if you want overdraft protection or access to ATMs that aren't your own bank's, you'll pay. Find out how much. Each of these services, and many others, are listed on the bank's fee schedule, so there's no excuse—other than laziness—for not knowing what these services cost before you use them.

If you use your bank account like a wallet—really? Have you NO planning skills?—make sure that you're banking with a company that has loads of ATMs everywhere you go. Using another bank's ATM can cost you $3 or more each time you pull that $20 to pay for lunch. (Beyond dumb!)

Keep in mind that the more accounts and services you have with one institution, the more likely you are to get a price break on the services you use. Banks love to be your sole provider.

TRACK YOUR MONEY

Do not use the ATM to keep track of your account balance. If you do, you may find yourself counting on a balance that isn't really there because a cheque you've written has yet to clear. Use a Spending Journal to keep track of your account—regardless of whether those transactions are cheques, debit card transactions, or credit card charges—and reconcile it monthly against your bank statement to make sure you're working with an accurate balance. Here's how:

- Buy a notebook. At the top of the first page, write the current balance in your chequing account. When you deposit money (your pay, an expense cheque, or a cheque from the government), add it to your balance. When you spend money (by writing a cheque, paying a bill online, making a debit card transaction, withdrawing cash, or making a credit card transaction), subtract that amount from the balance.
- If you don't want to carry the notebook with you, get a receipt for everything you buy and use those receipts to update your Spending Journal at night.
- Make sure you check your bank statement when you

receive it each month and compare it against your Spending Journal. I can't tell you how many times I've found extra fees on my statement that I've had removed with a single call. If you aren't watching the pennies, the dollars can go missing pretty quickly.

HOW MANY SAVINGS ACCOUNTS ARE ENOUGH?

Since a savings account doesn't cost anything, this is one product you can afford to have plenty of, assuming you can keep track of them all. Savings accounts are great places to accumulate the money you plan to spend on things like car or home maintenance, vacations, and big-ticket purchases—the things I refer to as "planned spending." By moving this money out of your regular chequing account, you accomplish two things:

1. You can't see the money, so you're less likely to spend it on something you really hadn't planned on, just because you have a high balance and are feeling "rich" (remember your money set-point?).
2. You can earn some interest on the money.

$ *Gail's Tips:* If you have a savings account at your bank, and that account is paying you less than you could earn elsewhere, you're letting your money languish when it should be working harder for you. If you were shopping for a mortgage, you'd negotiate hard to save a half or even a quarter of a percent on your mortgage rate, right? So why would you settle for next-to-nothing on your savings account, when you could be earning 1% to 2% more? Is it that you're so flush you don't need the extra money? Or is it that you're too lazy to bother hunting up a higher return?

• •

I have several savings accounts set up into which money is transferred automatically each month. There's my home maintenance savings, my vacation savings, and my planned spending. Since I budget monthly for things that I don't always have to pay monthly—things like property taxes, home insurance, car maintenance, clothes, birthdays, and Christmas—those monthly amounts go into my planned spending account. When I need it, I transfer the money back to my chequing account.

Some people find having several accounts confusing. They'd rather pile it all into one savings account and keep track of the various pots of money on paper. Do what works for you. The key to keeping your cash flow on an even keel is to figure out the system you're most comfortable with, find the products and services that make your system sing, and follow through consistently.

MAKE YOUR BANK WORK FOR YOU

If you find that your cheques are being held for several days after you deposit them, go in and speak with the bank manager and tell him you want the "hold" removed. Banks hold cheques for as much as seven business days—more if the cheque is drawn on a foreign account—to ensure the cheque clears before the funds are released. If you're a good customer, you shouldn't have to wait.

If you have a mortgage, a retirement plan, and other investments at several institutions, consolidating will let you throw your weight around. Banks love to have all your business, and you can use the economic power of consolidation to lower your mortgage rate, earn higher interest on investments, and reduce service charges on your accounts.

If you're charged for something that you think is unfair, complain. You'd be amazed at how many times fees will be waived because of your relationship with a branch staff member or because you have a big mouth.

Look over your financial services from time to time to see if the products you're using still match your needs. The banking world is constantly changing, and the banks are very competitive. Don't be tempted by "but if I need it." Review how you use your bank account, so you're only paying for what you're actually using. Don't be lured into buying a product just for the prestige. Shopping for financial services is like shopping for anything else. If you want to get the best deal going, you have to compare, and you have to negotiate.

15 STEPS TO GETTING ORGANIZED FINANCIALLY

1. Gather all your paperwork. Create file folders for your chequing, savings, retirement, and investment accounts;

credit card accounts, loans, and personal lines of credit; mortgage; insurance: life, disability, health, critical illness, home, and car; estate: wills and powers of attorney; and tax returns.

2. Welcome to 21st-century banking. If you don't already have it, set up online or telephone banking.

3. Reduce fees by setting up a buffer. If you can afford it, transfer a $1,000 float to your chequing account (pretend it isn't there), and use that to minimize your banking costs.

4. Save automatically. Set up an automatic withdrawal from your chequing account to a savings account that will not be touched.

5. Create a monthly bill summary. List your bills in order of the dates they need to be paid to prevent you from missing a bill. Write an "A" beside bills that are automatically withdrawn from your account, and remember to deduct them from your Spending Journal each month.

6. Set up your in-baskets. Create an in-basket with two folders, one labelled "1–15" and the other "16–31." When a bill comes in, look at the due date and put the bill in the appropriate folder. Create a second in-basket with three folders, and label them "bank statements," "bills paid," and "tax receipts."

7. Make a biweekly date with your money. On the 12th and 28th of each month set aside the time (you'll need 15 to 60 minutes) to pay your bills.

8. Always pay your bills in one place. Equip it with what I call an Office-in-a-Box: your file folders, Spending Journal, envelopes, stamps, pens, pencils, a calculator, tape, a stapler, return address labels, and a recycling bin. A shredder is good protection against identity theft.

9. When you pay a bill, write the cheque or transaction number, the amount paid, and the date you paid it on the bill. Put the paid bill in your "bills paid" file. Deduct the amount you've spent from your Spending Journal. If a bill has not been paid in full (tax bills are paid over several months, for example), put it back in your bills folder so you don't forget it.

10. Reconcile your bank statements every month. When your bank statements come in, put them in your "bank statements" folder. Make a date when all your statements are in (it'll depend on when you receive them) to review statements to make sure there are no mistakes.

11. Reconcile your Spending Journal. Mark the cheques and automatic withdrawals that have gone through your account, and highlight the ones that haven't. Go back to make sure all previous cheques have cleared.

12. Once a quarter, file all your paperwork.

13. Have a quarterly dinner with your partner, and talk about the bumps, your goals, and how you're doing.

14. Revamp your budget annually. Use last year's statements to see what you actually spent. If you spent more on a

particular category than you budgeted, make sure you know why, or look for ways to trim.

15. Clean up. Go through your files at the end of each year, and throw out bills and receipts no longer needed for auditing/budgeting purposes.

7

ESTABLISH YOUR CREDIT IDENTITY

Credit is a way of life. If we try to live without it, our goals become harder to accomplish. After all, does anyone you know have the cash to buy a home without borrowing? Credit isn't bad. But how we use credit can be a problem.

People who grew up during the '40s, '50s, and '60s believed that they had to save. They paid cash for almost everything they bought. They were willing to wait until they were well-established and had all the necessities before splurging on the extras. It wasn't that they were morally more highly developed than this generation, no matter what they tell you. They simply didn't have access to credit. So the fact that they didn't buy on credit is no biggie. The temptation to spend money they had yet to earn didn't exist. Now it does, and it's a tough devil to fight.

Not everyone succumbs to the credit-devil. There are people who would rather not eat than go into debt. When they are successful, we see their success, but we don't always see the effort they had to put in to get there.

Barbara talks about growing up in a strict European home. She says, "We saved all of our milk bottles. My father made his own wine and beer at home because that was a lot cheaper. We churned our own butter. We learned the value of every single cent. And when we did spend money, it wasn't on candy or pop, the non-necessities of life. It was on a good, sturdy pair of shoes." Even when she wanted the shiny new bicycle, her dad said, "You can't afford the bicycle until you have the good shoes."

The lesson was well learned. Barbara and her husband worked hard to buy their first car. "We worked every day in the office until 6:00 p.m. Then we travelled for two hours by bus to a factory and cleaned toilets. We did 200 toilets each night. We'd get home at 1:00 a.m. We did this seven days a week. We saved every single dollar. When we went into the dealership, we paid for the car in cash. I'll never forget that. We were just kids, in our early 20s. That, to me, was a much better experience than saying, 'Oh, put it on a charge card, or I'll pay for it over time.'"

Post-1985 saw a significant shift in people's attitudes towards borrowing, as credit became more accessible. People leveraged investments. They packed their purses full of credit cards. They were offered lines of credit at every turn. They wanted it all . . . IMMEDIATELY! And with credit they could have it. Saving before buying became a thing of the past. The result: huge debt loads that have kept growing year after year. We've swapped the responsibility of being able to take care of ourselves for the ability to scratch our consumer itch. We've given up our independence in the name of instant gratification.

Credit has become a commodity. When I first started in the money business, credit was something you had to prove you were worthy of having. Today, credit is heavily marketed, often to people who have no ability to handle it. While the instalment loan used to be the credit of choice for most people, the focus has shifted to revolving credit: credit cards and personal lines of credit. Unfortunately, when you choose to use revolving credit, you miss the checks and balances that lenders typically use to validate your reason for borrowing. Instead, because the credit is readily available, it's easy to use without giving thought to the consequences.

Most people don't understand how to use credit to their advantage. They react to their circumstances, and they keep reacting as they get further and further into debt. When the debt becomes unmanageable, they throw up their arms in despair and say that credit is evil. Well, it's not. Well-planned borrowing can be a useful way to realize dreams and achieve financial goals. Well-planned borrowing can get you where you want to be. But it takes a good understanding of how credit works, when to use credit, and which type of credit will make borrowing work for you.

ESTABLISHING A CREDIT RATING

When you sign a credit application form, you give the lender permission to check your credit rating. If you have no credit history, lenders don't know if you would be a good credit risk or not. You're an unknown commodity, and that's harder to deal with.

You can't develop a credit rating until you have paid back a loan. A credit rating is your reputation in terms of your previous behaviour in paying back money in a responsible and timely way. Been consistently late? You'll have a bad credit reputation. Missed a payment completely? You'll have an even worse rep. Always made your payments on time? Just about anyone will be willing to lend to you under the right circumstances.

....

$ Gail's Tips: One way to start building a credit reputation is to borrow some money to contribute to a retirement plan. You can pay back the loan over five or six months, and you'll have started saving for the future. And you don't have to worry about whether or not they'll give you the loan. As long as you take the retirement plan out with the lending institution, you'll get the loan.

....

A credit card is one of the easiest ways to build a credit rating. Apply for a card with a low limit, make small purchases, pay off the card each month, and become a credit star. Or you could take out a loan. If you are a first-time borrower, you may need a guarantor to get the loan. A guarantor is a person who has established a credit reputation and who guarantees to repay the loan if you don't. All you have to do is pay back that money promptly to establish your credit rating. If you have assets such as a car, investments, or a home to use as collateral, you can use that collateral to secure a loan. But be warned—if you don't repay the loan, the financial institution will seize the asset pledged as collateral and sell it or cash it in to collect its money.

Some people have difficulty establishing that they even exist when it comes to getting credit. If you are married and have been riding in the passenger seat as your partner has done all the financial driving, this could be you. If your credit cards are in your partner's name, even if you make the payments on the card, you're contributing to your partner's credit rating—not your own. The credit card company doesn't care who made the payments. Their reporting to the credit bureau is based on whose name is on the card. Women who are recently divorced or widowed often face the shock that they don't exist, simply because all the credit reporting was done in their partners' names. If you want to be independent and have your own financial identity, make sure you have at least one credit card in your own name. And use it. Initially, you may have to use a secured credit card.

. . . .

$ Gail's Tips: A secured credit card is fully secured by money left on deposit. There's no risk to the lender, because the balance is covered. Financial institutions typically want twice the amount of credit you're asking for placed on deposit. So if you want a credit card with a

$500 balance, you must put up $1,000 in cash. After you've made regular payments for about a year or so, ask the financial institution to drop the security requirement and return your deposit.

• •

As late as the early '90s, all credit reporting for a couple was done in the man's name. Now, however, credit bureaus have separated the reporting for men and women. To make sure you establish a credit history, borrow money in your own name. If you do borrow with your husband, insist that the credit granter report the information to the credit bureau in your name. Typically, credit granters report only in the name of the first person that signed on the credit application. So while banks and finance companies have come a long way by saying it doesn't matter who signs first, their reporting hasn't come a long way, because information is still only reported in the name of the first signer. If that happens to be the man—and typically, men are handed the paperwork first—all the credit history for that loan is reported in his name. Insist on signing first, so you'll be building a financial identity.

CHOOSING THE RIGHT CREDIT CARD

Credit cards may be the easiest way to build a credit identity, but with the hundreds of different cards available, there's nothing easy about choosing the one that will work for you.

If you usually carry a balance from one month to the next

(Really? Why?), then a low-interest card is your best bet. If you pay your card off in full every month, the interest rate won't matter. Look for a card that doesn't charge an annual fee. If you want to take advantage of some of the "rewards" available, you'll have a lot to choose from, but you'll end up paying for the privilege.

Every specialty credit card has a list of features as long as your arm. Wading through the options—points for travel or gift selections, cash rebates, and myriad insurance coverages—can bewitch even the most cautious shoppers into believing they are getting good value.

Some cards provide cash back up to a specified limit. Or you can use your credit card to work towards a rebate on the purchase of your first home, which is a terrific head start—as long as you're sure that institution will have the best mortgage deal when the time comes to sign the offer. Then there are all those promises of free travel, assuming there's a seat available. If you don't want to be disappointed by promised rewards that turn out to be less than those advertised, because of all the rules and regulations, make sure you read them thar rules and regs before you sign up.

The real test of the value of a credit card is in what it does for YOU. Collision damage waiver on car rentals can save you money. Trip cancellation or interruption insurance, baggage insurance, and emergency travel or medical assistance all provide you with peace of mind as you set off. And they save you having to pay for separate travel insurance. Free traveller's cheques eliminate the 1% fee normally charged. However, if you don't travel enough for these features to at least cover the cost of your card, take a good look at the other bells and whistles that are offered in return for the fee.

Most specialty cards offer to extend the manufacturer's warranty for an additional 12 months on items purchased with the card. Hey, you can skip the extended warranty. Some let you replace items bought on your credit card that were lost or damaged within 90 days of purchase. Both these insurance features are a good deal if you use them. If the only reason you have your card is to take advantage of the "rewards" (the banks' term for accumulating points to buy merchandise from a catalogue), make sure you claim your points. If you're looking for a card that will pay for itself, look for a card that will give you a cash rebate (and watch for limits on those rebates).

If you think you have to pay more for a snazzy credit card just to get a higher limit, save yourself some money. With a good credit history, you can write to or call your card issuer and ask for a credit increase, and it won't cost you a cent more.

Regardless of whether you are a binge shopper or a model of self-control, limiting your access to credit is a smart move. No one needs more than a couple of credit cards. If you carry a balance (Really? Why?), make sure it's on the card with the lower interest rate.

Keep in mind that higher credit limits will affect your ability to borrow money when you really do need it. If you're applying for a mortgage, the amount of credit you already have access to is considered when deciding how much more you can borrow. Even if your cards are completely paid off, because you have those seven cards with a $3,000 credit limit each, you have already been granted $21,000 in credit.

Should you choose to, you could run all those cards to the limit, severely affecting your ability to repay your mortgage. So don't accumulate cards indiscriminately—including all those department store cards offered at the cashier to save you an instant 10%. Instead, choose the card that does you the most service, and stick with it. You don't need store cards. They charge the highest interest. Go into your wallet now and cut them up, and then call and cancel the accounts. Everyone accepts Visa or MasterCard.

While credit cards allow you to take cash advances, I would say: **don't do this**. Advances accrue interest the moment they are taken. While there's a grace period for purchases, provided you pay your balance off in full each month, there's no grace period for cash advances. And often the interest rate on cash advances is higher.

Credit cards aren't for everyone. According to Equifax Canada, our total credit card debt was $78 billion at the end of 2009. So while credit cards can be a terrific tool for people who have the discipline to use them to their advantage, a lot of folks out there have fallen into debt traps using credit cards.

The smart way to use a credit card is to spend only what you know you can pay off when the bill comes in. Keep track of how much you're spending every time you whip out the card. (Hey, have you set up that Spending Journal yet?) Each time you use your credit card, deduct the amount you have spent— as if you'd made a debit transaction—from your Spending Journal. When the bill comes in, you'll have all the transactions already subtracted from your balance, so the money will be there to pay off the bill.

MAKING SMART BORROWING DECISIONS

Credit is a part of life. Whether you are financing the purchase of new appliances, replacing your furnace, or paying for your children's education, borrowing can offer real benefits. After all, it'd be tough on the family to have to wait it out a winter while you save the money you need to buy a new furnace. Borrowing money, putting in the furnace, and paying off the loan in easily manageable payments makes a lot more sense. The question isn't simply whether or not to borrow. Sometimes we have to. What you really need in this situation is to understand what borrowing will mean, so ask yourself:

- Do I really need it?
- What's the markup?
- What's this going to cost me in total (including all the interest I'll have paid)?
- What else do I have to give up to buy this?

Do I Really Need It?

If your furnace gives up the ghost in mid-January, my best guess is that your answer to the first question is a resounding yes. But you should question your borrowing motivation and rationale if:

You aren't sure the usefulness of a purchase will outlast the repayment period. It's bad enough when we spend cash on impulsive purchases, but when we have to pay for those beautiful earrings long after we've lost one of the pair, that's just dumb. Ask yourself, and answer honestly, "Will I be severely handicapped without the item?"

An instalment plan makes it too good to pass up. That's not the right place to start. Begin by deciding whether you need the item at all, and then calculate how much you'll be paying in interest.

You're adding more debt to your already-high debt load. Piling new debt on top of old is dangerous. It can lead you to the point where all your discretionary income is spent making loan payments.

You haven't told anyone you intend to borrow. Making unilateral decisions about financing is a great way to put a strain on your relationships. And if you haven't worked up the guts to tell the most trusted people in your life, maybe it's because you know you won't be able to justify the decision to them. Perhaps you'd like to reconsider?

You're buying something to cheer yourself up. Lots of people go shopping to lift their spirits. Unfortunately, shopping, like drinking, can create a hangover. Ask yourself how you'll feel when the bill comes in.

You're trying to impress others. Some people need to keep up an image. Others shop together to build or strengthen their relationships—my stepdaughter, Amanda, refers to this humorously as "female bonding." But when it comes to paying off the card or repaying the loan, it isn't so funny. Ask yourself if it's really worth it.

What's the Markup?

The cost of borrowing can vary significantly. Buy on your line of credit at 3%, and the markup is substantially less than if you'd financed using a credit card at 11%. Use a buy-now-pay-later plan and miss the payback date, and you'll be paying a whopping 36%! *The higher the interest rate you pay, the greater the markup.*

Also, *the longer the term of the loan, the more it will cost you.* And what could be worse that having your loan outlive the item you borrowed to buy? By negotiating the lowest possible rate and taking the shortest possible term, you can pay off the loan faster while reducing the overall costs. This leads directly to the next question.

What Will This Cost in Total?

It's a worthwhile exercise figuring out what that item will cost you in total before you finance it. Let's say that you buy a new car for $23,000, and your loan is for three years at 6%. That car will have cost you approximately $25,000. Take the loan for five years (because you want to have a lower monthly payment), and the car will end up costing you almost $27,000.

Do the same calculation on your credit card purchases, and you may not be quite so willing to charge ahead with your purchase. If you buy $2,500 worth of new furniture on a credit card that charges 17% interest, and you pay back $125 every month, the furniture will end up costing you almost $3,000.

Choose to make only the minimum monthly payment on your card, and that $2,500 in furniture will actually cost you almost $5,500.

There are heaps of loan and credit card calculators on the web. Do some number-crunching before you commit to the financing you're considering.

What Else Do I Have to Give Up to Buy This?

This final question relates to how pinched your cash flow is by your borrowing. The higher your monthly payments climb, the more the payments restrict your cash flow, and the greater the cost to you in terms of stress and having to go without other things you feel contribute to a comfortable lifestyle. If you choose to make higher payments over a shorter term, you have to be sure your other important living needs can still be met. Resist the urge to steal from Peter to pay Paul. Paying off your loan quickly won't do you any good if you run up your credit cards during the process. If you choose instead to take a slightly longer term, so that your payments are lower and fit more comfortably into your cash flow, remember this will mean a longer commitment and more interest over the full term of the loan.

LOSE THE HIGH-COST CARDS

Financial institutions have done research that shows most people will go out of their way to earn one-half to three-quarters of a percent more on an investment. Yet people will pay 7% to 14% more interest than necessary just because it's a credit card. If you have an outstanding balance of $1,000 on which you're paying 17%, that's costing you more than $14 a month, or almost $169 a year in interest. And that's after-tax dollars! You'd have to have a $1,000 GIC paying better than 24% to break even. If you can you find a GIC paying 24%, let me know!

Find a lower-cost form of financing to pay off your credit card. This is called refinancing, and there are many ways to do it. Take a consolidation loan and pay off all your existing loans, so you have a single monthly payment each month. Renegotiate an existing loan to a lower rate. Or apply for a lower-interest credit card and transfer your balance to the new card. It doesn't matter how you do it—DO IT!

This strategy only works to your advantage if you toss those credit cards behind the fridge until the loan is repaid. If you go out merrily charging away, in no time at all, you'll find yourself in an even deeper hole with both a loan and a balance on your cards.

If your debt is costing you more than your savings are earning, cash out and pay off. If it sounds like I'm repeating myself, that's because I am. This does not include retirement savings, since the tax bite to cash out would make the whole exercise far too expensive. And it does not include your emergency fund, because you don't want to leave yourself with no options if the worst happens. However, if you have an unregistered savings account, GIC, Canada Savings Bonds, or mutual funds that you've been putting aside, and you've racked up debt, pay off your debt and start saving again. I know I've explained this before, but if you're still not convinced, here's my last shot at getting you to see your assets and your debts as belonging in the same pot.

Let's say you have a $5,000 loan and $5,000 in a GIC. The loan has an annual interest rate of 9%, and you're earning 4% on the GIC. If you keep the GIC for a year, you'll earn $200 in interest. But you'll have to pay tax on that money. Assuming your average tax rate is 30%, you'll pay $60 in tax, so you'll end up with $140 in your pocket. Meanwhile, the loan will cost you $450 this year, so you'll end up paying more than three times as much interest on the loan as you earned on your GIC. By using the $5,000 GIC to pay off your $5,000 loan, you'll earn no interest, but you'll also pay no interest, and you'll end up ahead by $310 ($450 loan interest − $140 GIC interest). Got it? Gosh, I hope so.

HAVING TROUBLE MAKING PAYMENTS?

If you run into trouble making your credit card (or any type of credit) payments, you can get out. It may take some time, but you can do it. But you must act.

Begin by calling the credit company and explaining the problem. If you've lost your job or become ill, and you are not working, tell the credit company. If you are simply in over your head, tell the credit company. The important thing is to tell the credit company. They would much rather talk to you than send you nasty letters and wonder if they will ever be paid. You will probably be able to work out a repayment plan. You should be able to negotiate with them to reduce the total amount you owe if you make a full payment. Here are the steps:

Make a Plan

Without a plan, you're simply throwing money at the problem debt without a clear sense of what you're trying to accomplish. Make a list of all the people to whom you owe money—your creditors. Put the list in order from highest interest rate to lowest. Then put your greatest effort at repayment against the debt with the highest rate.

Call and Negotiate

If you have extremely high interest rates on your cards, it's time to put your negotiation skills to work. Call and describe the pickle you're in. Ask if the credit card company would be willing to eliminate the late fee and interest for a month or two. Try to get them to lower the rate on your card. If they won't, ask if there's another card that has a lower interest rate and transfer the balance. See if the creditor will take a smaller "settlement" amount if you agree to make a single repayment.

Get a Consolidation Loan

If your credit card company won't negotiate with you, and

you can't get your hands on a low-cost card to do a balance transfer, call your bank and see if you can get a lower-cost consolidation loan. Bundle all your debt together under a single loan, and set up a fixed monthly payment that will see you out of the hole within a specific time. Aim for 36 months or less.

Pay on Time

Pay at least the minimum on all your debts and make those payments on time. That will not only help you avoid fees, it'll stop the interest rate from bouncing up because you've broken the rules. And it'll improve your credit history, which will lay the groundwork for future rate negotiations.

Pay More

Get a second job, or a third job, or a better job. Do whatever it takes. You spent the money. Now it's time to pay it back. And the longer it takes you, the more painful and costly it will be, so bust your butt to make that debt go away.

Set Specific Goals

Set milestones that are achievable and for which you can pat yourself on the back. Maybe you'll have that department store card paid off in six months. Perhaps you want to be debt-free before your wedding. Whatever goal you set, write it down and hang it where you can see it every day. As you get closer to your goal, the motivation to hit your target will carry you forward.

Cut Up the Cards

You can't use those credit cards—or any credit cards—while you're paying off the balances you've racked up. You have to be living within your means. You better have a spending plan in place.

WHAT HAPPENS IF YOU DON'T DEAL WITH THE PROBLEM?

Debt collection practices vary from one creditor to another. Legal steps that can be taken are regulated by provincial law. As a general rule, repossession (seizure) of goods, garnishment of wages or bank accounts, and other court actions are covered under provincial law, while bankruptcy is covered by federal legislation.

If you default and have offered collateral, creditors have the right to seize the goods and sell them to try to recoup their losses. Even if you haven't offered collateral, creditors may be allowed to seize other goods to recover the debt. You usually have plenty of notice and are given one last chance to clear up the debt.

A creditor may also apply for a court order to garnish your wages or bank accounts. If a garnishment is issued, the creditor claims the money you owe directly from your employer or from the financial institution where your accounts are held. You may also be required to pay any court costs.

If the amount owed is quite small, the creditor may choose to sue you in small claims court to recover the debt. Larger amounts usually mean the lender may have to go to a higher court.

If you simply cannot carry on, you may have to declare bankruptcy, or you may be forced to do so by your creditors.

A FINAL WORD ON USING CREDIT WISELY

Sometimes it's easy to forget that you have to pay for what you buy, particularly when you use credit cards for the majority of your purchases. If you want to stay in control of your finances and use credit wisely, here are some guidelines:

- Make a spending plan and stick to it. Know how much is coming in and how much is going out each month. Include items that are paid less frequently (such as car and house insurance) or irregularly (such as dental bills).
- Get rid of extra credit cards. Everyone needs a credit card. No one needs four, seven, or 12. If you have a department store card, cut it up and cancel the account. The interest rate is staggering and you don't need the extra temptation.
- Avoid impulse shopping. Use a list. Ask yourself: Will I still want it tomorrow? Next week? Next month?

- Comparison shop for the items you're buying and the financing you're using.
- Read and understand any financing arrangements you are signing, particularly store financing arrangements. Are there any fees or penalties? How much interest will you pay in total?
- Don't co-sign or guarantee loans. If that person defaults, you will have to pay off the loan.
- Keep track of all your credit purchases. Save your receipts or keep a written record of credit card purchases, so you can compare them with your statement. Never just pay the statement off without checking it carefully. Mistakes happen, and you may be double-charged or charged for items you did not buy. In this day of fraud and identity theft, if you aren't paying attention, you're asking for trouble.
- If you are a good risk and have qualified to use it, it's credit. If you've used it, it's debt. It's funny how a single concept can have such different meanings depending on which end of the stick you're holding. If you've got credit, you're great. You're responsible. You're worthy. You're an up-and-comer. If you've got debt, exactly the opposite is true. Yet we're talking about the same thing: your ability to use someone else's money to achieve your goals.

8

PUTTING THE RIGHT ROOF OVER YOUR HEAD

Shelter is one of life's basic necessities, and it takes a variety of forms: apartments, townhouses, basement flats, bungalows, and condominiums. Most people start off by renting. Some people want to own a place of their own, so they save up some money and buy a home. There is no right or wrong way when it comes to sheltering yourself. Regardless of the pressure other people put on you to buy, buy, buy, you must choose for yourself the kind of place you want to live in—based on how much you want to spend, how much you want to work at maintaining a home, and your lifestyle. There's no point in strangling your cash flow and putting your financial health at risk just to own a home. You're a strong, independent woman who can choose for yourself what will best suit your needs. Don't let anyone guilt, bully, or tease you into becoming a homeowner. Sometimes renting is the best option. It's your money. Educate yourself on the options and then choose the option that's right for YOU.

RENTING

If you only hear one thing I say about renting, let it be this: ***Read your lease.*** Yes, I know that most of it sounds like gobble-dygook, but if you don't read the fine print, you may be in for a shock. Make sure any roommates are listed on the lease, and have them all sign it. This ensures you will all share legal responsibility in case of a problem. It also protects you if a roommate suddenly changes her mind and decides to move out.

Landlords sometimes ask for money upfront to protect themselves from the cost of repairing anything you might break. This is a security deposit, which differs from first and last months' rent. Find out how it works. The security deposit should not be used to pay for basic maintenance on the unit. Get receipts for any money you hand over in cash, and ask for a letter stipulating how the security deposit will be used. Check to see if you will be paid interest on the money while it remains unused. When your lease is up and you move out, the landlord should refund your security deposit if you didn't cause any damage. Take pictures of the unit before you move in and as you are leaving, so you have some physical proof should there be a dispute with the landlord.

Other key things to watch for in a lease:

- Can you have pets? Can you smoke? Can you have a party every Friday night?

- Can you have roommates?
- What are the rules for rent increases?
- What rights of entry does the landlord or his representative have?
- Is there parking? How about additional storage? Security?
- What about upkeep? Who's responsible for what tasks? Will you be allowed to paint?
- What's included in the rent? Will you have to pay your own utilities? Will the landlord throw in cable? How about an Internet connection? Will you have to supply your own appliances? Are laundry facilities available?

Know your rights. The law protects renters in many ways. But if you don't know your rights, you won't know when someone is taking advantage of you.

THE RENT-VERSUS-OWN QUESTION

At some point the rent-versus-own question may come up. The considerations are not all financial, so making the decision involves more than just comparing your monthly rent with the monthly mortgage you would pay.

Home ownership involves a commitment and responsibility not only in terms of money, but also in terms of time. Not everyone is up to the challenge. Once you own your first home, you'll quickly realize that there is always something that needs to be fixed: wiring, plumbing, or the eavestroughs, furnace, skylights, or pool linings. If it's not the inside of the house, it's the outside. It can seem like a constant onslaught of things to do.

Then, of course, there are the lifestyle issues. Some people are just too busy living to be bothered with the ongoing maintenance of a home. Painting, caulking, trimming, mowing, and shovelling are far from their minds. Avid travellers who are away from home for long spells may have security and insurance issues. People who move often because of work may see their equity eaten up by real estate and legal fees. If you end up selling your existing home in a down market and buying in an up market in your new location, you may have less of a down payment than you need to make an even trade.

If you like the idea of having your own place to do with as you wish, ownership might be right up your alley. If you're handy around the house and like puttering about, go for it. If you want to put down roots, if you want to become part of a community, owning your own home can be a very rewarding experience.

FIGURE OUT WHETHER YOU'RE READY TO OWN

When people start thinking about buying a home, their focus often shifts from simply providing shelter to making a profit. One home ownership myth is that a house is a good investment. This isn't always so. Witness all those people who bought into the market during the boom of the 1980s, only to watch their equity evaporate as the real estate market took a dive in early 1990. Many were left owing more than their homes were worth. Ditto the folks who bought a home in some parts of the country in 2009, who then watched 20% to 30% of their home equity evaporate when the housing market corrected.

While conventional wisdom says that renting is throwing your money away because you're building no equity, renters don't have to worry about taxes or major home repairs. And if you have the discipline to invest the difference you would have had to pay if you owned, you could end up ahead. On the flip side, no matter how small the principal portion of your mortgage payment (and it's incredibly small in the early years), as long as the market is stable or rising, every month you will be building equity and increasing your net worth. A short-term view often makes the owning picture appear somewhat bleak. But as you pay off more of your mortgage, more of your payments will go towards building equity.

If you're trying to work out whether you would be further ahead financially choosing one over the other, let me warn you that there is a lot that must be considered, so it's not a simple calculation. The standard calculation used for illustrative purposes typically uses the difference between the home's appreciation and the growth in the assets had they been invested in the equities market, but the answer is often misleading. There are a number of other things that have to be factored in to make the calculation truly realistic. You must consider the amount of interest you'll pay on the mortgage as a cost. And then there are the costs associated with home improvements and maintenance. When my good friend Victoria bought her new home in the Gatineau, she had to hire no less than eight repair people for plumbing, painting, heating, chimney cleaning, appliance repair, carpet cleaning, wiring, and floor replacement. A house is a constant source of expenditure. Also take into account the property tax and house insurance, as well as things such as the closing costs when you buy, the legal fees and real estate commission due when you sell, and the capital gains if the home is a second property.

This might sound like I am against home ownership. I'm not. But for almost everyone I've spoken with, the decision has been more than a dollar issue. It's been an emotional one: a decision based on a desire to put down roots, to have a place to call one's own. If all you think about is the warm fuzzy feeling you get when you think of owning your own place, you may not make the best decision. You must also think about how home ownership will fit with the rest of your life and your overall financial health. If it's a good fit, go for it.

BUYING A HOME

There are two questions to answer when you decide you want to buy property:

1. How large a mortgage payment can you handle?
2. How much of a down payment can you save?

A starting point in figuring out how much you can afford is to multiply your gross annual income (your income before taxes) by 3.4. Include only income you're sure you will receive, and if you and your spouse both have incomes, add them together. This is referred to as your household income. Let's say your gross salary is $32,000. Your honey makes $26,000 a year, gross. You could afford to buy a house with a price tag of $197,200 ($32,000 + $26,000 = $58,000 x 3.4) or less.

Remember, this is only an estimate. Not only do you have to think about the price of the house you can afford, you must also consider how you will come up with a down payment of at least 5% (which would be almost $10,000 in this case), and how you'll work those mortgage payments into your spending plan.

Let's say you and your partner make $6,000 a month before taxes. With a $10,000 down payment, property taxes of $2,400 a year, a monthly heating bill of $100, and a mortgage at 5% amortized over 25 years, lenders will happily give you a mortgage of $266,929. (There are heaps of calculators online that will help you figure out what lenders will let you borrow.) Add in your down payment, and you will know how much house you can afford to buy . . . according to lenders. But I have a word of warning for you: *lenders have been known to give borrowers enough credit rope to hang themselves.* You can't take what a lender says you can afford as gospel. You must do the math yourself to see how much house you can actually afford to carry.

WHAT CAN YOU AFFORD?

Lenders use a calculation called a "gross debt service (GDS) ratio" to calculate how much they'll lend you, based on how much you can afford to repay each month. They usually won't allow your GDS ratio to go above 32%. So you can use this as a starting point to determine how much you can afford. If you make $6,000 a month before taxes, 32% of that would be $1,920 a month, which is what the bank will say you can afford. With an interest rate of 5.5%, you could afford a mortgage of about $310,000. Add your down payment, and voilà, you've got the amount of house you can afford.

$ **Gail's Tips:** You can't look at the mortgage payment in isolation of everything else you're spending money on. This is how so many people squeeze their cash flows to the point where they're using their credit cards and lines of credit to buy food. You have to think about what you're spending on clothing, transportation, food, and entertainment to have the great life you want to have. So go back to your spending plan and start there. Add in the mortgage payment (in lieu of your old mortgage payment or rent) and see if your budget balances. If it doesn't, you'll have to cut something. Will it be entertainment, vacations, or the size of the house you're buying?

The amount you can afford to spend each month on a mortgage will depend not only on the size of your mortgage, but also on whether you have other debts, such as a car loan, credit card balances, student loans, or alimony and child support payments. To factor in these elements, lenders use another formula called a "total debt service (TDS) ratio." TDS ratios range from 40% to 44% of your gross annual income, depending on the lender and on Canada Mortgage and Housing Corporation's (CMHC) mortgage insurance rules.

Let's say you decided to buy a house and you'd calculated your GDS at $1,920. Let's also say you had some student loans that you were repaying at $300 a month, a car loan that was costing you $375 a month, and a couple of credit cards on which the minimum payments totalled $127 a month. You'd add together all the payment amounts and add it to your mortgage payment amount, for a total of $2,722 ($300 + $375 + $127 + $1,920 = $2,722). You'd then divide that $2,722 by your monthly gross income of $6,000 and multiply by 100 to come up with your TDS ratio: 45.36%. Too much! So you'd either have to get some of that debt paid off, or you'd have to find a way to reduce your mortgage payment.

Your mortgage payment amount is affected not only by how much you borrow and your interest rate, but also by how long you amortize your mortgage. Amortization refers to the amount of time you plan to take to pay the mortgage off in full. ***The longer your amortization, the lower your monthly payment, and the more interest you'll pay over the life of the mortgage.*** Take out a $200,000 mortgage at 5.5%, and over the life of the mortgage, this is how the numbers play out:

Amortization	Monthly Payment	Interest Cost
15 years	$1,627.60	$92,966.94
20 years	$1,368.79	$128,506.39
25 years	$1,220.79	$166,232.53
30 years	$1,127.82	$206,008.48
35 years	$1,065.93	$247,682.43

You can drop your monthly payment by almost $600 by extending your amortization from 15 years to 35 years, but you'll end up paying almost $155,000 more in interest. And your overall interest cost will be more than the original mortgage you took out, so you'll have paid for the house more than twice.

. . . .

$ *Gail's Tips:* People tend to underestimate what it'll cost to live in a home of their own. They like to think that as long as the mortgage payment is pretty much what they would pay in rent, things will be easy peasy. Not so much. You must consider what it will cost to live in your new home. Ask friends or family with similar homes what their heating, electricity, water, insurance, repair, and maintenance bills are like. A rule of thumb is to budget between 3% and 5% of the value of your home annually for maintenance, depending on how old your home is and how much work needs to be done. So if your house is worth $200,000, budget at least $6,000 a year, or $500 a month, for upkeep. If that makes you gasp, you're not ready for home ownership!

. . . .

DECIDE WHAT YOUR DOWN PAYMENT WILL BE

The amount of down payment you have will dictate the type of mortgage for which you will qualify. With at least 20% of the purchase price as a down payment, you can finance your new home price using a fixed-rate conventional mortgage. This is my favourite mortgage. You'll take the mortgage for a specific term, usually somewhere between one and five years, although longer-term mortgages are also available. And you'll pay a fixed rate of interest. No surprises with this mortgage. It's all laid out from the start and you just get in the habit.

Can't come up with 20%? If you can only arrange a down payment of between 5% and 19%, you'll need a high-ratio mortgage. These mortgages are insured through organizations like CMHC. You'll pay an application fee and insurance premium. This premium is calculated as a percentage of the loan amount, and the percentage ranges from 0.5% to 2.9% of the mortgage amount, depending on your down payment and its source, your employment status, your credit score, and the length of your amortization.

The lower your down payment, the higher the premium cost. If you're self-employed and don't have a third-party income validation of your income (like a corporate tax return), you'll pay more. If your credit score is lower than 600, you'll pay more. If you use non-traditional sources for your down payment—borrowed funds, gifts, lender cash-back incentives—you'll pay more. And if you go with an amortization longer than 25 years, you'll pay more.

You can pay the mortgage insurance premium in cash, or you can do what almost everyone else does and add it to your mortgage. Clearly, this is a more expensive option, since you'll now be paying interest on it for a long time, but it'll also get you into your home that much sooner.

Try to beef up your down payment to avoid mortgage loan insurance. Take a good, hard look at your spending for the last few months, and find places to trim so you can really save big. Brown bagging it once or twice a week can save you $40 to $100 a month. If you smoke, quit. If you hang out at the neighbourhood bar on Friday nights, nurse one beer for the evening or switch to soda.

Coming Up with the Down Payment

Once you decide to make the biggest purchase of your life, the next question you'll ask is, "How am I ever going to save enough for a down payment?" The answer is easy: *telesis.*

First, decide how much you are prepared to spend and how large a mortgage payment you can handle. Next, figure out how much of a down payment you'll need to save and how long you're prepared to wait before you jump into the market. The longer you can wait, the more you can accumulate. The less time you have, the more you'll have to put aside each month to meet your goal. Finally, get saving.

Make your savings automatic. Have the amount you've decided to save automatically transferred from your chequing account to your down payment savings account. Bam! It's gone. You can't spend it on dumb crap, and over time it'll build up to a nice little nest egg that'll get you into a home of your own.

While most of us live up to our means—we spend every cent we make—if you're determined to find the money for a down payment, you will. Review your spending plan to see where you can cut corners. You may be pleasantly surprised at how much you can set aside once you eliminate all the little frivolities that, in the long run, add very little to your life. There are dozens of things you can do to save money, but if you can't seem to find a place to cut, show your budget to your mother. In minutes she'll find a dozen places where you are wasting money. In lieu of your mom, turn to a close friend for help.

Get creative about it. If you've been paying premiums on a permanent life insurance policy, you've probably accumulated a cash value against which you can borrow. Check it out with your insurance company. Some people turn to parents, grandparents, or other relatives to help if they are able to. Getting married? Ask for cash in lieu of yet another small appliance. Explain that this will help you into your home, and be explicit about how important it is that your dream comes true. If you are buying a new home because you are divorcing, consider asking for your alimony payments as one lump-sum amount to get you back into the housing market as fast as possible.

Don't forget about the RRSP Home Buyers' Plan. As a first-time home buyer, you can withdraw up to $25,000 from your retirement plan as a tax-free loan towards a down payment on a home. The loan must be repaid in 15 annual instalments, or the amount not repaid will be included in your income for that year and taxed.

Consider a partner. Can you find a friend or relative who would also like to get into the housing market and with whose help you can manage the down payment? If your partner has the cash and you don't, you can assume a larger percentage of the mortgage as your responsibility. Treat this transaction as a business arrangement, and take the appropriate legal steps to ensure you are both well protected.

Practise and Save

There's nothing like a little practice to give you a taste of what home ownership will really be like. Let's say you decide you're buying a $250,000 house with 20% down, at 4% amortized over 25 years. Your monthly mortgage payment will be $1,052.05. Let's say your property taxes will be $2,400 a year, so that's $200 a month. And you'll have to pay house insurance, which we'll estimate at $100 a month. Then there are utilities, which we'll estimate at $300 a month. And home maintenance, for which we'll budget $425 a month. Your grand total: $2,077.05 a month. This is what it'll cost you to live in your new home. So now we come to the Gail's Great Advice part. This is where you figure out if you're ready for the responsibility of home ownership. If you can come up with $2,077.05 a month for your savings (less whatever you may be paying to keep a roof over your head right now), then you're ready. So if you're currently paying $1,200 for shelter, you'd have to be prepared to find another $877.05.

Hey, I'm not talking about whether you can *theoretically* come up with the money. I'm talking about taking that $877.05

and socking it away every single month in your home-buying savings account. Here are the two big benefits:

You'll learn to live on less disposable income. You better start practising before you buy your home, so you'll be ready for the adjustment to your lifestyle when you do take the big step. Loads of people buy a home and then keep on spending like they did before they became homeowners, racking up gobs of debt.

The $877.05 a month is going to get you to your 20% down payment in under five years. In the meantime, you could have friends and family gifting all the stuff you'll need for your New Home Adventure for all the birthdays and Christmases in between.

$ *Gail's Tips:* If you can't afford to comfortably work the mortgage payments into your budget and save the difference for your down payment, what makes you think you'll be able to afford to maintain a home, pay property taxes (yes, they will go up each year), and deal with the challenges of home ownership? Home ownership is a BIG responsibility. So spend a little time saving for a healthy down payment instead of locking yourself into a mortgage payment that strangles your cash flow, while you pay exorbitant amounts in interest and insurance premiums.

HOUSE HUNTING

When it comes to buying a house, do-it-yourselfers may think they can save a ton of cash handling the details on their own and negotiating away the commission the seller would have paid—but it ain't necessarily so. Home buying is a complicated legal and financial affair. A guide who has been around the block a few times can help assuage your fears, calm your nerves, and keep you on the straight and narrow in terms of your home-ownership priorities.

Your first step will be to choose both an agent and a mortgage person to work with. Ask friends and family whom they've dealt with that would be a good fit for you. You should expect great service from both these individuals as you go through this exciting and somewhat frightening experience. That means they call you back and you get lots of information. Get everything on the table before you start. Have your agent explain her commission structure. And remember, she won't get paid until the house closes. If you've never seen an offer before, have your agent explain about agent relationships—the relationship between the buyer and her agent (and the fact that the agent is obligated to look out for the buyer's best interests) and the seller and her agent, along with the other terms you need to be familiar with in the offer. And since the process of putting in and accepting an offer is VERY stressful, she should explain the whole thing to you before you have to do it, so you know what to expect.

Location and price are the two most important factors in home sales. You have to decide where you want to live and how much you're willing to pay. People always have priorities in terms of what they're looking for in a house. They usually write down a wish list. But they often don't have a specific picture of what the house should look like in their mind. That's for the best. Don't get too tied to the things people typically put on their lists: air conditioning, central vacuum, finished basement. You can always add in these extras. Even an open-concept feeling can be created post-purchase. The important things are the things that can't be changed. And these are the things you need to be very clear on when you go house shopping, so that you aren't unduly influenced by the nice-to-haves. The things that can be added or changed then become the conditions, in your own mind, that will affect which house you choose and how much you pay.

Even if you fall in love with the first house you walk into, look at 10 to 12 other houses so you can see what else you can get for the same money. The kitchen in the first house might be the best, but the second house may have a perfectly finished basement. You then have to ask yourself, what's more important, the kitchen or the basement? And what will it cost to remedy what's missing? If it costs twice as much to get the kitchen you want than the basement you want, then buying the perfect kitchen and doing the basement later probably makes the most sense.

Next comes the offer. Now, you might think as a buyer you would be involved in the offer process. Perhaps you've imagined negotiating with the vendor. Even if you expected to be present when the offer was presented, you'd be wrong. Here's how the process works: First, your agent reviews the offer with you, and you sign to make the offer. She then takes that offer to the vendor's agent and the vendor. If there is negotiating to be done, your agent moves between the seller and the buyer. When the vendor accepts the offer, the property is sold except for any outstanding conditions. Assuming all goes well, your agent will have you sign waivers for all the conditions of the offer, and the deal is done.

While getting a mortgage preapproved before house hunting means you can shop with a higher degree of confidence, because you've got your financing lined up, don't waive the financing condition until your financing has been approved by your lender. Sometimes in the heat of the exchange, sellers or real estate professionals suggest that a buyer put in an offer to purchase that is free of conditions, including foregoing the "financing condition." No matter how much you want that property, no matter how sure you are that everything will be fine, don't do it. Preapprovals come with the proviso that they are financing approvals in principal only; they can still be revoked by the lender if they are perceived to be a bad decision—for example, if your circumstances change, or if the house appraisal is lower than the purchase price. And that's why the "conditional on financing" clause is important.

Two other clauses every offer should contain are the "conditional on sale of existing home" clause, if you already own a home, and the "conditional on inspection" clause. The first eliminates the possibility that you'll end up desperate to find a buyer for your old house because it hasn't sold yet and you're carrying two mortgages. Your home may take longer to sell than you anticipated, and if you have to carry two mortgages for three or four months, you'll be motivated to accept less than your home may be worth. The second means you won't end up with a house that is likely to fall down around your ears, because in your desperation to buy THAT house, you ignored the potential problems inspections are designed to ferret out.

Even the closing date—the date you take possession of the property—is something that has to be negotiated. Flexibility is often the key to working this issue out quickly. Sometimes a vendor has no choice on the closing date. Other times, the purchaser is more constrained by time. Some agents believe that if you can give multiple closing dates, you have a better chance in a multiple-offer situation.

What else gives you an edge in the multiple-offer situation? Ultimately, the only way to win this game is to pick the right price. Lots of people say they don't want to get into this situation. In reality, it's not that big a deal. Go with your best shot, and resolve yourself to the outcome. You'll be no further behind than having made no offer at all.

Don't forget about your closing costs. From the home inspection to property tax adjustment, from the appraisal fee to the land transfer tax, every little thing costs. One rule of thumb is to estimate between 1.5% and 2.5% of the value of the home for closing costs to finish off the transaction.

PREPARING FOR THE MORTGAGE INTERVIEW

There's a great deal that goes into being prepared for the mortgage interview. When applying for a mortgage, particularly if you're looking for financing from someone other than your banker, you have to provide specific information about your financial circumstances. Take the following documentation:

- Personal identification, such as your driver's licence or social insurance card. Also bring a list of personal information, including your address, the name of your landlord or present mortgage holder, and the amount you are now paying in rent or for your mortgage.
- A list of all your assets and liabilities, with a realistic value set for each. And bring a list of all your credit cards, as you'll probably be asked for the numbers (to check your credit history).
- Written confirmation of employment income from your employer and confirmation in writing of income from any other sources, showing a consistent amount from year to year. Take your notices of assessment from Canada Revenue Agency (CRA) as proof of your income history.
- For self-employed people, the last three years' income tax returns and/or financial statements.
- A copy of the accepted purchase agreement, along with a statement regarding urea formaldehyde foam insulation (this statement is normally included on the standard offer of purchase forms used by real estate brokers), and a photograph of the house or a copy of the listing.
- Your lawyer's name, full address, and telephone number.

- Who to contact for access to the property for the appraisal (the person's name, full address, and telephone number). This may be the realtor or the vendor.
- Heating cost and property tax estimates (usually found on the listing) and condominium fees, if applicable.
- For properties that do not have municipal services, well and/or septic tank certificates.
- Confirmation of down payment. If it is a gift, you'll need a letter confirming that it is a gift with no repayment. If the down payment is to come from a second mortgage, a written confirmation of the terms and conditions of this mortgage must be provided by the second mortgagor.

CHOOSING A TERM YOU CAN LIVE WITH

Everyone wants to pay the lowest amount of interest they can on their mortgage. If anyone could accurately predict where interest rates were headed, they'd make themselves a fortune. Mortgage rates have been higher than 18% and lower than 2%. That's a big difference. Happily, rates tend not to zoom; they usually click up or slide down based on what's happening in the economy as a whole.

One of the first decisions you'll have to make about your mortgage is what type of mortgage—fixed or variable—to choose, and for how long. Mortgage variations are a little like Baskin-Robbins ice cream flavours: there's something for everyone. You can choose from one-year fixed rates right up to 10-year fixed rates. And then there are variable-rate mortgages that move with the market, so they reflect what's really happening, good or bad. If you choose to go variable, make sure you keep a close eye on the market, so that if rates start to move up, you can lock in.

So how do you decide which mortgage term to take? Ready for a little economics lesson?

If you want to know how to make this decision for yourself, you're going to have to wrap your head around an economic concept called the "yield curve." The yield curve is a graphic representation of the interest rates being paid on government bonds of differing maturities. If the one-year bond is at 5%, the two-year at 6%, the three-year at 7%, and so on, you can see that the longer the term, the higher the interest rate. The yield curve is curving upward from left to right. This is referred to as a normal yield curve because this is the way the curve usually looks. A normal yield curve represents investors' desire to charge more for the use of their money over the long term, because longer-term investments are inherently more risky. To encourage investors to plunk down their money for a longer period of time, a higher interest rate is offered as compensation.

Sometimes yield curves are inverted: the longer-term investments carry a lower interest rate. And sometimes the curve isn't a curve at all; it's flat, but it's still called a flat yield curve. That's when there is virtually no difference between the interest rates right now and those five years from now.

So what can the yield curve tell you about mortgages? Well, if the curve is normal, then the longer-term rates are predicted to be higher than the shorter-term rates. In other words, right now, Them That Knows say that interest rates are going to go up. All you have to do is look at the difference between the one-year and five-year mortgage rates to see where interest rates seem to be going.

If they are, in fact, predicted to go up (I say "predicted" because anything can happen), then the question you have to ask yourself when deciding which term to choose is this: how much will the increase in interest rates affect your ability to make your mortgage payments?

Find a mortgage calculator on the Internet. Put in the mortgage amount and the new higher rate. If you have 10 years to go on your existing mortgage, put that 10 under the amortization period. (Do not use a longer amortization period because you want to see a lower payment. That's delusional.) Look at what the monthly payment amount will be.

Let's take the example of a $350,000 mortgage amortized over 12 years. At your existing rate of 4%, your monthly mortgage payment would be $3,058. But if the one-year rate has jumped to 6%, your payment is $3,402, biting another $344 a month from your cash flow. If the five-year rate is 7.5%, your new monthly mortgage payment will be $3,672, a jump of $622 a month.

Here's the tough part. Now you have to decide: Are you going to take the "risk" of a one-year renewal where rates are lower—knowing there is no security, so rates may go up even further—to keep your increase to only $344? OR, are you going to bite the bullet and take the five-year term, coughing up another $622 a month, so you know where you stand for the next five years? Don't get so focused on trying to get the lowest possible interest rate that you end up compromising your overall financial health and your peace of mind. Ask yourself these next three questions as you're making your decision.

Do You Want a Fixed Payment Amount?

Some people choose a long-term mortgage to ensure they'll have a fixed payment amount they can live with for as long as possible. This makes it much easier to plan for your mortgage payments and everything else in your life—particularly when your cash flow is tight and even a small upward movement in interest rates would be disastrous.

Are You a Gambler?

Some people don't mind the stomach turning associated with fluctuations in rates. Others can't stand the stress. If you're not comfortable with the game, pick a payment amount you can live with and lock in.

Are You Prepared to Keep a Close Eye on the Market?

If you're going to choose a short-term, open, variable-rate or convertible mortgage, then be prepared to keep a careful watch on what interest rates are doing, so you can lock in when rates bottom out. If you're not prepared to do this, go with a mid- to long-term rate.

If you're mature enough to buy a house, you're mature

enough to decide your own term. Do the math, take your stress levels into account, and then decide what you're going to do. Make sure you negotiate hard for the best rate going. Just because the mortgage rate is posted at 5.5% doesn't mean that's what YOU have to pay. Lenders routinely discount their posted rate for customers who have shown they are trustworthy. If you've been a good borrower, then now's the time to use it to your advantage.

MANAGING YOUR MORTGAGE

Having decided on the amortization that will give you the payment amount you want, now it's time to think about what will happen if rates go up or down when it comes time to renew your term. Since the "up" is the one we all hate, let's look at it first.

If rates go up, you have two choices. First, you can work the increased payment amount into your spending plan. Second, you can increase your amortization to bring your payment amount back down. That may mean moving your mortgage to another financial institution, so be prepared for the cost of writing a new mortgage.

If rates go down, you could benefit from a lower payment amount. But think about this for a minute. You've already worked the payment into your budget. If you keep your payment amount the same, you'll be paying off your mortgage a lot faster because you'll be putting that extra cash against your principal. So, don't pocket the difference. Keep applying it to your mortgage.

One final point on managing your mortgage: rather than

locking yourself into a high payment amount that you have to struggle to make each month, do yourself a favour—choose a payment amount you find easier to live with. Then make sure you have prepayment options that allow you to make additional payments against your mortgage when you have the cash available. That way you'll have a payment amount you can manage comfortably, and you can still aggressively pay down your mortgage.

PAYMENT FREQUENCIES

Financial institutions offer a variety of payment frequencies so that you can choose when and how often you wish to make your regular payments. The traditional option is the monthly payment. If you're paid semi-monthly, biweekly, or weekly, you may wish to use a payment frequency that matches your cash flow.

Want to save on interest? Use a faster-pay or accelerated frequency. With this option, you make extra payments against your mortgage, but you do so in such small amounts that those extra payments fit easily into your cash flow. With accelerated payments, you make the equivalent of 13 monthly payments instead of 12. That extra payment reduces your principal, so you save big on your interest costs in the long term. On a $200,000 mortgage amortized for 25 years at 5.5%, using an accelerated weekly payment will save you $30,000 in interest and have you celebrating in just over 21 years. And since that extra payment is spread over the whole year, your cash flow barely feels the pinch, because it'll cost you only $23.48 more a week. Hey, you can find $23.48 a week to save over $30,000 in interest, can't you?

Many financial institutions allow you to change your payment frequency as your needs change. Be aware that there may be an interest adjustment from your current payment due date to the revised date.

MAKING EXTRA PAYMENTS AGAINST YOUR PRINCIPAL

The best way to pay your mortgage off fast is to pour any extra money you have into the mortgage whenever you can. This is one area in which all mortgages are not created equal. While some banks offer very flexible options, others still think you should fit with their schedules. If extra payments are a priority for you, shop carefully for the mortgage that offers you the level of flexibility you're looking for.

Some institutions let you make an additional payment every year. Some let you increase your monthly payment up to double the original amount. Almost every lender lets you make a lump-sum payment of 10% to 20% of your original principal once a year. While some institutions want it on your anniversary date, others will let you do it on any payment date.

Put one extra $1,000 prepayment against your mortgage principal, and over the life of a $100,000 mortgage, you'll save $4,000 in interest. Do it every year and you're in the money to the tune of almost $29,000.

BALANCING PAYING DOWN YOUR MORTGAGE WITH OTHER GOALS

Did you know that 58% of Canadians with a mortgage don't have a retirement plan? It seems that once that mortgage note is signed, getting rid of what can be the single largest debt we ever take on becomes of paramount importance. But the building of retirement assets is just as important as getting rid of that mortgage. It all comes down to time. The longer you have your mortgage, the more interest you'll pay. And the earlier you begin saving for retirement, the more money you'll have accumulated through tax-deferred compound growth.

There are other parts of your financial life that also need to be managed. In coming up with a down payment for a home, many people tap all their available resources. They even dip into their emergency fund (if they have one at all) to minimize the amount of mortgage they have to take or to qualify. But an emergency fund is an important part of being financially healthy; without one, you leave yourself open to all sorts of dire consequences. Doing anything to the exclusion of everything else is not healthy. You need an emergency fund for the near future. And you need to sock away money regularly for your long-term needs. If you're asking yourself whether you should contribute to a retirement plan or pay down your mortgage, here are some factors to consider:

If your income is particularly high one year, then your marginal tax rate will also be high, and a contribution to a retirement plan may significantly reduce your tax liability. But if your income is low one year, the tax savings from a small contribution limit and lower marginal tax rate might be outweighed by the interest savings from paying down your mortgage.

The further you are from retirement, the more valuable contributions to a retirement plan are, since the money has a longer period to benefit from compounding. The closer retirement is, the less impact a retirement plan contribution will have in terms of compounding and the more important it is to get rid of your debt.

The amount of time left on your mortgage amortization schedule is also important. The faster you repay your principal, the more interest you save in the long run. So, you'll save more interest by paying down a mortgage with a 20-year amortization remaining than one with a 5-year amortization remaining.

Avoid falling into the retirement savings carry-forward trap. Just because they can carry forward their unused contribution room for use in later years, some chicks believe this strategy is the right one. But delaying contributions means less compounded return. A $5,000 contribution delayed for just five years will cost your retirement plan over $16,000, assuming a rate of return of just 8%. So think carefully about delaying.

The answer to the question of whether to contribute to your retirement plan or pay down a mortgage does not have to be either/or. *Why not make your maximum RRSP contribution and then use the proceeds from your tax refund to pay down your mortgage?* Let's say you decided to contribute $3,000 a year to your retirement plan, and your marginal tax rate is 30%. You should see a tax savings of $900. Apply that refund against your $200,000 mortgage (with an interest rate of 5.5% amortized over 25 years), and you will save over $22,500 in interest and have your mortgage paid off in 22 years instead of 25. If your $250 monthly RRSP contribution grows at a rate of 5% on average, in 35 years, you'll build up over $280,000 in retirement savings.

This strategy lets you save for retirement and secure your future, earn tax-sheltered income, reduce the amount of current income tax paid, reduce the amount of interest to be paid on the mortgage, and shorten the amortization term. Use an online calculator to see how much you will save by applying your tax refund as a payment against your mortgage principal. It makes a lot more sense to work towards both objectives than to grapple with the issue of which should be a priority. With the right balance, you can have it all!

Buying your first home can be a thrilling and somewhat scary experience. Be careful not to overextend yourself when it comes to picking your home's price range. It's easy for the home-buying process to suck you in. Just add another $30,000 to your price range and your neighbourhood options become so much wider. Another $30,000 and you'll be looking at houses with finished basements, renovated kitchens, or landscaped yards. But if at the end of the day, you've added so much to your price range that you're house poor, you'll end up foregoing annual vacations, entertainment, and the other good things in life. Or you'll start using your line of credit or your credit cards to make ends meet. Dumb! Stay balanced and focused on what you can afford, so you stay healthy financially.

Being realistic about how much you can really afford is particularly important during periods of low interest rates. Tempted by manageable mortgage payments, buyers often push the envelope on the house price. Later, when interest rates rise—what goes down must eventually go up—they find their cash flow strapped, sometimes to the point where they must sell their homes because they can no longer afford to keep up with the mortgage payments.

Buying a home is a complex process. Don't rush into it, and don't rush through it. You'll likely have to live with your decision for a long, long time. Talk to some friends and family who have bought recently, and try to get a feel for the process. Pay attention to the details. And ask lots of questions. The more you know, the better homebuyer you'll be.

UPGRADING

If you're considering upgrading to a new house, you're also probably considering one or more of the following questions:

- Can I get the same great rate on my new mortgage as I have on my existing mortgage?
- Should I discharge the mortgage and take out a new mortgage? What will that cost me in penalty interest?
- Should I let the purchaser assume the mortgage and take out a new mortgage on the new house?

If you decide you want to take your mortgage with you when you move, then it's time to learn all about the portability option on your mortgage. By "porting" your mortgage, you can continue taking advantage of your existing mortgage rate. If you find you need additional financing, you can blend your existing mortgage with a new one, eliminating the need for a much costlier second mortgage.

The biggest benefit of porting your mortgage is that it eliminates the interest penalties that apply to an early discharge of an existing mortgage. This can mean major savings, particularly when the interest rate on your existing mortgage is lower than the rate currently available for a new mortgage.

You can port your mortgage in one of three ways:

1. If you're taking your remaining mortgage term, interest rate, and principal balance to your new property without increasing or decreasing the principal, that's called a straight port.

2. If you're downgrading to a less expensive home, you'll be interested in porting and decreasing. The mortgage is ported, but the principal is reduced. A penalty for lost interest, also referred to as an interest rate differential, or IRD, may be payable when a smaller loan amount is requested.

3. If you're upgrading and need more financing on your new home than originally existed on the home being sold, then you'll port and increase. The mortgage is ported, the principal is increased, and your interest rate is blended so that you still have the advantage of the original rate on at least a portion of the mortgage.

If you plan to port, you and the new property will still have to meet normal lending guidelines, so a full mortgage application and property appraisal will be done. And you can only execute your portability option if your existing mortgage is in good standing. Since a new mortgage document must be drawn and registered on title, expect normal appraisal and legal fees.

SETTING THE PRICE ON YOUR EXISTING HOME

Once you decide to put your house on the market, one of the first things you'll have to think about is where you'll set your asking price. This is probably the most crucial issue when it comes to listing your home. You should have a financial strategy to offset the emotion that accompanies selling a home. Price is the primary motivation for long hours of negotiation, signbacks, and the eventual decision to buy or not to buy.

Home prices soar and plummet on all sorts of factors, including inflation, where interest rates are and where they are going, and demand and supply. Buyers always want to know if the market has reached the bottom. Sellers want to know if prices are going up.

So where do you start if you're planning to sell your home and have to set a price? Begin by checking the market value of your property. Ask at least two real estate agents for appraisals. Check the listings for prices of homes in your area that fit the description of your home. Carefully assess how market conditions have changed in the last six months and how that may affect your asking price. Are interest rates rising or falling? Is it a buyer's or a seller's market? Then set your price within 3% to 5% of the average price you've come up with. If the market indicates that your home is worth about $189,000, set your price no higher than about $198,450. Of course, you could set your price at the bottom end of the scale—$179,500—if you want to get lots of offers and close quickly. You might even benefit from a bidding war that drives up the price slightly.

If you set your price high because you *feel* your house is worth more, don't be surprised if it takes a while for an offer to come in—or if you then have to drop your price once, twice, or several times to interest buyers. Don't be insulted by low-ball offers. And don't think that just because you need the money to get you into a more expensive home that buyers will be willing to fund your dreams. In a buyer's market—one where buyers set the tone for sales because there are fewer of them—buyers are much more likely to win in negotiations because there's so much available in the market, and they usually have time on their side. In a seller's market—one where sellers write the ticket and buyers often bid it up—buyers will go to great lengths to make their offers attractive.

Setting the right price may just be the most important aspect of selling your home. With the ideal location, the perfect features, and the home in tip-top condition, the price still has to be right for buyers to bite. And since most purchasers already have a price in mind when they set about house hunting, pricing too high could take your home right out of their "viewing" range. Also keep in mind that the right price means your house will spend less time on the market, so you'll have to spend less time keeping it in "show" condition. Setting a reasonable price that makes potential buyers want to venture into your home will, over the long run, save you money, disappointment, and time.

9

SET UP A PAY-YOURSELF-FIRST INVESTMENT PLAN

The single best investment you'll ever make is in yourself. It doesn't matter how much money you make in your lifetime, how much stuff you accumulate, or how rich you *feel*, if you don't have some money put away for the future, you'll be up the creek without a paddle sooner or later. That's where the pay-yourself-first investment plan comes in.

When I talk about a pay-yourself-first investment plan, I'm talking about taking money out of your cash flow (savings) and putting it somewhere it can work for you (investing). This isn't new money that you have to find. This is the money you've allocated in your spending plan to savings. Now you're going to put that money to work to earn a return.

Just because the financial press focuses on mutual funds, the stock market, and indexed investing, doesn't mean you must. Anything that earns you a return on your money is an investment. It can be Canada Savings Bonds. It can be GICs. It can be individual stocks or bonds. *It has to be something you are knowledgeable about and comfortable with.* And it has to suit YOU.

One of the biggest complaints I hear about the world of investing is that the jargon is stifling. Strips aren't malls. Convertibles aren't cars. TIGRs aren't wild animals.

$ Gail's Tips: Some of these acronyms, like GICs (Guaranteed Investment Certificates) and DRIPs (Dividend Reinvestment Plans), have become pretty well known, so most people aren't baffled by them. Others, like ADRs (American Depositary Receipts), PEACs (Payment-Enhanced Capital Security), and SPECs (Special Capital Gains Security), are still used only within the industry and are sure to boggle the minds of those less familiar with them. And new acronyms are coming along all the time as new investment alternatives are created. Do you know what a BOOM is? How about WEBS, RTUs, or REITs? Take heart. Even the people closest to the products find it hard to keep up sometimes. That's one of the reasons you may need a really good investment person by your side as you wade through the jargon and the proliferation of options available for investing your money.

To understand even the basics, you must take responsibility for educating yourself. This is one of my biggies when it comes to taking control of your financial life. If you don't know what you're doing, the answer isn't to do nothing—or worse still, to give the control to someone else. The answer is to find out, get educated, read and learn, and then read and learn some more. You can't expect someone else to take as good care of your money as you would yourself. And you can't blame someone else when your investments go awry. *It's your money, so it's your job.*

There are lots of good books you can use to begin your education. And there are also good people out there who are willing to help you with your money. Your job is to find someone who brings the experience and expertise, kindness and care, thoughtfulness and thoroughness you need to the client-advisor equation. Thankfully, there are also many investment options that are not complicated. So if you show a little interest and invest a little time in them, you can get a handle on them quite easily.

There's absolutely nothing wrong with starting out with the safe, tried-and-true, and well-understood investments that you're familiar with. But don't stop there. Branch out. Ask tons of questions of your banker, broker, personal advisor, father, daughter, or anyone who can give you more information and help you spread your investment wings. In this respect, women have it over men hands down. We're more willing to ask for advice. We're more willing to question, to think about how we feel about something, and to want to know more.

RETIRE RICHER SOONER PLAN (RRSP)

One of the best vehicles for long-term saving is a Registered Retirement Savings Plan (RRSP). An RRSP is a tax-deferral plan registered with the Tax Man. With an RRSP, you can contribute a portion of your earned income and claim the contribution as a tax deduction. The income generated by the investments inside an RRSP is not taxed until its withdrawn from the plan, so you can accumulate a much larger pool of money for retirement than you could by investing outside an RRSP.

Between the tax-deferred compounding return and the tax deferral on the contribution (often referred to as your tax refund), an RRSP puts your savings way ahead of the game. And you can use your tax refund to help supplement the growth of your annual contribution. Let's say you can afford to save $100 a month in an RRSP. Go ahead, put it away. At the end of your first year, you'll have contributed $1,200. Assuming a marginal tax rate of 30%, you could receive a tax refund of $360. When you get your tax refund, stick it in the RRSP for next year. At the end of next year, you'll have contributed $1,560 (your $1,200 plus the $360 refund you received). Assuming your tax rate hasn't increased, you could get a refund of $468. Roll that into an RRSP, and in year three, your refund will be $500.40 [($1,200 + $468) x 30%]. Now all you have to do is keep it going, girl!

Having decided to take the plunge into investing, you may not be sure where to start. You have to figure out why you're investing: that is, your purpose.

PURPOSE

Ask yourself, "What am I saving this money for?" Are you planning a holiday, planning to take time off work for school or to raise your family, or planning to make sure you have money for retirement? People often say one thing but do another. Take the example of Alison, who religiously put money into her RRSP every year because she said she was planning for her long-term future. But each time Alison had an emergency, the first place she turned was to her RRSP. Out came some cash. So Alison wasn't using the RRSP as she claimed—as long-term savings for the future. Instead, she was using her RRSP as an emergency fund. Alison told me how frustrated she was that no matter how hard she saved, and how diligent she was, her long-term savings weren't growing fast enough. She figured she was investing in the wrong things. She needed to be more aggressive, to take more chances.

I asked her to show me her statements for the previous six years. There, in black and white, were all those small cash withdrawals Alison had made. The problem wasn't what Alison was investing in; the problem was that she wasn't leaving the money invested at all. She kept dipping in. She hadn't firmly decided her purpose before deciding to invest in an RRSP.

To rectify the problem, I suggested that Alison put half her normal contribution into her RRSP and contribute the other half to an emergency fund. Now Alison has an emergency fund that she keeps at about $3,500 (less than recommended, but in keeping with her personal money set-point), and she is back to making full contributions to her retirement plan.

Interestingly, since she established her emergency fund, Alison hasn't dipped into her RRSP once.

When you're establishing your investment purpose, ask yourself, "Is this money touchable or untouchable?" This goes back in part to the purpose of the money (as in Alison's case). The answer to this question will depend on your personality. Let's take saving for a child's education as an example. Some people may say it's touchable—they can tap it if they need extra money—while other say it's not. Be honest with yourself.

TIME HORIZON

A time frame is also very important. If you're saving for a child's post-secondary education, whether your child is two or 12 will have an impact on the investments you choose. The longer you have until you will need to use the money, the longer your time horizon. That means the more time your investment has to even out its return, so you can withstand a higher level of volatility . . . the ups and downs in value some investments experience. *You must match your time horizon to the investment you are choosing.*

What does the time horizon of your investment have to do with what investment you choose? GICs have no volatility, and the return is guaranteed. You can't lose your principal, and you know exactly what you'll earn in interest on the day your GIC matures. The same holds true for a bond or mortgage investment if you hold them to maturity. So it doesn't matter whether you go long or short, you're guaranteed your return as long as you hold the investment until the end of the term you choose. Equity mutual funds and direct investment in equities are a whole different kettle of fish. They can be quite volatile, with some offering more price stability and others offering more opportunity for growth. Either way, they don't work as short- or medium-term investments, since they may be at a low just when you need the money and must sell. They work as long-term investments, because you have time to ride out the highs and lows and average out your return.

Less than five years is considered a *short-term* investment horizon. Five to 10 years is considered *medium term.* Beyond 10 years is considered *long term.*

Short-term investors should avoid putting the majority of their money in equity investments, because the risk of losing that money is greater. A better idea is choosing fixed-income investments that generate a steady return while offering a higher level of security. Long-term investors have the luxury of time and can, therefore, choose an asset mix that is weighted more heavily with stocks and stock-based mutual funds. They have the time to ride out the natural volatility associated with the equities market. If you're a medium-term investor, you must balance your need for the money with your willingness to put off selling if the time's not right. Having money in fixed-term investments means you can redeem those first, buying you some time on any equities you may have bought.

Since no single investment offers the perfect opportunity for the highest return, full liquidity, most security, greatest tax advantages, income generation, and convenience, keep your specific goals and investment objectives clearly in mind. As you get older, or as your personal circumstances or economic conditions change, and as your investment horizon shortens, you'll need to rebalance your portfolio's asset mix.

The proviso to all this is that you have to buy investments with which you're comfortable. You may have a long-term investment horizon, but if you're uncomfortable with the thought of your investment fluctuating in value, you may not be an equity investor.

THE RELATIONSHIP BETWEEN RISK AND RETURN

I'm often asked to recommend investments. (I never do this because there is no way to follow up when the person's circumstances change.) The request is always for something that pays a huge return with no risk. Wouldn't that be nice!

There is an old investment saying, "The greater the risk, the higher the potential return; the lower the risk, the lower the potential return." There is no such thing as "no risk." And the more return you expect to earn, the higher the level of risk you must be willing to accept. Nothing in the investment world is risk-free. It's really all a matter of degree.

Understanding risks and being able to come to terms with them will take you a long way towards being a smart investor. Here are some of the risks associated with some pretty traditional investments.

Stocks and equity-based investments can be volatile. *Volatility* is the investment's penchant for fluctuating in value over the short term. High-flying equity investments are typically associated with volatility, though you may be surprised at where volatility raises its ugly head. Industry-specific mutual funds, such as mining or technology, or funds that invest in small-capitalization companies (companies that aren't worth a bazillion dollars yet) can be very volatile. And even bonds can be volatile investments if you're trading them and interest rates start to swing up and down.

All equity investments have some capital risk associated with them. *Capital risk* is the potential for losing some or all of the original money you invested.

GICs and other fixed-income investments, such as bonds and mortgages, seem relatively risk-free, right? Think again. Interest-bearing investments suffer *interest-rate risk.* One such risk is that interest rates will rise and you will be locked in to a lower rate (or that you'll have to sell your bond at a capital loss). Another is that if you've invested at a high rate, interest rates may be significantly lower when it comes time to renew.

Well, at least there's your risk-free savings account, right? Wrong again! If your investment's rate of return is at the same as or lower than the current rate of inflation, this is called *inflation risk,* and the end result is that your investment will lose value year after year. Your money will be worth less.

Everyone measures risk differently, since it is relative to our personal circumstances. While one woman may think investing $5,000 in a stock is an okay thing to do, another may balk. If $5,000 represents the second woman's total savings, or if it represents a substantial part of her annual disposable income, she will be less willing to throw caution to the wind. On the other hand, if that $5,000 represents only 5% of an overall investment portfolio, the risks can seem a lot less life-changing.

When a loss would be deeply felt financially, the level of risk is much higher. Interestingly, however, the sense of risk decreases as the pot grows bigger and the odds improve. Would you invest $50 if you had the chance of winning $5,000? What about if the jackpot was $500,000? Or $5,000,000? See what I mean. The bigger the pot, the more willing most people are to take the shot. Now, what about the odds. Would you invest $50 to win $5,000,000 if your odds were 100 to 1? If your odds were 10 to 1? What about 2 to 1? Most people would have no problem investing $50 for a 2-in-1 chance of winning $5,000,000. What would you do?

It's human nature to measure risk against the opportunity to win. The bigger the risk or the potential downside, the bigger the opportunity for a higher return, which is what we need to persuade us to go for the gusto. But risk has another face that is seldom clearly seen or well-understood. What's the risk to you personally in not taking any chances, in always playing it safe? What's the risk in being so conservative that you end up losing ground year after year in terms of the real value of your money? The answer is entirely personal, so once you decide your purpose—What am I trying to achieve here? What is my goal?—then it's a matter of doing a risk profile. You have to find a profile that's comprehensive. Those quickie, four-question versions banks love to use to cover their butts in terms of "knowing their clients" don't do you any favours in terms of helping you to better understand yourself. After all, if a financial service's profiler tells you that you're growth-oriented and quite aggressive, you believe it, right? You want to believe. But what happens when you're challenged by a slip-sliding market or a change in personal circumstances? If you don't have confidence in the risk-profiling exercise you went through, you won't stay the course. You'll do exactly the wrong thing at the wrong time. You'll panic and you'll bail. If you're comfortable with your risk-profiling, you don't even look at the market. You're comfortable with your choices. Find a risk profile that takes you the extra step so that you are completely comfortable. (There's one in my book *Never Too Late* that'll really put you through your paces.)

$ *Gail's Tips:* Remember that everyone is a "person" first—even advisors. While we believe that those who we think of as being better educated, more in-tune, or anaesthetized to the volatility of the market should know better, they are people first and, therefore, they act emotionally. I remember speaking with an investment advisor once about how gold was doing. "It's in the toilet," she replied. I suggested that meant it was a good time to buy. (Remember the old adage, "Buy low, sell high"?) Her response, "But it's in the toilet." She couldn't get past her own personal bias—her emotional baggage—to look at the opportunity a low gold price offered.

DIVERSIFICATION

The key to building a healthy investment portfolio—one that gives a good return while minimizing risk—is *diversification*, which is a little of this and a little of that. Some stocks, some bonds, and some GICs. A touch of foreign investment and a little tucked away in a money market fund where it is easily accessible. By hedging your bets, you'll protect yourself from negative swings in any one type of investment. When the stock market dumps and bonds glow, your bond portfolio will pull you along. When bonds dive and the stock market soars, your equity investments will save the day. And when Canada spirals downwards while Europe, South America, or Asia skyrocket, you'll have enough invested internationally to keep your return balanced.

Whether you call it "asset mix," "investment mix," or "asset allocation," it's the same thing. It means dividing your money among a variety of investments, and it's what you do to diversify. Asset mix usually falls into one of three groups: conservative, balanced, or growth-oriented. But within each of those groups, there are many subgroups defined by very subjective criteria.

To illustrate my point: I consider myself to be fairly conservative. I'm more likely to buy blue-chip stocks (shares in a large company that's consistent in its profits) or a large-cap mutual fund (read "has a high capitalization ... or lots 'n' lotsa money") than an investment that focuses on emerging industries. Yet, if you put me beside a woman who wouldn't dream of investing in anything but GICs, I look pretty risk tolerant.

Stick me beside someone who considers herself to be some-what conservative but who believes small-cap U.S. stocks are the way to go, and you have to ask, "What does conservative actually mean?"

It's also interesting that men and women do not benefit from the same asset allocation models in the same ways. While these models typically lump men and women together, our needs are different, so our models should also be different. Women are more at risk of becoming the principal providers of elder care and child care; women live longer on a fixed income during retirement, and we have not historically had the income expectations of our male counterparts, so we *must* be more growth-oriented right off the bat. And we have to maintain a growth orientation for as long as possible. Equally as important is that we continue to save throughout our lives, using new savings to re-balance our asset allocation as we age.

If you want a diversified investment portfolio, spread your investment dollars over more than one type of investment. One misconception is that if you buy stock in several different companies, you will be automatically well-diversified. That ain't necessarily so. To effectively diversify, not only do you have to buy stocks of different companies, those companies should be in different industries and in different countries. Here are five factors to consider when diversifying a portfolio:

1. *Type of investment.* You can buy bonds, deposits, stocks, mutual funds, or real estate.
2. *Quality of investments.* The lower the quality, the higher the return offered to offset the higher potential for loss.

3. *Region.* Buy in Canada, North America, and globally.
4. *Currency.*
5. *Level of liquidity.* Hold some long-term deposits, such as stripped bonds or equity funds, along with some shorter-term investments, such as Treasury bills.

The asset mix you choose will have a direct impact on the return you earn on your portfolio. The more risk you are willing to take, the more return your portfolio may generate. A typical conservative investment portfolio might hold 20% in cash; 60% in fixed-income investments, such as bonds or mortgages; and 20% in equities. It's a portfolio that is more interested in capital preservation and income than it is in growth. A balanced portfolio would hold 10% in cash, and 45% each in fixed-income and equity investments. Investors who want both income and growth, and who split their portfolios 50–50, have a balanced asset mix. A typical growth portfolio would hold 10% in cash, 30% in fixed-income investments, and 60% in equities. Investors who hold these portfolios are not as interested in generating income and are willing to risk far more in capital to potentially earn a much higher return.

Of course, there are some who choose to stay at the bottom of the scale, never venturing into alternatives such as individual corporate bonds or equity mutual funds. If you're one of these people, and you're doing it for the right reason— you have no stomach for volatility or for the potential capital loss, or you have a short investment time horizon—then you should stay just where you are. Most tools for risk-profiling will emphasize the need for you to diversify, but there are always investors who need GICs because they just don't have the stomach for anything else. For them, the risk that their return may be less than needed is a risk they can bear. What they can't stand is the idea of losing any of their hard-earned money. Remember: know your purpose in investing, understand your commitment to your purpose, know your time horizon, and perhaps most importantly, know yourself (your investment personality).

After a media blitz during one RRSP season, I received a call from a woman who wanted some advice. She had seen me on television when I had been answering caller questions about mutual funds. She thought I was down-to-earth and wanted the real poop on mutual funds. "Should I be investing in mutual funds?" she asked.

"Tell me about your situation," I responded.

"I'm retired," she said, "and living on a fixed income. I have no dependants, no family at all. I'm getting about 2.5% on my money right now, and I'm not very happy with that."

"How much do you have to invest?"

"$400,000."

Wow, I thought. "How much are you falling short in terms of meeting your day-to-day needs?"

"Oh, I'm all right," she said. "I'd like more of a cushion, but I'm not touching my capital."

Again, wow. "Have you ever invested in mutual funds before?" I asked.

"No," she said.

"Why do you want to invest in mutual funds?" I asked.

"My friends are all into mutual funds. They think I'm stupid to be stuck in GICs at 2.5% when they're getting 15% or 20% in mutual funds. And my insurance advisor says that he can double my money in six years. He's recommending mutual funds really strongly. But I'm not sure about this at all. I need some help. Will you tell me what to do?"

"How old are you?" I asked.

"Eighty-seven," she replied.

I was stunned. She was 87 with $400,000 in capital and enough income to meet her everyday needs. Before I even realized what I had said, I asked, "And how rich do you want to be when you die?"

She laughed. "I knew you'd cut right to the quick," she said. "I guess I shouldn't bother with the mutual funds."

There are a few interesting things about this conversation. First, she was thinking about investing in mutual funds without knowing what they are or how they work. Like her, there are a lot of people who don't understand the basic premise of investing or the various types of investments. They don't understand how changes in market or economic conditions will affect those investments. They do know the results can be spectacular. They do know their brother, cousin, best friend, and next-door neighbours are buying them. They don't know that some of these people have no idea what they are doing. The result is that many people rush into investments and then rush out when the investment doesn't perform to their expectations.

People are always questioning whether they should change how they're investing because someone comes along and tells them they're doing it wrong. If you want to be able to sleep at night, and if you want your investments to work for YOU, you need to ignore all the blah-blah-blah you hear around you and stick with the plan you developed. Never mind what the media, the experts, or your cousin Larry is saying. Make a plan, execute it, and then stay the course. Chasing returns without taking into account the risks is dumb. So is blowing money just because you're trying to keep up with the Buffets. You've got to do what's right for you.

MY DOZEN GOLDEN RULES OF INVESTING

1. Know What You're Investing In

I can't stress this first point enough. There are hundreds of investment options from which you can choose when starting an investment portfolio. If you want to expand your investment repertoire, be sure that you learn all about the alternatives you're interested in before you buy them. Invest your time before you invest your money, and you're more likely to be successful.

2. Know Yourself

You want to be able to buy the right types of investments for your specific needs, so you must also understand your personal comfort level with regard to risk and volatility. If you don't know who you are, the stock market can be an expensive place to find out!

3. What You Don't Know Can Be Just as Important as What You Do Know

One of the biggest mistakes we make in choosing investments is that we base our decisions on too few facts. We assume that what we do not know is unimportant. But how do you know what you don't know? That's the Catch-22 most investors face when they are entering a new investment arena. The answer is simple: ask tons of questions and read masses of information. Investing isn't the breeze most people would like to believe it is. If it were that easy, all the people working in the investment world would be stinking rich and living in Bora-Bora.

4. Accept Responsibility for Your Decisions

If you can't live with a trade gone bad, don't make it. You can't expect other people to take care of your money as well as you would. Remember, it's your money. And you shouldn't blame others for decisions you make—because ultimately, they are your decisions. So make this rule the cornerstone of your relationship with all your advisors.

5. Have a Plan

It's surprising how many people invest by the seat of their pants. Perhaps they rely on a broker's advice. Maybe they follow the financial press and buy what's hot. Unfortunately, without a specific plan, many people may find themselves playing it safe or putting too much money in high-risk investments. Without a specific plan, achieving any goal at all is a hit-or-miss proposition.

You don't have to be a financial whiz to develop a plan. Take a good look at what your priorities are, and then make some decisions about what you'll have to do to meet those priorities. If you don't have gobs of money to invest, a plan is even more important.

Planning begins with setting some goals. Do *you* have a written set of goals for your investment portfolio? If you don't, you should. Once you've set your goals, the next step is to develop an action plan to meet those goals.

6. Invest Monthly

It's much easier to find $100 a month than it is to find $1,200 all at once. If you want to put $6,000 in an RRSP, instead of borrowing from the bank because you just couldn't save it all up—and then paying it back monthly with interest—pay yourself first. Open up a periodic investment plan and slide away $500 a month. Don't wait to save up "a decent amount" before you jump in and *Do It!* Most monthly investment programs will allow you to contribute as little as $25 a month.

7. Make Sure Your Objectives Are Realistic

There's a great saying on Wall Street: both bulls and bears can make money in the market, but hogs get slaughtered. People get excited when they see returns of 18%, 24%, or 36%. And the media love to highlight the big winners. But expecting to achieve those kinds of returns year after year is unrealistic. If you aim too high, you'll never be satisfied with your return. Part of making peace with money involves setting realistic, attainable objectives so that you can pat yourself on the back. If you're a conservative investor, a realistic objective is to earn an average of about 7% over the long term. That's not 7% every year—it's an average return of 7%. If you beat yourself up over a bad couple of years, or raise your expectations after a couple of stellar years, you're not being realistic. If you're a balanced investor, you can add two points: you're aiming for about 9%. If you're growth-oriented, you might aim as high as 12%.

Investing is hard work. To be good at it, you have to learn a lot of stuff, keep up-to-date with changes in products and economic trends, and have a strategy. By working hard, anyone can become relatively good at investing. By setting realistic objectives, anyone can feel good about investing. Remember, balance is the key to achieving financial freedom.

8. Don't Do It Just Because Everyone Else Says You Should

Another interesting aspect of the conversation I had with that elderly caller (remember the 87-year-old with $400,000 in capital and no dependants?) was that she was sufficiently swayed by her friends' ragging to be inquiring about mutual funds. If everyone else claims to be getting 12%, 15%, or 20%, how stupid are you for earning only 4%? Add the fact that every single financial advisor in the world seems to be saying that GICs have little or no place in your investment portfolio, and that GICs are archaic, GICs are sluggish. They claim that you'll fall behind inflation with GICs when what you need is growth, growth, growth!

If you follow the herd, you're sure to step in a lot of cow pies. If you make an investment simply because it seems like the right thing to do, you're making the wrong decision. If you make an investment just because people say you should, you're making the wrong decision. If you ask plenty of questions and listen carefully to the answers, understand the investment well, understand your priorities and weigh them carefully against the information you're getting, and make a decision that fits with your overall strategy, chances are you'll make the right decision.

9. Don't Try to Time the Market

Yes, there can be a right and a wrong time to buy most types of investments. Buying equity-based investments after the market has been steadily rising for some time may not be prudent. Similarly, when interest rates are poised to go up, that's not the time to buy bonds. But market timing is a risky business and far too sophisticated and time-consuming for us regular folk. Far better you invest regularly and average out the market swings. You can do that by dollar-cost averaging.

Dollar-cost averaging is a complex name for a simple investment technique. Rather than accumulating a large sum of money before making an investment, you invest small amounts at regular intervals. Dollar-cost averaging means you don't have to worry about investing at the right time. However, for it to work effectively, you should use it as a long-term strategy—and stick with it! Don't let market performance shake your trust. It's a great system.

10. Diversify

Don't put all your eggs in one basket. How sick are you of this saying? But it's true. If you spread the money around, you don't have to worry about losing it all in one fell swoop. By purchasing several different investments, you can build a well-diversified portfolio to reduce your exposure to investment risk—if one investment doesn't do particularly well, the others may make up the difference.

11. Stay the Course

If you find you are a little shy of the stock market, or you rank as a conservative investor, but you decide to go into the market anyway, get yourself a knowledgeable buddy (preferably a financial advisor) who can hold your hand through the rough spots. You want someone who will remind you of your initial objectives and reassure you of what is happening, so you don't make the fatal leap out of the market at just the wrong time.

And now, for the final and most important of my Golden Rules of Investing . . . wait for the drumroll . . .

12. Keep a Level Head

It's easy to get carried away, to forget the plan, to launch into an investment you don't really understand because someone else has made a killing. And it's easy to get scared, to want to run when everything seems to be turned the wrong way. It's good to keep reminding ourselves that the things we feel aren't real; they are just feelings. If you think your plan has gone askew, then sit down and review it logically. If you wish you were doing a little better, look at investments that might get you there: learn all about them, know the upsides and the downsides, and then make a level-headed decision.

10

MANAGE LIFE'S RISKS WITH INSURANCE

Part of the peace of mind that comes with being financially healthy involves preparing for the risks of everyday life. The ones we seem to deal with quite easily are the risks addressed by property insurance, car insurance, and contents insurance. The risks we tend to overlook are those associated with our earning power. If you or your partner were to die or become disabled and unable to work, would your family have the resources to meet their day-to-day needs? It's a tough question to face, but the consequences of not facing it can be even tougher.

Whether you're looking at disability insurance or life insurance, *what you are buying is a replacement for an income that's disappeared.* While your emergency fund will replace your income for the first six months, past that point, you'll need some other way to support yourself and your family. Insurance shifts the risk off your shoulders, and you pay a premium for that.

If you have no form of income-replacement insurance, you're betting that you'll just keep on chugging until you retire. Here's a scary stat: if you're 30 years old, there's a 23% chance that you'll die before you reach age 65. And there's a 52% chance that you'll be disabled for 90 days or more.

Unfortunately, people seem to be completely unaware of the impact of not having coverage, the right coverage, or enough coverage. When you compare the media exposure investments get, or the deluge of promotion that accompanies the RRSP season, life, disability, and critical illness insurance are pathetically underrepresented. One reason may be people's unwillingness to look at the potential downsides of life. This can't happen to me, right? Yet I know six women who are about my age who have been diagnosed with debilitating diseases such as multiple sclerosis and lupus. The phenomenal performance of the stock market, the growth of a retirement plan—these are happy stories. Thinking about getting sick or dying is a bummer—so we don't do it. But we should. It's part of our responsibility to those we love, and it's crucial to our own healthy financial life.

Think of insurance as protection against the financial loss resulting from an event that may not have a high probability of occurring, but if it did happen, it would be so devastating financially that it would be almost impossible to recover.

Most people don't appreciate the "asset" that they have in the form of their future earnings. If someone is earning $60,000 with a very modest annual increase, over 30 years, that's a multi-million dollar asset. It sounds corny, but *YOU are the goose that lays the golden eggs.*

You have fire insurance, right? You've insured your car, your possessions, and your home. Yet if you don't insure your ability to keep those home fires burning by insuring your income, your goose will be cooked. Quit procrastinating. You can't assume that it won't happen to you, because that assumption could be financially and emotionally devastating. And if your significant other is the primary breadwinner, you can't assume his continuing health is guaranteed. Men like to think of themselves as invincible. Like Superman, right? Yet every day we hear stories of men who keel over in the prime of their lives. You better make sure he has enough insurance so that you can take care of him, and the family, while he recovers.

If you're not convinced yet, here's one more statistic to blow your socks off: according to the Society of Actuaries and the National Center for Health Statistics, in one year, one in eight people become disabled. One in eight! What would your family do if one of the people bringing home the bacon couldn't do it anymore? Live on your savings? How long would that last, and what would the cost be to your future? Borrow the money? Your lender is more likely to call in your existing loans than to lend you more money. Put all the pressure on your spouse? That's a great way to get a divorce. Tap your retirement plan? What will you do when retirement arrives? Rely on the government? Yeah, right!

If you want to be independent, if you want to know that you can take care of yourself and your family, you'll put the pieces in place that will help you when the caca hits the fan. You'll do your research, and you'll buy enough of the right kinds of insurance to see you through whatever life throws at you.

DISABILITY INSURANCE

Nobody likes to think about becoming disabled. And being sick is much worse if you have no money. But as a woman, you're at higher risk, so you better take this seriously. According to CIDA (Commissioner's Individual Disability Table A), for the top occupation class, at age 35, the claim incidence rate for women is three times greater than for men. After 40, the incidence of claims begins to move closer, narrowing to 6% higher for women by age 60.

The other frightening issue for women is that the incidence of divorce seems to rise sharply for women who become disabled. Disability puts a strain on marriages; every woman needs to be prepared to cope financially with this devastating situation should it arise. That means facing up to the possibility that something bad can happen and taking steps to offset the challenges you may face. You owe it to yourself, so you don't end up sick, poor, and alone. You owe it to your partner, so your sweetheart has the means to get the help needed to make your life more comfortable. And you owe it to your children. How much more comforting will it be for them to see you deal with your setback with dignity? Being prepared will send them the right message: they must take personal responsibility for their own lives.

Choose four female friends who are all around the same age as you. Write their names on a sheet of paper along with your own. There's a 65% to 75% chance that one of the people on that list will die before they reach age 65. Worse still, there's a 92% to 98% chance that one person on your list will become disabled. And if that disability lasts 90 days, chances are it will last five years. How sure are you that it won't be you? Having enough insurance means you can keep a roof over your head and food in your stomach without having to liquidate investments and use up all your savings. Being prepared means those assets are protected, so you, your family, and your long-term financial future are protected.

What to Look for in a Disability Plan

You need the help of a qualified insurance advisor when you go shopping for disability insurance. Why? Because there are so many sizes and styles out there that it's very easy to buy one that looks good on the hanger but just doesn't fit. Remember that with insurance, as with just about everything else, you get what you pay for.

The most important thing to look for in a disability insurance policy is that it is *non-cancellable* and *guaranteed renewable*. It would be useless to buy a policy if the insurance company could refuse to renew it after one or two years. This is a fundamental issue, because you don't want your contract to be changed. The definition of disability might become more restrictive, premiums might increase, or entire benefits, such as cost-of-living increases, might be eliminated. You would have bought a pig in a poke, because despite all the comparison-shopping you did, you could end up with a policy that looks significantly different from the one you bought.

The *definition* of disability is also phenomenally important. The variables are almost unlimited as to what is or is not a disability, how you define it, and when it begins and ends.

Maria was playing field hockey with her daughter's team when she fell and shattered her left wrist, thumb, and index finger. After several operations, it became clear she would never recover the full use of her hand. As a left-handed endodontist, Maria was no longer able to perform dentistry, so she decided to take a position at the local university. How does the change of occupation affect her disability insurance? Is she still entitled to a monthly income benefit even if she is working at something other than what she was originally qualified to do? Well, that depends.

There are basically three definitions of total disability that are available, and they come with different price tags. The plan with the narrowest definition, and the one that carries the steepest price, is "own occupation," according to which an individual is considered totally disabled if she is unable to engage in her own occupation, even if she is working at something else. Next down the price scale is "regular occupation," according to which an individual is considered totally disabled if she is unable to engage in her own occupation and is also not working at anything else. "Any occupation" is the least expensive, along with being the broadest in terms of not paying you, should something go wrong. According to this type of plan, an individual is totally disabled only if she is unable to work in any occupation, regardless of the changes in duties or income.

While Maria may be earning a substantial income, under an own-occupation definition of total disability, she would be entitled to full benefits regardless of the fact that she is gainfully working in another occupation. If she had taken out disability insurance with a regular occupation definition, her university employment would preclude her from receiving monthly income benefits, because even if she remains totally disabled from her own occupation as a dentist, she is gainfully employed. She would have to not work at her own occupation or at anything else to collect. If she had disability insurance with a definition of "any occupation," she would not qualify for monthly income benefits unless she was unable to work at anything at all. If she could take tokens at a turnstile, there'd be no benefit payout.

Disability is a grey area. It is a matter of degree and debate. Are a fractured wrist and fingers totally disabling? It depends on your job. Will you receive monthly income benefits? It depends on the definition. So find out how your plan defines disability. Must it be total? Is the determination made by your doctor or the insurer's doctor? How long must you be disabled before you'll begin receiving benefits? Make sure you know what your insurance does or does not cover.

$ **Gail's Tips:** If you are self-employed, disability insurance is absolutely, positively, without question a MUST. It's unlikely that your business can survive a long-term disability, which means you'll have no source of funds from which to support yourself through the disability. Premiums are expensive, but disability insurance must be a priority. If you don't believe it can happen to you, remember the statistics: one in eight people become disabled each year.

Equally important is the *residual disability* feature. While some people become totally disabled, it is much more likely that you will be able to do some work but at a lower income. In the case of a slow recovery, or a slow deterioration from a progressive disease, this becomes very important. If you don't have residual disability insurance, it could take years before your claim can begin because you must be totally disabled.

My bestest friend was diagnosed with multiple sclerosis, but she was far from totally disabled. Some days she could walk better than others. It faded in and out. She seemed to get much more exhausted than the rest of us. And a flu bug affected her much more severely. But she wasn't totally disabled. If you're in this situation and do not have residual or partial disability coverage, you have no claim until you reach the point of total disability. Think of it in terms of black and white. If your ability to work whole hog is white, and total disability is black, residual disability represents all the shades of grey in between.

Since most group plans have limited or no benefits for residual disabilities, you can be up a creek even though you think you're covered. Check the fine print. Some individual policies require earnings loss only, without requiring any loss of time or duties, which is much more restrictive. The question becomes, "What is the definition of residual disability?" One company might say it requires a loss of time or duties plus income. Another might say it only requires a loss of income. Look for a contract in which the payout is based on a loss of your income. If you bought a policy several years ago that required both definitions at the time, as long as you're in good health, you should try to have the definition changed to "loss of income."

Make sure you also understand the *qualification period* in the plan. This is the number of days of total disability required before the insurer will pay residual disability benefits. A policy with a zero-day qualification period is best and means there is no requirement of total disability. Multiple sclerosis is a good example of an illness that may take years to create total disability. However, as the disease progresses, this could cause significant loss of income. The requirement for a period of total disability, such as a 30-day qualification period, would prevent you from ever being eligible for residual benefits and would make your policy almost useless.

. . . .

$ Gail's Tips: Do you smoke? Quit. If you don't smoke, you'll pay 10% to 15% less in premiums. To qualify as a non-smoker, you must not have used any tobacco products for 12 consecutive months prior to applying for coverage. Another good reason to give up the evil weed!

. . . .

Having an *inflation rider* or a *cost-of-living rider* is a good way to increase your monthly benefits. While this is an expensive "addition" to a basic policy, it is critical when you look at the long-term cost to your purchasing power and take inflation into account. At an inflation rate of 5%, today's $1,000 will be worth only $613.90 in 10 years, $376.90 in 20 years, and $231.40 in 30 years. So what looks like a healthy payout today may seem paltry in a couple of decades.

An inflation or cost-of-living rider is different from a policy that is indexed, although they sound much the same. The cost-of-living rider addresses increasing your claim cheques after you've been disabled. So once you've made your claim, the cost-of-living rider means the amount on your cheques will increase to keep pace with inflation. The indexing addresses keeping the protection level of your coverage up to what it should be while you are healthy. Sometimes called an update benefit, it is a way of keeping your protection level current. So if you buy your insurance at age 30 and qualify for $2,500 in coverage, it is the indexing that will allow you to increase your coverage to $3,000 and then $3,500 as your income increases and you need more coverage.

Another way benefits might increase is under a *future insurability rider*. With this option, once every year or two, the insurance company allows you to increase your benefits by quite large sums without additional health questions. This is important for the young healthy person who anticipates there will be significant increases in income in the future. While there are no additional health questions, and you don't have to disclose that you've taken on a more danger-ous hobby, the increases do have to be financially justified.

$ Gail's Tips: One way to reduce the cost of your premiums is to eliminate short-duration claims, or claims for periods when you are covered by an employer or by government benefits. Know that if you choose this route,

you will not be able to make a claim until the waiting period—
usually three or six months—has expired.

. . . .

There are a lot of *i*'s to dot and *t*'s to cross when it comes
to making sure you have the best policy for your needs. Here's
a case in point: When Maya bought her disability plan in her
early 30s, she checked on the definition, the residual disability feature, and the qualification period. About 10 years later,
Maya went through a difficult divorce and sought counselling from a psychiatrist. She was prescribed antidepressants,
and over time, everything fell back into place for her. In her
mid-40s, Maya decided to increase her disability coverage to
keep up with her increased income stream. She was in for a
shock. The insurance company felt Maya was too high a risk,
because she had been treated for depression, and her request
for increased benefits was declined. Maya couldn't understand
it. She was well past that rough patch. It had been almost five
years since she had taken any drugs. Why was this coming
back to haunt her now?

Insurance companies hate all kinds of psychiatric conditions
because they are so hard to define, so they routinely rule against
anyone who has ever been to a shrink for anything . . . even marriage counselling! This is also a reason to buy your insurance
when you're young and healthy. If you have fewer life experiences
and have faced fewer challenges, you're much more likely to present a nice, clean, and easy-to-approve application for insurance.

Are there exclusions for *pre-existing conditions* on the
policy? If you are a diabetic, how would that affect claims

for disability arising from conditions that could be linked to your diabetes? In the case of individual disability coverage, you must declare all your health issues, and then you will be covered—if you are accepted for coverage, that is. Nearly all group policies have pre-existing condition clauses. If you have a disorder before buying a policy, usually you will not be covered for disabilities related to that disorder. It's just as important to know what you're not covered for as what you are.

Another thing to look for is an *integration clause.* Some policies deduct the amount of benefits paid by Employment Insurance, Canada Pension Plan, or car insurance from the amount they pay out in benefits. This has advantages and disadvantages. It can mean that the premiums are lower. However, low-income individuals might end up with no benefits at all from their insurance policy until Employment Insurance sick benefits run out. Also look for the use of the terms "payable" and "paid." This might not sound like a big deal. But imagine being told, "We *think* that CPP is going to pay, so we'll wait to see before we pay you anything." That's what could happen with the "payable" option. It's in your fine print, so make sure you read it.

The Stats Man says that the number of people who are disabled increased by 21.2% between 2001 and 2006. Part of this is due to the population aging. The prevalence of disability is higher for women than for men. Men die. Women get sick. In both cases, we can end up significantly worse off. If we want to be able to maintain our independence, even when we must deal with physical limitations to our activity, we better make sure we have enough and the right kind of disability insurance.

$ Gail's Tips: How much do you know about your company disability coverage? Can you answer these questions?

- How much are you covered for? Will your income from disability be taxed? Group policies paid for by an employer generate income that is taxed. If you pay the premiums directly from your after-tax income, your benefits are tax-free. Is your coverage sufficient once tax is taken?
- Is there a maximum? Group plans usually cover a percentage of your salary, but some also have a specified maximum.
- For how long will your benefits be paid? Most plans cover you for only two years if you can't work in your own occupation, shutting off completely if you are deemed by the insurance company to be able to do any type of work at all.
- If you leave your company, will you be able to take the plan with you, or would you have to requalify at your new employer? If you developed a problem in the interim, would you qualify?
- Are your benefits indexed to inflation?
- What's your policy's definition of "disabled"? If you

can't do the job you were hired to do, will you be paid your benefits regardless of what other work you find?

- Can the insurance company deny your benefits because they see you as fit to do any other type of work? Let's say you're currently a salesperson who must drive as part of your duties. If you cannot drive because of a sight problem, can the insurance company insist you can do other work and deny your claim on this basis? Will partial benefits be paid if you can only work for a few hours a day?
- Can the company raise the premiums for one category of insured and not for another? How will you be affected?
- What are the exclusions on the policy? Travel outside Canada? Pre-existing conditions? Disclosure of mental health problems or a nervous disorder? Alcoholism?

Many people who benefit from company coverage assume that they're covered for any disability. And they figure that since the coverage is free, it's fine. Remember, you get what you pay for. The question you should be asking yourself is, "Does this come anywhere close to meeting my needs?" If you find your group plan lacking, look to an individual policy to supplement it.

CRITICAL ILLNESS INSURANCE

Critical care insurance is intended to reduce the financial impact of a critical illness. It provides a lump-sum payout to deal with expenses not covered by traditional health programs, such as the costs associated with lifestyle adaptation, transportation, and in-home care. You are insured against the likelihood of being diagnosed with any one of a list of serious medical conditions, ranging from cancer to AIDS to heart attacks. The insurance pays when you are diagnosed, so it is not tied to your ability to work and the benefits are tax-free.

When one spouse doesn't work outside the home, people often don't think about the cost to the family of replacing the efforts of that person. Should mom get sick, the kids still need child care. Mom may need nursing care. There may be extra transportation costs, as well as the extras that will make life easier for the whole family. This money really makes a difference, and it doesn't fit into either life insurance or disability. It is a category all unto itself. What's unique about critical illness insurance is that it will pay on diagnosis. You could be diagnosed with a critical illness and not yet be disabled from it. Or you could be someone in a wheelchair who uses the lump-sum payout to make your home more accessible.

LIFE INSURANCE

The term "life insurance" is a misnomer. After all, you're not insuring your life; you're insuring the economic value of your life, or your ability to earn an income in the future. It's a matter of taking care of one of the most important details of your life: your responsibility to ensure that those who count on you have been wise in their judgment.

People seem far more willing to spend money insuring their

stuff than to spend money insuring their future economic sta-bility. Look at car insurance as just one example. My young friend, Judy, pays approximately $300 a month for her car insurance. Because she is just 23 years old, Judy could buy a universal life policy for $300,000 for a premium of just $50.50 a month. If she did so, by the time she reached 60, Judy would have accumulated $235,350 in assets through her plan.

There are four main reasons for the resistance to rolling up our sleeves and picking out a plan. First, people don't want to face their own mortality. It's the same story with wills. People don't want to make a will because they superstitiously believe that once they take care of the details, the hand of fate will strike them down.

Second, life insurance is an intangible. It's not like buying an investment, where you walk away with a share certificate or an investment statement that shows what you have. The idea of creating a source of income to replace your contribution to the family coffers should you die seems far less concrete for many people.

Third, people are very suspicious of the product, the indus-try, and of the people within the industry. People are afraid they are going to be hounded into doing something they don't want to do. Insurance is often sold on the fear factor, which is just the kind of tactic that makes people run away from the product.

Fourth, life insurance seems complicated. Will you need to have a physical? What special terms and conditions do you have to watch for? Will the amount you buy now be enough for the future? How much should you buy?

In combination, these concerns form a wall over which many people cannot climb when it comes to protecting their financial health. Everyone pretty well accepts the fact that the worst time to buy something is when you need it. It is ALWAYS more expensive—or worse, unavailable. Life insurance fits this truism to a T. *The best time to buy life insurance is when you don't need it: when you're young, when you're healthy, and when it costs less.*

The thing about insurance—whether it is life or disability—that makes it different from any other financial instrument is that you can't always get it when you want it. With practically everything else, you can go out and buy it when you need it. With life insurance, if your health should deteriorate, as it tends to do when you get older, you may not qualify. Health underwriting is also more rigorous for higher value plans.

The most important part of buying insurance is sitting down with a financial advisor that you trust. Because life insurance is a fairly complicated product, you need someone who can explain the differences. Be suspicious of anyone who starts off with a set amount you should have: "You need $100,000." You need someone who begins by trying to understand your needs and concerns. What are the risks you are trying to cover? What are your issues? This person should be able and willing to guide you through the alternatives.

Kathy and her husband first bought insurance when they purchased their home and wanted mortgage insurance. Kathy says, "At the time, I wondered if I had been swindled because, in my mind, we only had a short-term need. Our insurance representative was considered to be one of the best in the industry. He said it would give long-term value, and we would always have a need. I more or less just went along with him, always questioning it in my own mind. Now that we're at this point in our life, it has very significant cash value. What I like best about it is that if our best-laid plans are sideswiped because we end up with unexpected financial needs, we can always access that policy. It's something we can literally take to the bank and they will give us 90% of the cash value. Or we can borrow against the cash value."

Think of the concept of investment diversification and relate that to the issue of insurance and its place in your financial plan. We know it makes sense to hold a variety of investment types within our portfolios, so that the underperformance of any one asset type doesn't have too much of an impact on our entire portfolio. Insurance is such an important part of that diversification formula, because we are protecting our most important asset: our ability to make a living.

Whether or not you need to buy life insurance depends on a lot of things, such as:

- how much you currently have in the way of assets
- how much debt you have
- how much your family will need to make ends meet
- whether you're concerned about minimizing the tax impact on your estate.

Do I Really Need Life Insurance?

You may not. However, if your death would cause economic hardship to others, you probably do. As a quick test, read through the following questions. If you answer no to any, you'll likely need some insurance.

Will your estate have sufficient funds to pay for your funeral?

In 2007, the average cost for a traditional funeral was $9,000. It's surprising how many people make no preparations for their funeral expenses. The more carefully planned this is, prior to your demise, the less stressful the whole episode will be for your family. Remember that funeral costs rise over time, just like everything else, so review your needs from time to time.

Will your estate have enough money to pay your accounting, legal, and probate fees?

There are costs associated with the winding up of your estate. (There are also ways to minimize or even eliminate these costs, but that requires careful planning and the advice of an estate specialist.) You'll have to decide if you want those costs paid out of your estate, or if you want them covered by insurance so that your estate remains intact for the benefit of your family.

Will your estate have enough money to pay the taxes you owe at death?

At death, the Tax Man considers all your capital assets (except those assets that pass directly to your spouse or beneficiaries) to have been sold. If you had an investment that was sold for a profit, that profit would be taxed. Any money in registered plans, such as Registered Retirement Savings Plans (RRSPs) or Registered Retirement Income Funds (RRIFs), is also included as income unless it passes directly to a partner. If you have a whopping income reported on a final return, more of that income will be taxed at the highest marginal tax rate. That may significantly affect what's left for your family. Again, careful planning and sound legal and accounting advice can help minimize the Tax Man's grab. See an estate specialist to plan how your estate can be distributed with the least tax impact.

Will your estate have enough money to provide the income required to meet your family's day-to-day needs?

If you want your family to continue having the lifestyle to which they have become accustomed, you must make a plan. It's difficult enough dealing with the death of a loved one. Adding financial pressure to the picture—expecting your family to struggle to satisfy their day-to-day needs—only worsens the impact of the loss. Make sure that your death benefit is large enough.

Once upon a time, by the time we began actively planning our retirement, our children were usually grown. But times have changed. With later marriages, remarriages, and second families, we're having children at later stages of life. Not only do we have to plan for ourselves, we have to consider the ongoing care and education of our kids.

Even if you don't have a young family, as a surviving spouse, your financial security may be threatened when your partner dies. Corporate pension plans (and many annuities) often pay a reduced income upon the death of the primary pensioner/ annuitant. That would mean a significantly reduced income from sources you'd come to count on. Insurance can make up for the shortfall in income.

Will your estate contain sufficient funds to eliminate any debts you have at death?

Can you imagine the impact on your family if they lost you (or your partner) and their home at the same time? How would you feel if you were left to cope with caring for the kids on your own and on top of that your home had to be sold because your partner died and you didn't have enough money to keep making the mortgage payments? Insurance is one way you can minimize the impact of your debt. Take a look at your mortgage, credit cards, loans, and personal lines of credit. If you have sufficient insurance to eliminate those debts, you also eliminate the worry and financial strain on your family.

Will your estate have sufficient funds to provide for such priorities as the education of your children/ grandchildren?

Once you've figured out all the other costs you need to address, you may want to consider the "exceptional" costs—those short-term or one-time costs such as education, vacations, or the cost of replacing a big-ticket item such as a car.

How Much Insurance Will I Need?

Here's a quick formula you can use to calculate how much insurance you'll need:

A − (B + C + D + E) = Insurance needed

A = Your family's Assets and income

Including existing insurance, a spouse's income, government benefits, pension income, income from investments (e.g., GICs, Canada Savings Bonds, mutual funds), income that could come from the sale of assets, etc.

B = Your family's monthly Budget needs

Including shelter, food, household supplies, clothing, utilities, car maintenance, insurance (home and car), child care, entertainment, etc. You will have to have enough money invested to generate the annual income to meet the budget needs that you define.

C = Costs associated with your death

Including funeral expenses, accounting and legal fees, probate costs, estate taxes, etc.

D = Debts to be paid off

Including credit card balances, mortgages, loans, etc.

E = Exceptional expenses

Including educational costs, vacations, major purchases (e.g., new car, medical equipment), etc.

Begin by adding up the income your family would have, based on the existing income (from pension, spouse's employment, and the like). Add the income that would be generated from your assets. A $35,000 GIC at 3% would generate an annual income of $1,050. If you have an existing insurance policy that would pay out $100,000, and that money is then invested, earning a return of, let's say, 5%, it would provide an annual income of $5,000.

Once you know how much income your family will have, you then have to calculate the expenses they will face. Some of those expenses are one-time costs, such as your funeral or the pay-off of existing debt, while others are ongoing, such as monthly expenses and educational costs. The discrepancy between what your family has and what it will need must be covered in some way if you wish to minimize the financial impact of your death. That's where the insurance comes into play.

This can be a complicated calculation, and having an insurance broker you trust to guide you through it is a very good idea. A good broker will be familiar with the types of things you must think about, such as rates of return and the amount of capital needed to produce a specific amount of income. He or she can make the process of figuring out how much insurance you need a lot easier.

What Type of Life Insurance Should I Buy?

Whether you buy "term," "whole life," or "universal life" insurance will be dependent on two primary factors: the amount of insurance you need, and how long you need that insurance to be in place.

Term insurance provides protection for a predetermined period of time (perhaps five, 10, or 20 years) or until a certain age. However, many term insurance plans automatically end at a specific age, such as 65, 70, or 75. With men and women living considerably past that age, if you're looking for longer-term protection, term insurance won't cut it.

With term insurance, when the term of the contract expires, your coverage ends unless you renew the term. Each time the term is renewed, the premium is adjusted, usually upwards.

$$\textbf{\$ }\textit{Gail's Tips:}$$ **Gail's Tips:** Consider using "decreasing term" insurance as an alternative to bank-offered mortgage life insurance. With traditional mortgage life insurance, while the premium remains the same for the term of the insurance, the benefit goes down as the mortgage balance decreases. As well, since mortgage life insurance is always paid to the mortgagor (usually the bank), you give up control of how the money will be used. Maybe mortgage life insurance should be called "group creditor insurance," since the creditor is the person that is protected by the policy. If you want to be in control (and why wouldn't you?), skip the bank's plan and buy your own decreasing term insurance.

Think of term insurance as an expense. While it will give you comfort and peace of mind, it accumulates no residual value. If you're only after peace of mind, term insurance may be the ticket. But if you want coverage to last your lifetime, or you want to use insurance to build assets, you'll need to look at permanent insurance.

Whole life and universal life insurance are permanent,

remaining in place until death. With whole life policies, the insurance company does the investing. With universal life, you have much more control over the types of investments the money is going into. With both types, the premium is generally the same for the life of the policy, so the annual cost can be low if taken early in life (when the risk of death is low), or very high if taken late in life. Most whole life policies have a "reserve," which can be refunded if you cancel the policy before your death. This reserve is referred to as the cash value of the plan. You can also borrow against this cash value at an interest rate set in the policy. However, if you haven't paid it back, the money owed will be deducted from the death benefit.

At a certain point, both whole life and universal life may become self-funding: the assets built up in the policy can be used to pay for the policy so that the cost to you is eliminated. That was one of the reasons why I bought my whole life policy at 30. I wanted to set the rate before I got any older or any sicker, and I wanted the benefit of having a policy that would eventually pay for itself. Since I had no idea at the time that I would end up with two children eight years later, in retrospect, my decision was brilliant. But over the years, I've taken a pile of flak for having bought a whole life policy. Mostly the criticisms have centred on how much more I am paying for my insurance than I would be if I had purchased a term policy.

When I purchased my $200,000 policy back in 1989, the premium came in at just under $1,200 a year. Compare that with the quote of $4,800 a year for term insurance that was given to Denise, who was shopping for coverage for her husband because they had just started a new family (her first, his second). And if he renewed the term at 62 (his children would then be just 15 and 18), his annual premium for the next 10 years would be approximately $14,000 a year. Wowza!

So, back to the question "What kind of insurance should I buy?" The best place to start is with the amount of coverage you need. Let's say you'll need $125,000 to pay off your mortgage, $5,000 to cover your funeral expenses, $15,000 to cover legal and accounting bills, and an additional $100,000 to cover the capital gains your estate will be hit with. All told, you'll need about $245,000. Buying a policy with a lower payout clearly won't serve your needs.

The next thing to look at is how long you'll need the coverage. Some of your needs may be short-term. Declining term insurance is often the most cost-effective way to cover this debt. On the other hand, the need to meet your funeral expenses, minimize the tax hit on your estate, or protect a partner is permanent. So permanent insurance will be your best bet here.

Remember, the premium on your permanent policy will remain the same, while the premium on term insurance will rise each time the policy is renewed. So while the cost of term insurance will appear far less expensive in the early years of a policy (if taken at an early age), you have to look at the long-term costs. Have your insurance salesperson compare the lifetime cost of both types of policies (remember to compare similar features and benefits—apples and apples), and then make your decision.

Another interesting fact: with some policies, you can buy the right to convert your term policy to a whole life policy at a later date. So if you decide to start off with term insurance to protect your young family, and then decide to convert to a permanent policy when your needs change and you have more money, your health won't be a factor in setting the premiums. However, your age will be a factor. And the older you are, the more your insurance will cost.

Gail's Tips: One of the critical differences between your work life insurance coverage and an individually owned plan is that with a group plan, you don't own the plan (your company does), even though you're paying a taxable benefit on the policy. Since you don't own the plan, you can't take it with you, and you can't convert it. So while you're covered for as long as you remain with the company, if you're wholly dependent on your group policy, you may find yourself out in the cold if you are terminated from your job, unless your group plan has a provision that allows you to purchase your insurance privately upon termination.

Shop around when looking for life insurance. Get several quotes. Compare apples with apples. Buy the policy that best meets *your* needs. Resist the urge to overbuy, but don't sell yourself and your family short either. Evaluate your future earning potential and your family's ongoing needs realistically, and then buy enough.

When deciding which options or riders to add to your policy, remember that each option will increase the cost of your premiums. Here are a few to think about:

Waiver of Premium

If you become disabled (sick or injured), this option will waive your premiums, yet keep your coverage in place. Often this option is of little value, since the definition of "disabled" is extremely restrictive. Before you buy this option, make sure the definition of disabled meets your needs. Also, see how the option is priced. If it is not classified by occupation or health, it will be very expensive. Rather than purchasing this option, consider buying disability insurance coverage—which you should have anyway—that makes allowance for maintaining your life insurance premiums.

Accidental Death Benefit

This is often referred to as "double indemnity," because it doubles the benefit if your death is caused by an accident. However, since your family needs a certain level of insurance coverage regardless of how you die, double indemnity often creates a false sense of security. Don't be tempted to buy only half as much insurance as you need, relying on the fact that if you die it will be by accident. Less than 8% of deaths among people aged 25 to 65 are the result of an accident.

Guaranteed Insurability

This is a guarantee that in the future, you will be able to buy more insurance at standard rates despite a change in your health. The amount you can buy, and when, are spelled out in the policy. Your option to purchase additional insurance usually cannot exceed the original face value of the policy. Remember that while you have the option of buying more insurance, you should only do so if your circumstances have changed and you need more insurance.

Increasing Face Value

This option allows you to increase the benefit of your policy by a set amount each year; your premium increases with each increase in the benefit. Since the increases are provided automatically, you can rest assured that your coverage has some inflation protection. And since there is no need for proving your insurability, even if your health circumstances change, you can still benefit from an ever-increasing face value. As well, with a locked-in schedule of premium increases, you can take advantage of competitive rates or decline the option if you feel you can arrange separate, less-expensive insurance. This rider usually has an annual administrative fee, so it's only economical on larger policies.

Insuring the Cash Value of Your Plan

If you choose this option, the death benefit paid will also include the cash value of the plan. This means that the policy provides an increasing benefit over time, which is good for inflation protection.

● ●

($) Gail's Tips: If you've decided that insurance is an important part of your basket of goods, but you just can't get your better half to move towards the solution, you may have to take matters into your own hands. Did you know that you can take out insurance on a spouse? (This sounds like the plot for a murder mystery, as opposed to a tip in a financial book, doesn't it?) Yup, as long as your spouse is aware and is in agreement, you can take out the policy, name yourself the beneficiary, and pay the premiums. You'll own the policy, so any cash value will accrue to you. It is simply his life that is insured.

• •

If you haven't yet considered the importance of insuring your future earning potential from the rigors of disability or death, I hope you're convinced now. Find a professional to help you assess how much and what type of insurance is just right for you. Remember, you'll need a person who is knowledgeable and experienced in the type of insurance you are seeking. That person should be willing to provide you with quotes from more than one insurer, and should be willing to explain the ins and outs of the variety of features available.

Ultimately, we all hope to live long, healthy lives that are full of joy. When circumstances change in ways that threaten to rob us of that joy, or present us with challenges we never imagined, the last thing we need is to be financially challenged at the same time. If you haven't yet faced the possibility that you might become disabled or die, the time has come to take a long, hard look at the statistical realities. The cost of insurance is a mere drop in the ocean compared with the cost to your family, in peace of mind and financial security, if you are not insured and your worst nightmare becomes their reality.

11

TAXES, TAXES, TAXES

Everyone pays too much in taxes. In 2006, we paid over $222.2 billion in total tax, $103.7 billion of which came from personal income tax. In Canada, everybody who earns income above a certain level is taxed on their Canadian income, as well as on any income received from outside the country. Knowing how to deal with taxes is the ticket to ensuring you keep more of your hard-earned money in your own pocket.

While we report our taxes on a calendar-year basis, the deadline for filing a personal tax return is April 30 of the following year. Scads of people leave it to the last minute. You shouldn't. Give yourself some breathing space before you do your final check of your return to make sure you've claimed everything to which you're entitled and to confirm your arithmetic. And if you owe money, you're going to need to figure out where that money will come from. Minimizing your taxes isn't something you do on April 30. It takes planning. Tax planning should start in January, not April. While you may have to deal with last year's taxes in a few months, you still have all year to plan for your next year's tax bill.

Canada uses a graduated tax rate system, so as your income increases, you pay more income tax. You calculate your taxable income by adding up all your sources of income and then subtracting certain deductions and credits to come up with your net income. We pay tax both federally and provincially. For 2011, the federal tax rates were:

- 15% on the first $41,544 of taxable income, plus
- 22% on the next $41,544 of taxable income (on the portion of taxable income between $41,544 and $83,088), plus
- 26% on the next $45,712 of taxable income (on the portion of taxable income between $83,088 and $128,800), plus
- 29% of taxable income over $128,800.

Each province and territory in Canada has a different tax structure, and you'd do well to find it on the Tax Man's site (it keeps moving) by searching for the words "income tax rates" at www.cra-arc.gc.ca.

There are a number of deductions and credits you can claim to reduce the amount of tax you have to pay, and by taking advantage of these, you can avoid tax. *Avoid* is a very important word. While tax *avoidance* is a perfectly acceptable way to minimize tax, tax *evasion* is a violation of the law. Since tax laws become increasingly more complex with each passing ruling, check with an expert to ensure you're on the right side of the Tax Man.

$ *Gail's Tips:* Just because you get advice from the Tax Man doesn't mean that you can go ahead and follow that advice, assured that you're well within the rules. CRA's representatives can't be held accountable for the information they provide. (Isn't that the stupidest thing you've ever heard!) The idea of seeking advice from those closest to the whole process seems like a logical one. If you aren't sure if your business set-up or your deductions are within the confines of the Tax Man's rigorous restrictions, it would seem natural to go straight to the horse's mouth for the answer. You would then assume, of course, that the answer given would be one you could bet the farm on. However, there is a long-established principle of law that disallows taxpayers from seeking refuge from a negative assessment simply because they were guided by CRA's advice, since comments from officials are not binding. Crazy! So, if you're not sure where you stand, you had best check with someone who really knows the answer: an accountant or an experienced tax lawyer.

The way to pay less tax is to keep more of your taxable income in the lower tiers so you pay a lower percentage of tax. You do that by maximizing your deductions. One of the best ways is to contribute to an RRSP. If you made $60,000 in 2011, and you stuck $9,000 in an RRSP, you essentially reduced your taxable income by that much. Your $9,000 would be working on a tax-deferred basis inside your RRSP, and you would have an additional $2,880 (assuming a marginal tax rate of 32%) that you kept out of the Tax Man's hands to do with as you wish. You can take a well-deserved vacation, make a principle prepayment on your mortgage, start a non-registered investment plan, or boost your next year's RRSP contribution. Whatever you decide, you'll have been smarter to keep the money for yourself. I bought my first car using the tax refund from two years' worth of RRSP contributions. From my perspective, the government bought me the car. I paid cash. No finance charges. The cost to me: a little deferred gratification. The benefit: I still have the retirement plan, which provides a nice little nest egg for the future.

The most common mistake people make when filing their returns is not claiming all the deductions and credits to which they are entitled. All the information you need to make sure you pay as little tax as possible is laid out in the tax guide. Take the time to read it from cover to cover, highlighting those things that are applicable to you. If you don't read the whole thing, you won't know what you may be missing. It's not the most stimulating reading in the whole world, but you have lots of time if you start now. Keep a copy in the bathroom, along with a highlighter pen, and when you get 10 minutes away from the kids, start highlighting. If you're not a bathroom reader, pick another place where you spend 10 minutes a day and work through the guide slowly. If you have read through it at least once, you're more likely to identify opportunities for taking advantage of the credits and deductions that come up when you change jobs or make changes in your personal circumstances. Don't want to do this? Hire a tax expert to do your return, or use one of those tax preparation packages that'll prompt you to check for tax savings.

$ **Gail's Tips:** Suppose you did your return and then found out that there were credits or deductions you could have claimed but didn't. Check your notice of assessment to see if the Tax Man caught your mistake. You should always review your notice of assessment in case a mistake was made. Remember, those guys are human too. If the error wasn't caught, the next step is to call CRA to see if you can recover those deductions or credits. This may mean filing a notice of objection—a time limit of one year applies, so heads-up. Ask the Tax Man to guide you through the process, or consult a tax specialist for help.

A tax deduction reduces your income. So if you claim an RRSP contribution of $10,000, your income is reduced by $10K, which means any tax you may have paid on that $10K is coming back. Deductions behave differently than tax credits, which are "non-refundable," so they aren't used to calculate a refund. Tax credits simply reduce your taxes owing, so you won't get extra money back if you have more tax credits than taxes.

FILE A RETURN EVEN IF YOU DON'T OWE ANY TAX

People often think that because they don't have to pay any tax, they shouldn't bother to file a tax return. If you're one of those people, you may be losing out on an opportunity to build RRSP contribution room, so that if and when you do pay tax, you'll have a deduction you can use to offset that tax. It doesn't matter how small your income is, and it doesn't matter that you don't owe any tax. As long as you have earned income and you file a tax return, you will have eligible RRSP contribution room that you can carry forward. That can translate into a deduction when you do have sufficient income to pay tax.

Making the contribution is even better. While there's little point in claiming the RRSP deduction when you owe little or no tax, you will benefit in two ways. First, any contribution can compound to produce what can seem like a magical amount. Second, the tax deduction can be carried forward and claimed when your tax-bracket goes up, so you get the biggest bang for your buck. Most young people who are just starting out at their first jobs have little extra income to make a retirement plan contribution in their first few years of working. It can be a challenge just making ends meet. But small amounts are all you need.

WAIVER OF INTEREST AND PENALTIES

Believe it or not, there are times when the Tax Man leads with his heart instead of his hammer. CRA recognizes that despite a person's best efforts, there may be a time when, due to extraordinary circumstances, he or she may be unable to comply with the *Income Tax Act* and, as a result, will incur penalties and interest. So, at his or her discretion, the Minister of National Revenue (and, of course, his or her representatives) may waive interest payable. What qualifies as extraordinary? Natural disasters, civil disturbances, disruptions in services—read postal strikes—and the like. It could also include more humanitarian issues, such as a serious illness or accident, or serious emotional or mental distress, such as that caused by a death in the immediate family. It also applies to situations where the tax department messed up, such as processing delays, errors in publications, incorrect written information, departmental errors, or delays in providing information to taxpayers. It's also interesting that if the Tax Man thinks you won't be able to pay your back taxes because you just don't have the bucks, he may waive the penalties and interest as part of his collection efforts. And if the penalties and interest are sooo big that they present an enormous barrier to payment, voilà . . . they can be wiped away, providing the taxpayer keeps to the agreed-upon repayment schedule.

INSTALMENTS

Lots of folks don't realize that they may be required to remit tax in instalments during the year. Since the tax most people owe is deducted at source, they figure they're always on the right side of the Tax Man, and they are astounded when they are charged interest on tax owing. After all, how did they know they were going to owe tax before they completed their return? Under the law, you have to remit instalments if the difference between the amount of tax you owe and the amount of tax that's been withheld at source is more than $2,000 in both the current year and either of the two preceding years. So if you have alternate sources of income on which no tax is deducted—let's say tips earned, a second job, income from self-employment, or, in my case, royalties—it's your job to make sure the Tax Man has his fair share on time. And on time doesn't mean when you file the return. It means quarterly: on the 15th of March, June, September, and December.

To figure out how much your instalments should be, calculate how much income you'll have from your other sources on which tax hasn't been withheld. Let's say that you earn an additional $15,000 a year at a part-time job and that your marginal tax rate—the rate at which you pay tax on the last dollar you earned, or your highest rate—is 32%. Then you'd owe $4,800 for the year. Divide that by four, and you'll see that your quarterly remittances should be $1,200. Another alternative is to take the balance you had to pay last year, and pay that amount in four equal instalments. Remember, no matter how it shakes out, if you owe, the Tax Man collects. So if you guess wrong and still owe taxes, you'll still have to pay interest on the difference between the amount you owed and the amount you paid, based on the three-year rule. The only time you won't owe interest is if you made instalment payments according to the notices sent to you.

VOLUNTARY DISCLOSURE OF NON-FILING RETURNS

The tax department, in an attempt to encourage taxpayers to come forward and correct deficiencies in past tax filings, has a set of rules relating to voluntary disclosure. If you've never filed a tax return, and you do so voluntarily, you will only be required to pay tax owing on your reported income along with interest. In other words: no penalties and no prosecution. You'll have to pay the total amount of tax and interest owing according to an agreed-upon schedule.

WHAT TO DO IF YOU ARE AUDITED

Could there be any word that strikes more dread in a taxpayer's heart than the word "audit"? Almost everyone has heard a horror story of a friend of a friend being reviewed with a fine-tooth comb. And, unfortunately, even people who have received advice directly from CRA can find that advice overruled when the Tax Man cometh.

So what exactly is an audit, and should you be petrified? What we think of as an audit can be as simple as a request for additional documentation to support a deduction, or as complex as a full-fledged review of your taxes for the previous five years. In fact, the audit can start long before you're contacted, such as when doctors' incomes are compared with provincial health plan payouts, or waiters' tips are compared with the average tips on credit cards slips in the restaurants where they work. If something looks suspicious to the Tax Man, an audit ensues.

If you're informed that your taxes are being reviewed, the first thing to do is ask for a letter of notification from the CRA's audit group, so you can see what they want. If you have a tax advisor, get advice immediately. Respond promptly to your notification, since CRA allows a specific number of days for your response. Need additional time? Ask for it. Whatever you do, don't ignore the request. It won't just go away. And if they think you're obfuscating, watch out.

If it comes down to a meeting with the auditor, your behaviour will be a critical factor in the outcome. Don't be confrontational. Co-operation and credible presentation of the facts will go a long way in your favour. Be frank and open in your responses, but do not volunteer information. Give the Tax Man what he asks for and no more.

If it ends up that CRA disallows a deduction and sends you a notice of reassessment stipulating the amount you owe, you can challenge the reassessment by filing a notice of objection with the CRA's appeals division. You must file your appeal within 90 days of the date on the notice of reassessment, or within one year of the original filing date for your return, whichever is later. However, you'd be wise to pay the amount for which you've been assessed in the interim to avoid the accumulation of interest should things not go your way. Don't worry, paying up is not an admission of any sort, so it won't prejudice your appeal.

Back to the question of how scared you should be. That depends on how honest you've been thus far. You're not likely to be prosecuted for tax evasion if your claim has been based on an honest difference in opinion on how the rules apply.

But if the Tax Man concludes that you deliberately under-reported your income or overstated your deductions, you're in for it. Tax evasion is punishable by a fine of up to twice the amount of tax evaded—that's in addition to the tax you owe—and a prison sentence of up to two years.

Paying more tax than you absolutely have to is dumb, Dumb, DUMB! And getting big tax refunds is almost as dumb. It may be exciting to fill out your tax return and find that the Tax Man is going to send you back a whopper of a refund. You want to get up and do a little dance, right? Well, you're a dope. And here's why. If you're getting a refund, it means YOU PAID TOO MUCH TAX. That means you gave the government an interest-free loan.

Some people say that they like getting a refund because it's "forced savings." Are you kidding me? Savings on which you earn nothing for the year, while you struggle to come up with the money to achieve the goals you've set for yourself?

If you're serious about your financial independence and being in control of your money, today's the day to make some changes. Get yourself a copy of Form T1213 (you can find it online), and use it to request permission from the Tax Man to have your employer reduce the amount of income tax taken off every paycheque.

If you can demonstrate that you're eligible for certain recurring deductions that will reduce your tax bill at the end of the year, then you can trade in your tax refund for more take-home pay. Do you make monthly RRSP contributions by way of preauthorized withdrawals? You're eligible. How about child care expenses? If you're tithing monthly, you can do it for your charitable donations. If you have rental losses, interest expenses on investment loans, or carrying charges, those are eligible too.

Since you'll be paying less tax on an ongoing basis, you'll have more cash to use to pay down debt, build an emergency fund, save for your kids' education, contribute to an RRSP, save for a down payment on a home, or whatever it is you want to achieve.

You'll have to fill out the form and send it to the Tax Man each year. You can do it at any time, but the best time is in October or November for the following year. Once you're approved, the Tax Man will provide instructions by letter to you, which you then give to your employer, who will adjust your pay for the remainder of the year.

Getting a tax refund may feel good, but when you think that the government has been using your money without paying a red cent in interest, you'll realize that taking control is way more satisfying. Get the form, fill it out, and keep your money!

12

WILLS AND POWERS OF ATTORNEY

Almost everyone should have a will. Unfortunately, many people think they don't need one. Some people think their wishes will be carried out by a family member. Others feel they don't have sufficient assets to justify the cost of making a will. And some people simply avoid making a will because personal circumstances—marriages, divorces, and accumulated children and stepchildren—just seem too complex to unravel. If you've delayed seeing a lawyer about a will because you believe it's not worth the expense, let me assure you that dying without a will is far more expensive than the cost of drawing up a will.

Few people understand the rules, implications, and costs associated with dying *intestate* (without a will). It is enough to say that if you die without a will, trying to figure out who gets what and when is often an unholy mess.

If you die intestate, your estate is distributed according to the laws of the province in which you were domiciled. (Your

domicile refers to the place where you had your chief residence and the intent of remaining for the rest of your life.)
Your assets are frozen until the court appoints an administrator to oversee the sale of the assets and distribution of the
estate. Your assets can be frozen for months while the estate
issues are being resolved. In the meantime, your family can't
use what you've left behind (even in your personal chequing
account) to pay the rent or mortgage or buy food.

Consider making a will as soon as you begin to accumulate assets. This will ensure that your assets are distributed as
you would wish. Whether you are married or living together,
you and your buddy may want to have your wills drawn up
together, so that they reflect an integrated estate plan. Review
and update your will every three or four years, or when:

- Your family circumstances change. Weddings, divorces,
  births, and deaths all result in changes in family structure.
- Your financial circumstances change. Increases or
  decreases in your financial assets may necessitate
  changes to the will.
- New legislation is implemented. This may have a significant impact on your existing will.
- You change residences. If you move to another province, update your will to ensure compliance with the
  rules and regulations of your new province of domicile.
- You decide to change your executor or beneficiaries.

A will can minimize delays in the administration and distribution of your estate, since your executor can begin to take

action immediately. You can specify who gets what and when. (In some cases, the provincial family law legislation can override provincial distribution formulas or even override your will, so get professional help with this.) Choose the best person (or trust company, which are the only organizations eligible to act as executors) to represent you as executor of your estate.

Your executor or estate trustee is the person (or trust company) you appoint in your will to ensure your testamentary wishes are honoured and your instructions are followed. He or she must be of sound mind and must have obtained the age of majority to act. An executor can be a beneficiary or a witness. However, *a beneficiary should not also be a witness because, while the will is still valid, the gift to the beneficiary will be void.*

Your will is also the place to appoint guardians for minor children. While an appointment is only temporary—the courts have the final say—without it, some government agency may become the guardian of your children until an application to the court is made to appoint a relative or other person. Yucky for the kids, and a sure cause of fights within a family.

To make a will, you must have reached the age of majority—among the exceptions to this rule are people under the age of majority who are married or who have been married—and have "testamentary capacity." This means that you must have sound mind, memory, and understanding, and you must clearly comprehend that you are making a will that is disposing of your assets. You must understand and recollect the nature and relative value of your assets, and understand the claims of those you may be excluding from the will.

There are several circumstances that may affect the validity of your will. Your will may not be valid if:

- You are under the influence of alcohol or drugs when you make it, such that you no longer have testamentary capacity.
- Undue influence is exerted on you in making it, or if it was executed under duress or coercion.

WHO SHOULD DRAW UP THE WILL?

Although you can draw up your own will, or use a standard form, don't. While some people may feel that lawyers are simply being protective of their industry when they say, "you need professional help," the fact is that estate law is a complex beast.

In many cases, home-executed wills have been invalidated because of the way they were executed. While a holograph will (one that is completely in your handwriting and signed by you) does not have to be witnessed, a formal will must be witnessed by at least two people. There have been cases where a preprinted will form has been filled in and signed, but has not been witnessed. It is neither a formal will, because it has not been witnessed, nor is it a holograph will, because it is not wholly in the person's handwriting. There have even been cases where people have signed what they believed would qualify as a holograph will, yet it was not binding, because they typed it so that everyone would be able to read it! Here's another common mistake: nothing written after the signature forms part of any will, so a postscript doesn't count.

The language of a will may seem cumbersome, but it has been around for years, and its effect is tried and true. While the language can seem opaque and redundant—that is a shortcoming of the profession—there is a move afoot to put the language of wills into plain English. Until then, however, you're still best off letting a professional who is familiar with the technical rules and requirements draw up your will so you can be sure it is valid. An estate lawyer can also help you sort through many of the issues you should think about, so that your real intentions are translated into the legal language required.

The mistake made most often is that the testator's wishes are not clearly expressed, and the time it takes to sort them out can be interminable. Let's say I draw up my own will and indicate that I want my kids to have all my money by writing, "I want all my money to go to my kids." What do I mean by "money"? Do I mean cash? Do I intend to include the money in my retirement plan? If I mean all the money in my Royal Bank chequing account, what happens if I switch banks? As you can see, "money" can have myriad meanings. That's where the guidance of someone who does this day in and day out can be invaluable.

Just as "money" can mean a dozen different things, so can the term "household contents." Do you mean to include your grandmother's antique pearl brooch? Perhaps you don't mean to include the car in your garage as part of your household contents. What about the collection of paintings hanging on your walls? One person's financial status may be such that those paintings are simply considered as part of their household effects. For another, the collection may be their primary investment—in effect, their "money." Either way, intentions must be clearly stated to avoid ambiguity.

The naming of a beneficiary is another area where lack of clarity can cause problems. If you haven't seen your sister Laura for 20 years, and choose to leave a bequest to your sister Martha, but in your will you simply refer to your "sister" without using her name, guess what? You can't assume that it is implied that you are leaving the bequest to Martha just because you haven't seen Laura in donkey years. With an experienced estate lawyer at your side, you can avoid ambiguities.

An estate professional will also assist you in focusing on the issues you need to think about. Here's a for instance: when you use a term like "children" or "issue" in your will, it applies not only to your children and remoter descendants born within marriage, but to those born outside marriage as well, even if you don't know about them. And it applies to children who have not yet been born at the time you draft your will, unless you state otherwise.

An estate lawyer will also help you to work through some of the issues that relate to how beneficiaries will respond to the will. If you have two children to whom you are leaving your family cottage, will one want to sell while the other wants to keep the property? How will you structure your will to eliminate the fighting over what should be done with the property? The same holds true for a business that is being passed on to children. If only one child has taken an active interest in the business, but you leave it to all the children equally without further clarification, who will decide if the business is to continue being run or to be sold? How will the child who has invested time and energy in running the business feel if the business is "sold out from under her"?

If you're well-prepared for your meeting with a lawyer, the process should go smoothly, and the cost should be quite manageable. Before you start, do a little research. Most estate planning firms have a will booklet that will guide you through the process. These booklets often include a list of the information you need to bring with you.

In preparing for your meeting, you and your partner should discuss your financial details before you sit down with a lawyer. You each have a right to know where you stand, and you should both have a say in how your joint assets will be distributed. Make a list of your personal information, including your full legal name, any other names by which you are known, your address, social insurance number, date and place of birth, name and date of birth of spouse and children, marriages (all of them), and existing wills, trusts, and powers of attorney. List your assets, estimating their value. Indicate assets for which you've named a beneficiary (such as when you named your honey as your beneficiary on your RRSP, or your children as beneficiaries of your life insurance), or assets that are held in joint tenancy (like your joint bank account or your home), since these will be distributed on your death independent of your will. If special bequests are to be made, prepare a list of items to be left to particular individuals or organizations. List your liabilities and any insurance provisions you've made to eliminate those liabilities.

Of course, the majority of your focus will be on how your estate will be distributed. This used to be pretty straightforward.

But with divorces and remarriages, half-siblings, step-siblings, and all the other family permutations that are now part of almost everyone's life, the question can be considerably more complicated. Who will be your heirs? When will they receive their bequests—immediately or in the future? How will the bequest be handled if your beneficiary predeceases you?

NAMING YOUR EXECUTOR

Before the meeting, think about who your executor should be. Your executor is the individual appointed to administer the terms of your will and is responsible for assembling and protecting your assets, handling tax requirements and filings, and distributing your estate, among other things.

You can appoint a sole executor to act alone or two or more co-executors. And you can make a contingent or alternate appointment in case the first appointed executor cannot act. Some people choose to name a friend or family member because these people are familiar with the personal details of their lives. Since Aunty Val knows and loves the kids, she's the perfect person. However, rather than being an honour, being named as executor can be quite an imposition. It can be an extremely time-consuming job. Some executors feel out of their depth because they lack financial or investment knowledge. If your executor is too emotionally involved, that can impede the whole process. Also, get the agreement of the person you plan to name before you name them, since an executor can give up the right to act at any time before the will is probated and before he or she begins administering the estate.

The person you select must be of sound mind and must have obtained age of majority in order to act (i.e., a minor may be appointed as an executor, but he or she can act only after having attained the age of majority). Here are some folks you might want to consider:

- *Your partner.* Your spouse or life partner may be a good choice if the assets being transferred under the will are relatively uncomplicated. An estate made up of bank accounts, term deposits, a house, a retirement plan, and pension benefits would not be difficult to administer if it were going directly to the surviving spouse. With complex assets (unless your spouse has special skills), or if there are testamentary trusts involved (particularly a trust that will last during your spouse's lifetime), consider appointing a co-executor with expertise in investments, accounting, and tax. Remember that this will be a very stressful time for your partner. Think about how able he or she will be to deal with the emotions stirred up by losing you while handling the legalities of managing your estate.
- *Your children.* Appointing adult children, either alone or with the surviving spouse, can have some advantages. Mature children may be familiar with the assets. Keep in mind, however, that unless they have had specific training in a profession such as law or accounting, children may lack the expertise to complete the administration of the estate. As well, appointing one, but not all, could lead to friction, even if you have good reasons for the decision.

- *Friends and business associates.* Age is a factor in choosing friends and business associates. Inevitably, these individuals tend to be about your age and may find themselves acting as executor at a time when they themselves may require help to manage their own affairs. Older friends may die before you, leaving you to name a new executor—another trip to the lawyer. Worse still, your executor may die during the administration period, in which case his executor—someone you may not even know—would take on the administration of your estate if you have not made provision for an alternate. So a complete stranger who hasn't got a clue about what you wanted, and doesn't care one way or the other what really happens, will be making some big decisions for your family. Hmm. Maybe not the best idea.
- *Your family lawyer or accountant.* The family lawyer often seems a logical choice for either an executor or a co-executor. Lawyers may be an appropriate choice if they have a sound knowledge of estate law and enough time to devote to the estate. However, unless they are set up to carry out estate administration, these professionals may not be equipped to manage investments and run complex trust accounting systems. Plus, some lawyers prefer not to act as executors.
- *Corporate executors.* The only organization that can act as an executor is a trust company. Corporate executors have the expertise to handle all the necessary obligations; they also remain neutral, which allows them to

make objective decisions with regard to beneficiaries. Company representatives are available 52 weeks of the year, so the estate administration won't be delayed because the executor is ill, has gone on vacation, or has other business commitments. However, unless you have a pre-existing relationship with a trust company, they won't know your family. You may feel that a friend or family member would offer a more personal touch. Where there's good reason for a corporate executor, don't let the lack of a relationship deter you.

$ **Gail's Tips:** When you name an executor, also name a backup in case that person is unable or unwilling to act.

Choosing an executor requires a high degree of trust. You must be sure in your own mind that your executor will carry out your wishes as you intended them. And regularly re-evaluate your choice as your life progresses and things change. Choosing the wrong executor can have horrible ramifications.

GUARDIANS FOR YOUR CHILDREN

Think about the person you feel would be the best guardian for your children. A guardian is someone who assumes responsibility for your child until he or she reaches the age of majority. Hopefully, the person you name will never need to do the job, but that's no reason to ignore this detail. While your children may be minors, this is anything but a minor consideration. If you are a single parent, or if you and your spouse were killed in a common disaster, who would care for your babies?

The guardian you name is granted temporary guardianship of your kids. To make the custody legally permanent, the guardian must apply to the court. While the court is not required to appoint the guardian you have named, it usually does, unless there is a challenge to the appointment or a valid reason not to. If your kids are old enough to express their opinions, the courts will often ask them where they would like to go before a final decision is made. If you have strong feelings about whom you would want or would not want as guardian for your children, make those feelings clear in your will. That may help the court reach a decision that more closely reflects your wishes. And check with your intended guardian before you write his or her name into your will to be sure that person is willing to accept the responsibility.

Think about the kind of home life this guardian would provide. Would your children want to live with this person? Can this person afford to raise your children, and will your estate provide sufficient financial support to ensure there is no stress on the guardian's own financial resources? Remember, raising your own children is tough enough. Raising someone else's is an act of supreme kindness. This is particularly true in cases where children are physically or mentally challenged. Check back from time to time to see if the person you have appointed remains willing and able to do the job.

PLAN YOUR FUNERAL

Just as making a will can be difficult for many people, so too can be making funeral arrangements. Funerals are a rite of passage. They bring a conclusion to an episode of life. While you may not want an elaborate funeral that rivals a wedding, think about the fact that there is little time to prepare for a funeral—at most, a few days. This is a time when your family is most vulnerable both financially and emotionally. The last thing you should want is for them to be spending money without direction while in an emotional state. Better you spend a couple of hours thinking about it and putting it on paper, so there's no debate about how fancy or simple the whole thing should be. If you want a party, plan the party. Some people even identify the guests with prepared invitations. They choose the music to be played and the food to be served. Others want to keep the whole thing simple. I want to be cremated. It's fast and cheap, and it doesn't use up valuable land resources. I find the whole idea of spending gobs of money to plant me in the ground abhorrent.

Your funeral instructions aren't binding, but they're likely to be followed in most cases, and they will ease the burden on your family members. Don't simply leave them in your will. Leave separate instructions where they can be easily found, since your will may not be read (or your safety deposit box opened) until after you've been planted.

If you haven't thought about these things yet, now is the time. If you don't have a will, make arrangements to make one. If you haven't designated a guardian for your children, start thinking about who is worthy of the job. Don't allow your emotions to get in the way of your responsibility.

Hilary talks about redoing her will when she was pregnant. "Just before John was born," she said, "I redid my will and had to think about issues like guardianship. I sat and cried. How could I be thinking about my own death when I was awaiting the birth of my baby? It gave me a whole new appreciation for how difficult it is to go through the exercise, but how absolutely necessary."

It all comes back to the responsibility issue. If you don't arrange the details, the financial and emotional repercussions can be horrible for those you leave behind—those who have to deal with your death. The point of constructing a well-thought-out, well-executed will is to make the whole process of tying up loose ends as neat, clean, timely, and painless as possible for those you love during this most emotionally exhausting time.

EXECUTE POWERS OF ATTORNEY

While lawyers and financial planners have been calling attention to the importance of having a power of attorney for years, for many people the question remains, "Do *I* need a power of attorney?" *Everyone* should take the time to execute this relatively simple document.

A power of attorney is a legal document that authorizes another person to act on your behalf. The most common type of power of attorney deals with property and gives the person you choose the legal authority to deal with your assets. If you become mentally incapacitated, a *continuing* power of attorney would allow your representative to act for you. Note that it must be "continuing" to be binding if you become mentally incompetent. By executing a continuing power of attorney, you eliminate the likelihood of your family facing a cash-flow crisis because they cannot access your chequing or savings accounts, or liquidate investments in your name, in the event that you cannot act on your own behalf. If you become incapacitated without a power of attorney, certain family members could obtain authority to act, but they might have to post a security bond first and would be required to file a management plan for your assets.

The person you choose to act for you can be your spouse, another family member, your lawyer, or a trust company. Since the person who has your power of attorney can do anything you can do (except make your will), you should have implicit trust in this person. If a relationship is shaky, don't test it by adding the burden of a power of attorney to it.

A power of attorney can be "general" or "restricted." With a general power of attorney, all your assets are covered. With a restricted power of attorney, you set out the specific conditions you want met.

Since a power of attorney is legally binding, consult your lawyer to have one prepared.

In the spring of 1995, Ontario introduced new legislation to allow you to also make your wishes known with regard to medical and non-medical care. While this had been the domain of the "living will" for some time, living wills were not legally binding. The powers of attorney for personal care as executed under the *Substitute Decisions Act* are binding.

Within the power of attorney for personal care, you can appoint someone to make decisions on your behalf, and you can establish in written form your instructions regarding medical treatment and non-medical personal care issues. You can also establish the specific medical treatments you do or do not want, including the specific circumstances in which you want medical treatment to cease. You don't have to include instructions—you can leave it up to your personal care power of attorney to make the appropriate treatment decisions based on your wishes and preferences.

Hard as it may be to think about, putting your wills and powers of attorney in place is the only way to ensure that your money is handled the way you want it to be. Sticking your head in the sand may create huge problems later. Stop being an ostrich! Get them done!

PART THREE

ADAPT YOUR PLAN
AS YOUR LIFE
CHANGES

There is no greater constant in life than change. No matter how well you plan, how carefully you prepare, or how tenaciously you hold on, at some point, everything nailed down comes loose. That's life.

Many years ago, I came across a beautiful saying that I've held close to my heart. I can't remember where I read it or who to attribute it to, but it goes like this: *To grow is to change and to change often is to have grown much.*

I really like the idea that I'm not fickle (as Virgil would have us believe), scatterbrained, vacillating, shifty, warped, flip-flopping, or bent. I'm much happier thinking of myself as growing, metamorphosing, remodelling, reorganizing, moving, improving, and bettering. The bottom line: I'm changing. It's a good thing too, since my life continues to evolve, and if I didn't keep up, it would sure be a funny picture. Or a sad one.

While the pursuit of money in and of itself is a fool's game, having money in the bank means you have options when things must change. It's much easier to deal with those changes if you've got some resources. A sound financial foundation means you've got a steady place from which to operate as you adjust and adapt.

As my girlfriend, Brownie, says, the golden rule is, "Get up!" No matter how often you're flattened, you can only move forward if you get up. Of course, it's easier to get up if you have some tools at your disposal. And it's easier to stay financially healthy if you have a road map of the things to check for as you move along life's glorious, muddy, winding, uphill, rocky path.

That's what this section is all about: change.

Since your priorities as a young adult will not be the same as your priorities when you have kids or retire, it's important that you repaint your financial canvas to reflect the changes in your life. No one thinks about saving for their kid's education before they actually have a child. And few people can contemplate retirement at the sweet young age of 24. But as you progress, morph, move forward, you need to reorganize and remodel. If you don't take the time to reassess, you may waste a lot of time working to old plans.

So now it's time to look at what you'll have to think about as you move through life and your needs change. Next, I'll walk you through the major life cycle events and how to adjust each of the elements in your financial plan. Here we go!

13

WHEN YOU PARTNER

Whether you plan to tie the knot, or you're cohabiting for the first time, hooking up with a buddy comes with some surprises. It's an adventure as you learn to negotiate each other's space, figure out how you'll work as a team, and start to dream together. It'll be less stressful if you take some time to chat about what's important to each of you and to you as a new family.

My first experience with a joint account was negative. I was the only one working. My husband planned to return to Australia, where he felt he would be in a better position to contribute to the family coffers. I was to join him shortly thereafter. Before he left, he emptied the joint account of the $600 we had managed to save and bought me a television to keep me company. I was aghast! It may not seem like much money now, but in 1979, $600 was all the money we had in the world. And it had been hard to scrape together. My security was gone. I was going to end up alone, and without a safety net. From his perspective, he was doing something nice for me. From my perspective, he had placed me in a horrible position. From his perspective, money was for spending. From my perspective, money was for saving in case something dreadful happened and you needed it. For him, $600 wasn't a lot of money. For me, it was a fortune.

The point of this story is that you have to talk about what you expect of your partner and what he or she expects of you, if you plan to have a successful relationship. You have to talk about it all. How you will live together. How you will share responsibilities. How you will cope with challenges and deal with financial issues. Things one partner does shouldn't come as a shock to the other. That's not to say that as you live together, you won't uncover new, wonderful, challenging aspects of your spouse's personality and ways of seeing things. That's natural. What's destructive is to not have an open line of communication so you can discuss the things that make you sad, mad, crazy, and over-the-top frustrated. While the early months of shared life can be very exciting, they can also bring some very interesting discoveries. Talk about them. And that goes double for financial matters.

If you can't talk about money, you're in trouble. Since every family is faced with challenges, the ability to put the issues on the table, talk openly about them, and come to some resolution is absolutely crucial to your relationship.

Historically, money and power have had a very close relationship. Husbands who made more money were far more likely to control most of the key decisions in the relationship—from which house to buy to where the kids would go to school to who would stay home with a sick child. Women often ended up taking a back seat in major decisions, simply because they were not contributing in a significant way to the family coffers. Some of that's changed. I've worked with families where the woman is the primary breadwinner. But the money-power relationship hasn't shifted. Within these less traditional circumstances, she who makes more money has a tendency to throw her weight around, while he who makes less feels powerless. Do I have to say that this is no way to have a strong, long-lasting, and secure relationship? Regardless of who is bringing home the bacon, joining your lives together means you agree that you are equals in the relationship. Money is a tool you use to achieve what you both want, not a stick to beat your buddy into submission. By working together, you can achieve far more than if you're constantly struggling to prove who is top dog.

Assuming you and your partner agree to communicate openly about money, your first task will be to set the ground rules. Set aside an hour or so when you will not be interrupted—no kids, no friends, and no background distractions. Your first order of business should be to agree on the time and place for your next meeting. Some couples run these meetings like board meetings. Others use them as an excuse to get out of the house for a quiet dinner. Whatever your choice, start your meeting by setting the time, date, and place for the next meeting, so no matter what the outcome of this one, you will have already agreed to continue the process.

Begin by talking about the things you agree on, so you set a positive tone. Decide how you are going to arrange your money matters: who will pay the bills, save towards the down payment on the home, make the contributions to the kids' education funds, and make the investment decisions. If you've already identified a habit your spouse has that makes you nuts, put it on the table. Ask your spouse to do the same. The rule should be that anything is up for discussion, providing it is being handled without acrimony. Your discussion should also bring clearly into focus the things that are very important, somewhat important, and a little important to each of you. This may take some thought and may be deferred to your next meeting, but don't skip this step. If making sure you maintain a $500 safety cushion in your chequing account is important to one spouse, and the other runs the account to within a hair's breadth of zero every month, you'll drive each other nuts. Knowing the rules will help you both not to break them.

One reason many couples fight about money is that each person has different priorities. One wants to save madly, the other is a shopper; one wants to pay down debt, the other continues to charge purchases and take out loans; one wants to own a home, the other wants to invest the money in the market. And as time goes by, each position becomes more polarized as the individuals attempt to balance the other's "wrong."

Another reason couples fight is that their expectations are not met. Implied promises are hard to escape. A new mother may feel she was implicitly promised time to stay home and take care of her baby, but her spouse may insist she return to work. A husband may believe his wife should stay within the household budget, while his wife continues to use her already-stressed credit card to buy clothing and toys for the kids. One spouse may be disappointed that the other doesn't make more. The other may feel embarrassed, ashamed, or angry at not being able to live up to her partner's expectations.

Over time, the issues related to merging your lives and your money will evolve. The issues you have to deal with initially will be very different from those that arise if you start having children together. Some of the things you should talk about may take some time to get to. And you may never be joined at the hip financially, because you may choose to maintain your individual independence even as you work together as a family. But as long as you keep talking, keep sharing information, and keep listening, you should be fine.

YOUR SPENDING PLAN

The most challenging part of your early conversations about money management may be coming to terms with the fact that you have different money personalities. Your partner may be a charge-ahead spender. You may be a careful saver. Your partner may be illiterate when it comes to investing. You may be well-read and enthusiastic. Both you and your partner may be take-charge money managers who struggle over the power to make decisions. Whatever the case, you better get to know each other and come to some agreement about how you will handle this aspect of your relationship. The worst thing you could do is to simply settle into a financial relationship that pleases neither of you. In the end, fights, tears, and resentment will be the dividend of your unwillingness to talk it out.

So, today, it's time for a chat. Talk about your attitudes. Talk about your expectations. Disclose. I know this isn't easy for everyone, but if you can't trust the person with whom you are partnering, think twice about this life-changing decision. Talk about what you own and what you owe. It may be difficult admitting debt and listening to someone else's asset-building saga, but you have to know each other's circumstances fully to start off right. And don't assume you know your partner simply because you've been acquainted for years. You don't know a thing about a body until they choose to tell you. So there may be some significant gaps you aren't aware of. Talk about your goals. Do you want to buy a house? When? Do you want to have children? How will you share the care, nurture, and rearing of your babies? How much will you put away for the future? How will you decide where that money will be invested? If you are starting a blended family, how will you discipline together? How will the children's various activities be divided financially? How will support payments be integrated into the new family budget? If you and your partner have different expectations as you start out, it would be a good idea to come to an understanding of each person's position. Talk through your financial arrangements, so that the process and the outcome are fair for each person.

Once upon a time, men were the primary breadwinners in a family. But times are changing. One of the most dramatic changes in Canadian society has been the increase in the number of women who are employed. In 1994, 52% of all women 15 and over had jobs—up from 42% in 1976. In 1994, women represented 45% of all paid workers in Canada, up from 37% in 1976. By the fall of 2009, women had passed men in terms of employment statistics; they made up 50.6% of Canada's 14 million waged or salaried workers. There are more women working now than ever before. And the younger they are, the more likely it is that they are working—regardless of whether or not they have kids. This change is a sign of how the economics of family life have changed. For many women, the question of whether or not to work isn't really a question; they have to work to help their family attain or maintain a certain standard of living. For women who are now better educated, the choice to work is also a personal one. Women want the option of being able to contribute to the world at large in a meaningful and productive way.

Consolidating your spending plans will be one of the first challenges you face when you begin living together. Will you pool your money, or will you manage separate accounts? Who will pay which bills? Who will be in charge of saving? Who will maintain the emergency fund?

When it comes time to set up a joint household, the fact that many women come into the relationship already financially responsible for themselves is something both they and their significant others have to deal with. For many partners, this is a welcome change. For others, it is a challenge to their ability to take care of the family ("Don't I make enough to support us?") and to maintain their primary-breadwinner status.

The tack you take in consolidating your households will be a reflection of how similar or different your circumstances, attitudes, values, and objectives are. Here are five approaches:

1. Pool Your Resources

All your income goes into a joint account, and all bills and spending money are paid out of this pool. The remainder is invested for the benefit of the entire family: retirement planning for the grownups, educational savings for the kids. Some people say this won't work for them because one partner makes way more than the other. From my way of thinking, if you're partnered and committed, the money shouldn't have anything to do with the decision—money is simply the tool that let's your family do what it wants and needs to do. Who made it is of no significance. And what to do with it should never be a unilateral decision. However, if income disparity is a bugaboo for you, there are other options.

2. Contribute Proportionately

Each person puts part of his or her income into the common pot that covers the things you both have decided to pay for together: housing, food, the car you share. If both choose to contribute 50% of their income, the actual dollar amounts can be quite different. If you earn $60,000 a year after taxes and your partner earns $35,000, then your share of the pool would be $30,000 a year, while your partner would contribute $17,500.

3. Split Expenses 50-50

Let's say you determine that your joint living expenses will be $50,000 a year, and you decide to split that 50–50. Assuming the same incomes as in the previous example, you would each end up paying $25,000 a year. This would leave you with $35,000 a year to do with as you wish, while your partner would end up with only $10,000 in his or her pocket. This is one reason why I think proportionate is fairer than 50–50.

4. Split the Bills

You decide who pays what bills. Perhaps you'll pay the mortgage, while your spouse pays the utilities and entertainment costs. Often, people choose this route to split the financial responsibility, as well as the responsibility for getting things done. (There's nothing more aggravating than the confusion of an exchange like "Did you pay the phone bill?" "No, I thought it was your turn to pay the phone bill.")

5. Go Month by Month

If you particularly enjoy keeping the records or are an absolute control freak, this method may be for you. You would pay all the bills each month, total them up, and then give your partner the total of his or her share.

$ *Gail's Tips:* The fact that women are marrying later means they may bring assets—sometimes considerable assets—to the family. The question of how those assets should be identified in the event of a relationship breakdown is becoming more of an issue. The same is true for people who are remarrying and integrating their families and their family assets.

Everyone has an opinion about marriage contracts. Some people wouldn't dream of visiting the minister before visiting their lawyer. Others see a marriage contract as an act of pessimistic fatalism.

A marriage contract is simply an agreement about how assets will be divided should the marriage break down. Unfortunately, those people who have signed marriage contracts without being aware of their rights, or what they were giving up, have made the concept seem more like a negative than a positive. But think for a moment. If you were entering a second marriage, after your previous husband had died, and you had children from that first marriage, wouldn't you want to protect your children's interests in the assets you had prior to remarrying, just in case?

Even if you are both entering the relationship with no significant assets, think about how you want to keep your records straight as you accumulate your assets. After all, if you pay the rent every month, and your partner buys the furniture, will your spouse want all the furniture if the worst should happen and the relationship fails? How will you decide who gets that beautiful antique armoire that your partner bought at an auction and that you lovingly and painstakingly refinished?

. . . .

YOUR EMERGENCY FUND

True or false: Once you partner, you only need to cover one person's income so you can cut back on your emergency fund. FALSE. If you think that your spouse's income is your safety net, might I point out that there are many couples that have found themselves both out of work at the same time. Might I also point out that with most people living on the edge each month, it's unlikely that any one salary would be able to take care of all the costs associated with your joint lifestyle. Partnering should not be your excuse for giving up your financial responsibility.

Both members of a partnership should have emergency funds established to ensure that should the worst happen, they'll be covered. Trying to accumulate an emergency fund when your spouse has been laid off, during a divorce, or when the world has come crashing down on both of you is next to impossible. If you haven't already done so, start today by putting a little away each week towards your emergency fund. You'll sleep better for it.

MANAGING YOUR MONEY

Once you've set up your joint spending plan, you'll have to decide how you will deal with the day-to-day transactions. If you've decided to set up a joint account, might I suggest you use it only for your joint expenses. When couples pool their money and things go wrong, inevitably one spouse is shocked when the other empties the joint account. You shouldn't be shocked. Anger, bitterness, and resentment make people do things they would never do when they are happy. The first rule of coexistence is to maintain your financial identity. That means having your own accounts, your own investments, and your own credit. It also means not losing touch with the financial world.

I often hear from couples in which one person does all the money management and the other hasn't a clue about what's going on. This is often reported of women, particularly women of a certain age. But I've met women who worry about their husbands' lack of attention. They worry that if something should happen to them, their hubbies would be lost. So it's not strictly a gender thing. And I've met young people who were shocked to find that when their partner left, they had no idea of where anything was, or how much they had. So it isn't an age thing. It's a matter of taking personal responsibility for your own financial well-being.

Naturally, there are some things you can benefit from as you consolidate your lives. Throwing double your weight around in terms of your overall business could get you a lower rate on a loan. And joint bank accounts may let you keep a higher balance on a single account to avoid service charges. The flip side of this is that if your spouse bounces cheques on a joint account, the NSF (non-sufficient funds) charge will be reported in both names, and it will affect your credit record. It can be extremely frustrating to be meticulous about your record-keeping and ensuring you have enough to cover cheques, only to have your significant other take a more laissez-faire approach that results in a rotten credit history for both of you. If this seems to be a routine event, then separate your accounts to protect your credit history.

··

$ **Gail's Tips:** I'm not a fan of joint credit, but there's nothing wrong with one partner giving the other a leg up when it comes to establishing a credit history. Co-signing for a short-term loan (one year or less) will establish the credit history for a newbie. Once established, you can separate your credit accounts and build individual identities.

··

KEEPING A HEALTHY CREDIT IDENTITY

Now that you are two, in some instances, you'll be perceived as one—unless you do something about it. I once read a story on the Internet entitled, "Married Women Beware." I was intrigued. The story was from a young woman who had asked her mother to co-sign a loan for her. She chose to ask her mother because her mom made more than her dad, so she figured she stood a better chance of getting the loan. Imagine their surprise when they found out that mom had no credit history whatsoever. Even though she had been using credit cards and paying them off on time for years, all her credit history was under her husband's name, because her cards were secondary cards on his account.

"Married Women Beware" indeed. If you do not apply for

your own credit cards, loans, or personal lines of credit, you're not building your own credit history. And no matter how well you manage your money, it won't be reflected anywhere. In essence, you won't exist from a credit perspective. Don't let this happen to you. You have to take care of yourself and your credit identity now, so that you can take care of yourself in the future should you find yourself on your own. Your best bet is to have your own credit card, in your name alone. When you borrow money, make sure you borrow it in your own name. If you borrow with your husband, insist that the credit granter report the information to the credit bureau in your name. Better yet, be the first one to sign on the application form, so the reporting is applied automatically to your file.

Call your credit card company and make sure that *your* accounts are set up in *your* name only. You're not Mrs. Edward Johnston. You're Jane Johnston. Make sure you keep your nose clean, so your credit bureau report is a shining example of good financial management. And check your credit report every year or so to make sure no mistakes have been made that might tarnish your credit glow.

● ●

$ *Gail's Tips:* I can't tell you how many women I've dealt with who have signed unlimited guarantees for their husbands' businesses. A smarter approach would be to limit your exposure to half of the debt or to a specific time period. Get independent legal advice—have your own lawyer tell you the implications and ramifications—so that you can make unbiased, informed decisions. The bank should require this as part of the process. If no one has told you to get independent legal advice, consider yourself informed as of today.

Getting the advice is only half the equation, though. The other half is taking it seriously. If you don't understand what an unlimited guarantee is, ask. And keep asking questions until you're quite sure you do understand. After all, you should not be finding out for the first time that you are primarily liable for your husband's debt should he go bankrupt. There you are in the house with four children and the bank trying to sell the house, because you are the fall guy.

. . . .

Throughout the marriage, you must know what's going on. Marriage is a partnership. This isn't snooping. It's your right to know. It's healthy. Each partner should have equal knowledge. If they don't, should the partnership come to an end, one partner is at a disadvantage.

KEEPING A ROOF OVER YOUR HEAD

Where will you live? Your place? His place? A new place? Once upon a time, couples lived in apartments, flats, or rental units for years and years as they accumulated a down payment for a home of their own. It wasn't unusual for people to buy their first home in their 40s. Now, everyone wants a house, a bigger house, and all the stuff to put in the house as soon as they get hitched. But taking on a big mortgage can be daunting for new couples. And it is often done at the expense of other parts of their financial lives: emergency funds, insurance, pay-yourself-first investment plans, retirement savings. The thing about having a healthy financial life—and a balanced life over-all—is to have reasonable expectations that are in sync with your overall objectives. That's not to say you shouldn't buy a house. But it should be part of the equation—not the sum.

YOUR PAY-YOURSELF-FIRST INVESTMENT PLAN

As you start out together, keep your eye firmly on the future. Without kids, your living expenses are probably on the low side. You don't need as much living space as you will when the little mites start arriving. You're young, healthy, and, very likely, focused on your career. With two incomes, you have more disposable income now than you will once you start a family. While you can enjoy that discretionary spending power to travel, accumulate stuff, and have fun, you should also be using part of it to establish an asset base. Invest in your future.

Plan to have kids? Plan on a considerable drop in your dis-posable income once the babies start arriving. Your early years are the perfect time to establish a savings plan that will help bridge this gap. Whether or not you intend to become a full-time mother, those savings will come in handy. They can also cushion the financial shock that occurs when you hold your warm, cuddly bundle and decide you can't leave her to go back to work—at least for a year, two years, six years. Invested wisely, your savings can protect your family's standard of living, create more peace of mind, and offer you options for how to live your life.

REVIEWING YOUR INSURANCE

If either you or your spouse has health, life, or other insurance benefits at work, partnering is a good time to take another look at the plan. Most people have no idea what their company plans cover. Remember your first day of work? Remember receiving that little handbook of benefits? Where did you put it? Most people never bother to look at it until they need it. But not knowing what you're covered for may mean you're missing several things you could be claiming.

If your partner is paying independently for coverage, adding him or her as a beneficiary on your plan is one way to save some money. A spouse is usually covered under an employer's benefit plan for just about everything health-related that the employee has coverage for.

If both you and your spouse have benefits, pick the best plan and opt out of the other if it'll save money. Since most plans allow you to claim only the portion not covered under another plan, dual coverage often means you're paying more than you should. Read the fine print—under some plans, common-law couples must be residing together for a year before a partner can be named on the plan.

A common perk for most employees is life insurance. If you have no children, the minimum may be enough. However, if you plan to have children, or one spouse will be dependent on the other, trying to get insurance when you need it could be harder than you anticipate, since even a small change in health may disqualify you. And it will definitely cost more as you get older. If one of your company's plans offers you the ability to buy more insurance at the group rate, take the time to compare the rate with insurance you can buy on your own. And make sure before you purchase insurance through your company plan that you can take that insurance with you when you leave your employer.

The same rules apply to disability insurance. While many companies offer disability insurance as part of their package, you may want to consider topping it up with a private plan to ensure you are covered even if you are laid off. If your employer allows you to opt out of the company plan, consider buying your own plan with your after-tax dollars, so that your disability income will be tax-free. And remember, if you are self-employed, disability insurance is a must-have.

TAX IMPLICATIONS

Before 1993, common-law couples received different tax treatment than married couples. Now, under the *Income Tax Act,* unmarried couples are treated exactly the same as those who have signed the license. As far as the Tax Man is concerned, you are considered married if you have lived together in a conjugal relationship for at least 12 months, or are the natural or adoptive parents of a child. Even if you haven't taken a trip down the aisle, you can contribute to a retirement plan for your spouse, lump your medical and charitable donations together, and transfer credits between your returns. You can also leave assets to a common-law spouse without capital gains attribution.

Here's a question just about everybody in financial planning hears: "How do I minimize my taxes?" Once you've partnered, you have some more options. You can combine the claims for medical expenses incurred by both you and your spouse (including your premiums for health and dental insurance), along with your eligible dependants, for any 12-month period to maximize your tax savings. The lower-income spouse should make the claim. You can also maximize your tax credit for charitable donations by combining your claims on one return.

Income-Splitting

Remember how I told you that Canada has a progressive tax system, and the more money you make, the more you pay in tax? Well, this is the very reason people seek to split their income with their partners (and sometimes their children). By moving money into another body's hands, you can reduce your own taxable income and pay tax at a lower rate. It's a good idea. And the Tax Man has given us a couple of ways to make it work.

Use a Spousal RRSP

A popular way to split incomes is to use a spousal RRSP to accumulate retirement assets. A spousal RRSP makes oodles of sense for income-splitting if your projected retirement income will be significantly higher or lower than your spouse's. It is a good way to get more income into the lower-income spouse's hands, where the tax paid will be at a lower marginal rate.

Too often people are reluctant to use a spousal RRSP because they are concerned about marital breakdown. What they don't realize is that under family law, each spouse owns half of the other's RRSP anyway. So just because your name is on the plan, it doesn't mean it won't be divided when you divorce.

Use a TFSA

When the government introduced the Tax Free Savings Account (TFSA), it provided another income-splitting tool. The money you give to your spouse to put into his TFSA is his to keep without any tax implications.

REVIEWING YOUR ESTATE PLAN

When you marry, your will is automatically revoked unless you made the will in contemplation of marriage. So whether you are marrying for the first time or the fourth, you will need to make a new will.

Common-law relationships are recognized as legal marriages for certain purposes, but not for others. So you can contribute to a spousal RRSP as long as you have "cohabited in a conjugal relationship for a period of at least one year, or less than one year if the two individuals are the natural or adoptive parents of a child." However, under estate law, if you're in a common-law relationship—no matter how long it is—your partner has no rights on intestacy. So if you die without a will, your partner of 20 years would have no rights under the succession laws.

The common-law spouse's only course of action is to make a claim against the estate for support as a dependant, providing he or she has been in a common-law relationship for not less than three years, or for a lesser period if there is a child from that relationship. So, the common-law spouse would have to go through the process—and the cost—of making a claim against the estate through a formal proceeding in court. That's a rough road to walk emotionally, but particularly when you're also dealing with a family from a first marriage. To protect your spouse, or to ensure you are protected, a will with specific designations must clearly state who gets what and when.

In terms of property rights, legally married spouses can opt into the "elective regime," which is legalese for "since I don't like what I am getting under the will, I choose to go for an equalization," which is a 50–50 split of the property amassed during the marriage. Common-law spouses don't have this option.

Power of Attorney

While you don't need independent legal advice to sign a power of attorney, don't do so without: a) knowing what you're signing, and b) keeping a copy for your records. You wouldn't believe the number of women who arrive at their lawyer's office to talk about divorce with absolutely no idea of what they've signed. You trust your partner, right? You love him or her. Why wouldn't you do it if asked? There's no reason, as long as you know what you're signing and you keep a copy. If you don't, then you're a dope.

PARTNERING AGAIN

Remarriage brings its own complications. There may be one or two ex-spouses. Perhaps there are children. Maybe you plan to have children together. Then there are all the habits you've each established and want to keep, but that drive each other nuts.

Combining families brings additional complications to a new relationship. Older children can feel resentful that their parent's assets are now going to be used to support someone else or someone else's children. New babies may increase that sense of resentment. Parents, siblings, even nieces and nephews can feel angry because of being denied what they feel is rightfully theirs. (I'm not sure why anyone thinks a penny they haven't earned is theirs, but it happens all the time.)

Dying intestate is just about the worst thing you can do to your family at this point. Let's say your partner has children by a previous marriage. You have no children. Now let's say you have a terrible car accident. You die first. Your partner dies shortly after. If you don't have a will, your spouse will have been deemed to have survived you. All your assets will pass first to your spouse, and then to his family, leaving your siblings and parents completely out of the loop.

If you have children from a previous marriage, it is important that you safeguard their interests, and you have to talk about this in a calm and rational way. It may be difficult at first, but you have to work through it. Just as important is that children of the new relationship be protected. You have to weigh the responsibilities you have to the older children against the responsibilities you have to the younger children to come up with a fair deal. This can be particularly difficult if only one spouse has children from a previous marriage.

In complicated family situations, the best thing to do is seek professional advice. Whether you are thinking about setting up educational savings plans, transferring assets through a trust, or writing a will, only a professional will be close enough to the law and have enough experience to help you clarify your options. And don't choose a generalist. For complicated issues, you need someone with a wealth of experience. Choose a specialist. It may cost more, but it will save you time and aggravation, and it will give you peace of mind. What's the going rate on peace of mind these days anyway?

REVIEWING YOUR GOALS

Whether you're getting married or moving in together, hooking up can be both exciting and scary. The key to doing it successfully is to sit down and talk about it. Don't keep secrets. Make a plan for how you'll deal with your money as individuals and as a family, and make sure you both stay connected to what's going on with the money. Taking turns managing the accounts and having regular conversations, so that both of you are clear about what's going on, means you're both in the know and working to the same ends.

If you haven't yet talked about your goals as part of your financial discussions, it still needs to be done. When you partner, you have a whole new set of inputs—financial and otherwise—that need to be accommodated. While you would hope that you have similar goals towards which you're jointly working, that doesn't mean giving up your own dreams. Perhaps you'd like to go into business for yourself one day. How will marriage affect that? Will you move towards your goal more quickly or more slowly? Perhaps your goal is as simple as getting away for a couple of weeks every winter. Will you go together? Will you go with friends? Maybe your goal is to move to the country. Does your partner share your love of nature? Will your partner still work in your present locale? What about the commute?

Partnering requires a series of negotiations to work. But that doesn't mean compromising your own dreams and desires. Your personal goals are important. What you want to achieve is important. Giving up your life-long dreams, or trying to change yourself to make the marriage work, only ends up causing resentment. When my second marriage ended—he was a lovely man, but our different objectives were too much to overcome—I realized that I had compromised my way right out of our relationship. To make him happy and keep him happy, I kept changing who I was. There was a significant difference in our ages, and I had to compensate so people would stop referring to me as his daughter. I wore different clothes. I always wore make-up. I gave in and gave in and gave in, until I had nowhere to move. I had compromised myself right into a corner: I didn't like who I was, and I didn't like where I was. When it suddenly occurred to me that we were on different paths—I was just getting started with a wonderful career, while he was beginning to wind down and wanted to spend more time out of the city—I realized we weren't going anywhere together.

I'm not the only person with a story like this. I've met scads of people who suddenly realized they had to change. They were losing themselves. It comes as a huge shock to the partner. It seems like a betrayal. The only way to avoid the you-don't-know-who-I-am-or-what-I-want outcome is to talk. Talk about your dreams: what you want from life, what's important to you, how you feel, and what you would like to change. And keep talking about your dreams and goals until you feel they are being recognized and accommodated. You have them, whether or not you realize it now. And if you don't share them, they'll overtake you. It's a matter of riding the wave or being completely washed away by it.

14

WHEN YOU HAVE A BABY

Perhaps the largest source of internal conflict for many women is in reconciling their roles as caretakers and nurturers with all their other needs: keeping a job, furthering their careers, and achieving financial independence, to name just a few. I know that until my children were born, I had no trouble deciding what my priorities should be: Me! While a lot has been written about women's innate need to nurture—to put others at the centre of their lives and before themselves—little can prepare us for the impact of a baby.

My career track got broadsided when Alexandra was born. Until then, I could work 17 hours a day, seven days a week when the situation demanded it. With a sweet angel waiting for mommy, I was loath to make those kinds of commitments anymore. When Malcolm came along, I was hit by a two-by-four, never to be the same again. My priority-shift was final and, without question, the kids came first. That's not to say that I didn't still want a career. I did. But now I was going to have to fight with myself each time I contemplated a job of any size. It was no longer a case of, "What do I do to get this job?" Now it was, "How badly do I want this job, and what am I willing to give up to do it?" Often, what I was willing to give up was sleep. I've spent hundreds of mornings from three to seven o'clock trying to get a decent amount of work done before the kids got up. Thank goodness those early months of motherhood and the accompanying lack of sleep prepared me so well for the rest of my life.

YOUR SPENDING PLAN

Kids are expensive. They need diapers, cribs, carriers, child care, and "big beds" when they outgrow their cribs. They damage and break things. There are medical and dental expenses and clothing. And let's not forget about food! Then there are birthdays, school field trips, summer camps, holiday seasons, and all the parties they'll attend for which you will have to supply a gift. Take a vacation with two children and suddenly your travel costs double. Go out for a meal, and, *wham*, there's another bill that just went up. Add in enrichment lessons such as music, ballet, or gymnastics, or sports such as hockey, skiing, or anything competitive that requires travel, equipment, and gear, and you're looking at a whopping bill. And when kids become susceptible to the triple whammy of advertising, brand power, and peer pressure, watch out! Did I mention allowances?

While the costs of raising kids can be daunting if looked at all together, it's surprising how you manage to get by with a little less of this or that, so Molly can have that new stuffed toy. There are strategies you can use to minimize the cost of things such as toys and clothing.

When you get pregnant, you'll be overwhelmed with the desire to provide the best of everything for your new lassie or laddie. The first thing to do is hunt up all your old friends who have had kids and ask them what you need. Check a baby book. Make a list. Then start shopping—slowly. Put the word out, and you'll be amazed at the number of people who will offer things you'll find useful. Mommies are the most sharing of all creatures.

If you want an idea of what it will cost to raise your child, talk to your friends. Do up a budget for your new expenses, and then confirm your figures with those who are in the know. When it comes to shaving dollars off your kid budget, buying second-hand can save you scads of money. Find the second-hand stores in your neighbourhood, or ask friends for the names of good stores. Shop the garage sales. When Alexandra was about 18 months, I was an avid garage-sale shopper. It got me out of the house on my own for a couple of hours on Saturday mornings, and for just a few dollars, I participated in a great shopping experience. I got an enormous bucket of Lego for $30. We got a $200 climber for the backyard for $65. I bought toy cars, books (one of my favourites came from a garage sale), clothes, and dress-up supplies, such as beads, necklaces, and scarves, at a fraction of the retail cost.

Second-hand stores are also a great place to recycle stuff your kids have outgrown. When Malcolm no longer fit his crib, I took it to a second-hand store and got 60% of what I paid for it. That's not bad. And I used the money from his crib towards the cost of his new, big-boy bed.

Probably the most money I have saved has been in clothing my daughter. Her cousins, who live in Florida, are two and four years older than Alex. The timing couldn't be better. Twice a year, my cousin boxed up her girls' outgrown clothes and sent them to me. Alex wore the most beautiful dresses. I had to do winter, but summer was sealed.

YOUR EMERGENCY FUND
....

Now that you have a baby, your emergency fund is even more important. You're not just responsible for yourself anymore. You've got a baby to feed, clothes to buy, and a roof to keep over baby's head. If your partner were to die, you were to become unemployed, or you were to become disabled, you would need your emergency fund. If your roof were damaged in a storm, your furnace were red-tagged, or you separated from your spouse, you would need your emergency fund. This is no time to give up your safety net.

If you've already established an emergency fund, you may have to top it up to cover the additional expenses associated with your kids. Major changes in lifestyle such as divorce, widowhood, and illness have their own traumas. You and your children do not need the additional worry about where the groceries will come from next week, or how you'll pay the phone bill.

MANAGING YOUR MONEY

If you're planning to have a baby, there are steps you should take to prepare for the interruption in your income to assure your financial health, just as you would take steps to ensure your physical health. Women who want to get pregnant often change their life patterns in anticipation of creating a new life. They change the way they eat, how much sleep they get, take extra vitamins, stop smoking and drinking—lots of stuff to prepare for the blessed event. However, fewer women take into account the cash-flow crunch they'll experience during their maternity leave. Fewer still are prepared for the strong desire to remain at home caring for that sweet little bundle of joy, even after the maternity leave has expired.

If you want your maternity leave to go smoothly, if you want to be able to focus on the baby without having to worry too much about money, then you have to do some planning. It's like everything else in life. Look ahead, see what has to be done, and just do it.

You'll have to start by guesstimating how long you'll be off. Check with your benefits department at work to find out how much you'll receive in maternity benefits, as well as what benefits you'll be covered for during your maternity leave. If you'll receive only a small portion of the money you'll need to meet your commitments, you'll have to save aggressively while you do have an income to compensate for those months when your income is reduced. (Keep in mind that there are circumstances in which you may receive no maternity benefits. I was self-employed. Other women may not have worked long enough prior to their maternity leave. Don't assume you will qualify for benefits. Check!)

Lots of women think of this as the prime time to dip into their retirement plans or line of credit to support themselves while they aren't earning a regular income. If you've contributed to your retirement with this in mind, then you've been using your RRSP as a savings account with special tax advantage, and you haven't really been planning for retirement (which you'll still have to do). So don't fool yourself. Every cent you take out of your retirement plan is out for good. There's no way to get that money back into the plan. And the long-term growth? *Poof.* It's non-existent if there's no money in the plan to grow.

I received an e-mail one day from a woman who was in a panic. She was about five months from her maternity leave, her husband was not working, and she had no idea how much income she'd have while she was off work. She hadn't checked to see what her maternity benefits would be, but she was already sure they wouldn't be enough to cover rent, never mind food and everything else that comes with a new baby. Obviously, she didn't have a plan.

It's not unusual to see a woman surprised by the fact that the strip turned pink, blue, or whatever the going colour is. The thing is, panicking won't help. It'll add stress to your life and your partner's. It'll stress out the baby. But it won't solve anything. It's time to sit down, have a talk about how you're going to cope—what you're going to DO—so that you can move from panicking to planning. Remember, a little creativity will go a long way to getting you through the tight spots. Women aren't the only caregivers in the world, y'know. If a child has two parents, both are equally capable of nurturing, cuddling, and caring for that child. And no, he doesn't have to do it the way you'd do it; he just has to do it well. You may have to go back to work early and leave your partner to the job of caring for baby if your financial circumstances demand it.

KEEPING A HEALTHY CREDIT IDENTITY

In the best of all worlds, you'll have enough set aside to stay in the black while you're off work having your kids and caring for them. But most people don't live in that world, and credit becomes one tool for helping to make ends meet. I have a girlfriend who is a single mom. She's chosen to work only part-time so that she can be at home with her daughter as much as possible. She has seen her income plummet and her debt rise as she works only three days a week. She's frustrated. She's worried. She's sometimes angry. And she's always looking for ways to get to the end of the month without getting any further into debt. But there's always something. When she came to me with the problem, she was $12,000 in debt, including her car loan and several credit card balances. We talked about what she could do to ease the pain.

She was carrying a lot of money on a credit card that charged 17% interest. The first thing I told her to do was apply for a cheaper card and transfer the balance. "You can do that?" she said. "Yes," I replied. "I didn't know that," she said. Many people don't. (A caveat to balance transfers: don't fool yourself into thinking you now have access to double the credit, or rationalize that you can carry more credit with a lower interest rate. That defeats the purpose.)

Sometimes, when people get into debt, they can see no way out, and everything they do gets them in deeper and deeper. They don't know the rules, so they don't know how to play the game to their advantage. They start to bounce cheques. They miss making minimum monthly payments on their credit cards. They skip mortgage payments or car payments, figuring it won't have any long-term impact or that they'll catch up later. Out the window goes the emergency fund, followed very closely by the spending plan. Unfortunately, the long-term impact can be quite severe, since our credit history tends to show all our financial indiscretions. And it can take a long time to repair the damage we've done.

It's important when you hit any financial crunch that you keep your credit picture in mind. Credit mistakes aren't quickly erased, so you must be careful about what you do and how a lender will perceive it in the future. Bouncing cheques may only carry a small penalty now, but the blemish on your record can have significant consequences when it becomes really important to qualify for a loan.

In my girlfriend's case, her car died. She needed her car to do her job. When she went to the bank to get a loan for a new car, she was astounded to find that she was denied the loan. It wasn't a huge loan, but her credit history was blotchy, and she was already in debt to the tune of about $20,000. She felt trapped. Thankfully, her wonderful parents stepped in and co-signed for her, so she could get a car and get back on her feet. But she felt ashamed and embarrassed in having to turn to them.

KEEPING A ROOF OVER YOUR HEAD

One decision most new parents face is how to make room for a new baby. If you're already in a house or a large apartment, chances are you can just clear out that room you've been using for storage. But if you're out of space or starting to consider things such as school locations and recreational facilities, you'll be planning to move.

One of the things you must think about carefully is how to time your move. Will you need to be in your new place before the baby is born? Can you wait a few months, a year, or even more before moving? Check your rental agreement to see when you can move without penalty. If you are in your own home, you likely have a mortgage. When will it renew? Do you have the option of porting the mortgage to a new property? Will you be able to add on to the existing mortgage without penalty?

People often use the birth of their first child as an excuse to upgrade their home. But unless you're currently living in a shoebox, you can probably incorporate a baby without needing a whole lot more space. If moving to a new place makes sense financially, then have a plan so you're not going off half-cocked.

MANAGING YOUR RISKS

The arrival of a little one brings added responsibilities, not the least of which is your financial responsibility to ensure your child can be cared for in the event you are no longer around, or are unable to earn a living because of a disability.

Babies are beautiful, aren't they? Thank goodness we have the good sense to take steps to protect them. Or do we? Ask yourself these questions: If you or your spouse were to die tomorrow, would there be enough money available to raise your sweet innocent to maturity? Would there be enough for food, clothing, a roof over her head? Would he be able to take piano classes, travel, get a university education? Or are you depending on the kindness of family and friends?

If you don't have enough protection for your children, NOW is the time to do something about it. It would be bad enough having to deal with the loss of a mom or dad—or even worse, both parents. But to deal with the financial repercussions of not having any money is too much for any child to have to bear. It's too much for a single spouse to have to deal with too. Mom has to abruptly return to the workforce to put food on the table. Dad has to find the additional income to hire a caregiver for his precious little ones. The stress can wreak havoc on the family's life.

Money doesn't solve all the problems of the world. But having sufficient insurance to protect your family gives your loved ones the breathing room and financial resources to cope, adapt, and move forward. And it takes the jeopardy out of the future.

Now, more than ever, you must insure your ability to generate an income. Think about the impact of losing your income for just five years. If you net $30,000 a year, that's $150,000. Clearly, the risk to you and your family is huge. Besides the mounting debt as you watch bills go unpaid month after month, there are also all the increased costs associated with being treated for your condition. With the appropriate coverage, not only will you be able to meet your financial commitments, you'll be protecting your assets.

TAX IMPLICATIONS

It can cost between $150,000 and $250,000 to raise a kid today. There are lots of deductions and credits you can claim that will help make ends meet each year.

Claim all your child care costs. Child care expenses include everything from a nanny, daycare, and camps, to occasional babysitting and swimming lessons. Regardless of your babysitter's age, as long as you get a receipt, you can claim the expense. And child care expenses can be claimed for children under the age of 16. While you don't have to submit those receipts with your return, you must keep them for seven years in case they are requested by the Tax Man for verification. Make sure that all your payments for the year will be made by December 31.

For kids in private school, check with the school to see if any of the tuition is eligible for the tuition-fee credit. For children in university, make sure they file their own returns. If they do not need all their tuition fees to reduce their federal tax payable to zero, those fees may then be transferred to you. But this is only possible if your children file returns.

Here's a tax tip to consider when planning your maternity income: just because you make an RRSP contribution doesn't mean you have to claim the deduction in the same year. You can claim that deduction when it suits you most. That's usually when you're in the highest tax bracket, because that's when you'll get the biggest refund. Choosing the right time to claim is particularly important for people who are planning on having a family, anyone who has left the workforce for a period of time, or anyone who has income that rises and falls from year to year. Let's take the example of Sue, who worked all through 2000 and had an income of $55,000. In 2010, Sue was eligible to make an RRSP contribution of $9,900. Smart Sue was on a periodic investment plan and had socked away all her eligible contribution. In June of 2010, Sue gave birth to Michaela and did not work for the rest of the year, so she only earned $25,000 that year. If she had claimed her full deduction, she would have gotten a deduction of only 20% based on her much-reduced income tax rate. But let's say Sue held on to the deduction for another year. When she returned to work in 2011, she was back to her higher income, so she could claim the deduction at a much higher marginal tax rate, and her deduction was worth way more. Planning when to take the deduction is an important part of using an RRSP as a tax-reduction strategy. Plan carefully, and you'll get a bigger bang for your buck!

REVIEWING YOUR ESTATE PLAN

At no point is it more important to have a will than when you have children. If you don't have one yet, go and get one. The peace of mind it brings is well worth the money.

I remember the first trip I planned to take away from the children. A friend asked me how I was feeling about going. I answered that the only thing I was worrying about was the flight (I'm not a frightened flyer, just a dumb mom), and what would happen to my children if both my husband and I were to drop from the sky. She smiled. "Do you have a will?" she asked. "Yes," I replied. "Then nothing can happen," she said with a huge grin. "You only die without a will. Once you get a will, you'll live forever!" I laughed myself silly and felt much better. The point: if you take the right steps to protect your family, you have much less to worry about.

$ **Gail's Tips:** I believe strongly that educating children about money—what it is, how it works, its value, and its place in our lives—is a vital part of raising healthy and responsible children. Without your guidance, how will your children learn to do it right? Where will they learn to do it at all?

There's no safer place to learn about money than at home. And there's no one better equipped to teach it than you. Never mind that you're not a financial expert. You can learn too. What's important is that you know your child. You know how she learns best. You understand what motivates her. And you know what won't work. You are her best teacher.

To experience money, children need to get their hands on some first. Hello allowance! When is the right age to start an allowance? At about six. How much? Try one dollar for each year of age—so your nine-year-old would get $9 a week.

Once your child has some money, your next step is to help her set expectations about what she'll do with her money. Since every wealthy barber in the world will tell you to save 10% of your income, start your child off on the road to financial success with this simple rule: out of every dollar in allowance, she'll put 10¢ towards a long-term savings program. Then there are the weekly or monthly expenses your child has assumed responsibility for, such as bus fare, lunch money, and, as she gets older and more responsible, her clothing, school supplies, and extracurricular activities. Finally there must be some mad money—that's the go-out-and-blow-it-on-anything-I-want money.

The idea of an allowance isn't to give your child scads of money above and beyond what you spend on him. Rather, you should be moving the money you would normally spend on your child into his hands so he can learn to manage it.

Once you've established the allowance routine, keep your hands out of your pocket! If your kid blows his stash, makes unwise loans, or loses his money, he needs to experience the real consequences. Let him wait until his next allowance or find a way to earn the money he needs.

The most constructive thing we can do as parents is allow the natural consequences that teach the important lessons. It's tough to bite your tongue as your little one sadly watches his friends go off on an outing he can't afford because he blew all his money on the latest fad going, but that's life.

Learning about money doesn't rob children of their childhood, and it doesn't steal the magic. By teaching your children what money is, how it works, and the role it plays in life, you're giving your kids one of the most useful lessons of all. It's a lesson that will serve them for a lifetime. It prepares them for the future. And it gives children an opportunity to make their own magic.

. . . .

REVIEWING YOUR GOALS

Now that you have a new dependant, this is a natural time to review your goals. Things like retirement planning and vacations tend to take a back seat to the costs of raising a baby. But it's not always a good idea to put your own financial goals on hold completely. After all, raising kids is an 18-year proposition.

Let's say you can currently contribute $7,500 to your retirement plan. You decide to forego your contribution for the next 18 years. At just 8%, that'll cost you $296,000—and a whopping $161,000 in growth (translation: money you didn't have to contribute).

While you will have to trim expenses in some places, and your retirement plan may be one of them, it's worthwhile to continue contributing as much as you can because of the Magic of Compounding.

Saving for Your Child's Education

If you think raising kids is expensive now, wait until you see what it's going to cost to educate them when it's time for them to go off to university. While you may believe it is at least partly your child's responsibility to pay for their education, no one likes to think about their children graduating from school with an albatross of debt around their necks. So what can you do to ensure your little ones have all the educational advantages you think they should have? Start planning, and start now!

One of the most popular ways to save for future educational costs is with a Registered Education Savings Plan, or RESP. With an RESP, all income earned within the plan is tax-deferred and taxed in your kids' hands when they use it. There is no deduction for money going into an RESP, but contributions do earn a bonus from the government in the form of the Canada Education Savings Grant (CESG). The CESG only applies to children under 18, and special rules apply for children who turn 16 or 17 in a year an RESP contribution is made.

While there is no maximum that you can put into an RESP each year, there is a $50,000 lifetime limit per child. And you can catch up for the years you did not make a contribution. The basic CESG room is $400 per year from 1998 to 2006, and $500 from 2007 onward. The maximum grant that a child can receive in a calendar year is $1,000, provided grant room is available, so don't be tempted to catch up too much at once. Each year, you can catch up for roughly one year of missed contributions.

Let's say you made no RESP contributions for Molly, who was born in 2000. The total CESG room Molly would have accumulated for contributions you haven't yet made would be $5,300 ($400 per year from 2000 to 2006, and $500 per year from 2007 to 2011). If you set up an RESP for Molly this year, you can contribute up to $5,000 (that's the regular $2,500 you're allowed, plus $2,500 for one year you didn't contribute but could have) and grab a grant of $1,000. Yup. You put in $5 and the Feds give you $1 . . . that's an automatic 20% return on your money, before it's even invested. Have I got your attention now?

RESPs must be collapsed within 25 years of the starting date. That expiry date is sometimes a bummer for parents who have kids who are far apart in age. If you want to get around the 25-year limit, avoid family plans and open up a new RESP every five years or so. With several RESPs, you won't have all your money in one plan. If there is a delay in using your RESP because your daughter decides to take time to travel or work before entering university, you won't have to forego all the income earned because the 25-year time limit has expired. You'll still have two or three other plans to draw on.

While many of your goals will now focus on creating the best possible life for your wee one, you can't push away your own dreams and desires completely. You will be modelling for your children what life can be. If it is just service to others, that's what they'll learn. Or they'll rebel and become selfish and self-centred. As a mom and a woman, you must demonstrate balance: today's desires with tomorrow's needs, individual desires with familial needs, making money with making time for everything else. What you show your children will have far more impact than anything you say, so make sure you're living the life you want your children to emulate when they take charge of their own lives.

15

AS YOU APPROACH RETIREMENT

Retirement is just around the corner, and you can hardly believe it. Just a few years ago it seemed so far away. Now, with five years or less left working full-time, you've got to start thinking about a lot of the issues you thought you'd have plenty of time to contemplate. Where will you live? What will you do with your time? How will you structure your finances so you don't have to spend the next 22 years worrying about money?

Twenty-two years? That's right.

Many Canadians retire before age 65. In fact, the median retirement age for women is just 60. There's some debate about whether this will reverse because of a combination of a shortage of women in the workforce and the fact that they don't have enough savings, but that's still the future. For now, women are retiring earlier, and they're living longer. A woman aged 50 today can expect to live to about age 82, while her male counterpart can expect to live to age 76.5.

Retiring early requires some careful planning. When you combine early retirement with longer life spans, the result for most people is more time to fill, more inflationary pressure on fixed incomes, and greater concern about how to make the money last at least as long as you do. Your savings will have to last longer, and you'll have less time to accumulate the money you'll need.

But retirement shouldn't be a time of stress and worry. There are many things you can do to plan and put your mind at rest for the financial impact of retirement. By looking ahead, you can adapt your plan while there's still time to accumulate and organize assets, and you can ease the transition to the next phase in your life.

Taking maximum advantage of all the choices retirement offers requires some planning. By developing new skills as a rehearsal for retirement, you can set the stage for a more orderly transition. Consider the non-financial impact too. What will you do with your time? How will you maintain your friendships? Where will you live? Look at the big picture as well as the individual pieces of the puzzle. So if you happen to be forced into retirement before you're ready, you'll be better able to deal effectively with your change in circumstances.

YOUR SPENDING PLAN

To retire when you want and live the way you want, take a good look at what retirement will cost. One rule of thumb is to estimate that you will need approximately 70% of your income just prior to retirement. Another way to figure out your expenses is to look at your current spending plan, and project what it will cost when you retire. Some costs will go down. You'll likely spend less on clothing and transportation. And if you've planned carefully, you'll have made all your major purchases (such as a new car, new appliances, etc.), and you should have eliminated all of your debt. But some of your expenses will increase. Insurance premiums, costs for medical and dental care, and travel and entertainment costs may rise. Don't worry about being too precise in your projections. The point of the exercise is to gain some insight into what your retirement lifestyle will cost compared with your current costs.

The second step is adding up how much income you'll receive. Your retirement income will come from a combination of sources, including government pensions, employer pensions, RRSP savings, and your non-registered assets.

The final step is to determine if there is a gap between income and expenses. If you have a positive gap (your income is greater than your expenses), you're in fine shape and can let your retirement savings continue to grow tax-sheltered. If there is a shortfall, you'll have to look for ways to supplement your income.

Determining whether or not you have enough will also be a reflection of your money personality. Retirees seem to fall into three distinct groups: those who are fearful of not having enough and spend little or nothing, those who want to maintain their capital and strive to live on the return their investments generate, and those who plan to draw on their capital to enjoy their retirement.

Sticking your head in the sand isn't the answer to the queasy feeling in your stomach about whether or not you'll have enough. If you think money will be tight, now's the time to adjust your expectations . . . and your spending.

Review your current spending plan to ensure your expenses are nicely in hand and that you are on target with your savings goals. If you're not, do some belt-tightening to accumulate the extra savings you need. Brown bagging it, cutting down on dinners out from three times a week to one, and taking the bus or carpooling are all ways of taking money out of your cash flow so you can put it into your retirement nest egg.

You might also decide to delay your retirement. The later you retire, the more time you have to save, the higher your company and government pensions will be, and the more time your money has to grow before you have to start pulling on it. And if you also plan to work during retirement, you'll stretch your retirement savings even further. Do you have an interest or hobby you could turn into a money-maker? My friend, JD, decided to build websites as a sideline during retirement. What do you like to do that you could use to bring in a few extra bucks? It doesn't have to be a BUSINESS in the grand sense of the word. But if you can bring in $100 to $200 a week, that would offset your grocery bill quite nicely, wouldn't it? Would you consider working part-time in a completely new field? Be creative. Don't underestimate the value of your skills. If you're in a position to take an extra job, you can boost your savings by increasing the money currently coming in.

Remember that your retirement income comes from both the income earned on your savings as well as your principal.

Does this sound obvious? Many people resist drawing on their principal during retirement for fear that they will outlive their money. Or worse, because they want to leave it to someone. For those of you who deny yourselves even the smallest of pleasures because you are hell-bent on leaving an estate for your children, who was your benefactor? It'll be tricky enough getting to the end of the trail before you get to the end of the money. Don't make it tougher by becoming a principal hoarder. If necessary, take your figures to a financial advisor who can show you exactly how long your principal will last.

When it comes to figuring out what your income will be in retirement, the key is to gather lots of information. While we often take for granted our entitlement to government pensions, neither Canada Pension Plan (CPP) nor Old Age Security (OAS) benefits are automatic. You have to apply for them. Send in your application about six months before you wish to receive the income (age 65 for OAS and as early as age 60 for CPP), so you can begin receiving your benefits when you need them. Get a quote from CPP to determine your benefits should you decide to take them early or late, to ensure you have some real numbers to work with. If your CPP benefits are lower than your spouse's, consider splitting your benefits to receive more income. This may help eliminate or reduce the OAS clawback—the Tax Man's grab at your universal pension benefits if you make over a certain amount of money each year. And it may also put each of you in a lower tax bracket, so you'll lower your total family bill.

Next, look to your company pension plan if you have one. Find out exactly how it works. If your spouse has a plan, make sure you understand the benefits of that plan too, especially the death and survivor benefits. Pension plans often pay out more when a woman signs away her survivor benefits. You may think that makes sense in the early years. But how will you cope if your husband dies before you do—which statistics show he very well might. Don't just sign away your rights. Do the math. Understand the implications. Stay in control.

Check to see if your or your spouse's company plan is integrated. This is important, because an integrated plan means the company pension is reduced when government pension benefits kick in. This can affect your decision to take CPP early or late. And it can throw a real spanner in your budgetary works if you have not made an allowance for it. For integrated plans, when you get pension income estimates from your employer, make sure these are the "integrated" amounts, so that you don't double-count your CPP benefits. If the plan promises to provide $1,200 a month and is integrated with CPP, and your monthly CPP benefit is $650, you'll end up receiving one cheque for $650 from the government and another from the pension plan for $550—for a total of $1,200. If your integrated-plan benefits are reduced once you start receiving OAS, make sure that OAS is not clawed back, so you will not lose out. Have a chat with the plan administrator to check the likelihood of this, and then discuss how to avoid the problem with your employer. Find out if your pension is indexed to provide protection against inflation. While most pension plans have eliminated this feature, there are still some people who will benefit from indexing. Find out how it works. Also check to see if your existing benefits programs continue into retirement. Will your health and life insurance remain intact? Do your benefits include a dental plan? Extended health care? Find out where you stand, then make provisions for these items yourself if you are not covered when you retire.

Ask your employer's pension plan administrator for quotes at a variety of ages. Find out year by year what your pension will be, approximately, so you can decide on the right time to retire.

The role your RRSP savings play will depend on your other sources of income during retirement. For some people, RRSP assets will be supplemental to the income they'll receive from other sources, such as government benefits, a company pension plan, or rental property. If you are one of these fortunates, wait as long as possible to convert your RRSP, so you aren't forced to take income before you need it. If you find that you need some income to make ends meet, you can always make a withdrawal from your RRSP.

With sufficient income from your company and government pension plans to meet your basic needs, you'll be able to use your RRSP for special needs, such as for travel, to supplement your family's income when pension benefits are reduced due to the death of the primary pensioner, and to offset the impact of inflation on your retirement purchasing power.

Once you have to mature your RRSPs at age 71, you'll need to find ways to minimize the income you withdraw and, by extension, the tax you pay. More on that later.

If you'll be depending on your RRSPs throughout your retirement, you'll want a steady stream of monthly income that will last as long as you do (and perhaps as long as your spouse). But you'll also need flexibility, so you can change the amount you take or how often you receive your income, or gain access to additional funds, as your needs change. Since this will be your primary source of income, inflation protection will be important. Choose investments that will help you preserve your capital (to protect your future income) while maximizing your yield (to cover inflation).

If you aren't getting pension income on which you can claim the $1,000 pension income tax credit, don't let the credit go to waste. Roll as much as you will need each year from your RRSP into an RRIF (it'll be the $1,000, plus the applicable withholding taxes if the $1,000 is above your minimum annual payout amount), and take the full amount as a lump-sum withdrawal.

If you find that you have enough money to meet all your retirement-income needs, you won't need to draw on your RRSP savings at all. Once you have to mature your RRSP at age 71, it's time to find ways to minimize the income you withdraw and the tax you pay. One way is to use a younger spouse's age for the minimum annual income payment calculation. Another is to take the income from the RRIF annually at the end of each year.

As you can see, there's a lot to consider when you're managing the income and expenses for your retirement spending plan. Don't try to do it all too quickly. You'll need time to noodle, to figure out the best ways to make it all gel. If you need some help, get some. Talk with family and friends, speak with your banker, or hire a retirement specialist to go through your plan with you and point out what else you need to think about. Moving into retirement is a big step. Start planning early and take your time.

YOUR EMERGENCY FUND

Don't forget your emergency fund. A big unexpected bill can put a serious crimp in a spending plan that is based on a fixed income. The size of your emergency fund will depend on your financial commitments and the amount of income you have regularly flowing in. If it looks like things may be tight during retirement, establish a fairly significant emergency fund before you retire. If you know for certain that you will have more income than you'll need, your emergency fund can be smaller. Also consider the source of your income. A pension that is indexed is more reliable than income from interest-bearing investments, since a decline in interest rates could mean significantly less income. Make sure you build an emergency fund into your budget for unforeseen expenses. Even if you plan a tranquil retirement, unexpected expenses can mess up your budget.

MANAGING YOUR MONEY

Holding joint bank accounts with your partner or with a responsible child is one of the first things you should consider as you move closer to retirement. It's one way to simplify your life and your estate plan. Another way to simplify is to consolidate all those savings and chequing accounts into a single account. People who have moved into retirement often say, "I cannot be bothered with watching the money anymore. I am retired. I have other interests. I need this to be as simple as possible." Other people see themselves spending more time charting their growth or monitoring their portfolios on their computers. But eventually, even these people find the whole thing overwhelming and move to simplify.

One of your primary objectives in planning for retirement should be to do go into retirement debt-free. Ongoing credit card or loan payments can create a real strain on a fixed income. And if interest rates should rise, you could find more and more of your food money going to interest costs. If you have outstanding debt that is not tax-deductible, make sure you're working to pay off that debt as quickly as possible. Your investment strategy should balance your need to reduce your debt with your need to grow your assets. If you have a low-return investment (say, a GIC earning 5%) and a high-cost credit balance (your department store card has a balance, and you're paying exorbitant interest), you'll be way better off cashing in your pre-tax GIC to pay off your post-tax department store card.

KEEPING A HEALTHY CREDIT IDENTITY

You're likely to be well past your major borrowing needs at this point in your life. Now you're looking to get rid of all your debt. But a healthy credit history and the ability to borrow money when you need it are still part of a sound financial plan. You just never know when you might need a bridge for your cash flow. If the car suddenly needs major repairs and your GIC doesn't mature for six months, being able to access credit could tide you over. Since one of the only sure things in life is change—and the most significant changes are seldom predictable—having the flexibility to adapt will give you a greater sense of control.

Keeping a healthy credit history as you approach retirement means continuing to borrow money and pay it off to maintain your credit history. Use your credit cards to make purchases, and pay them off every month on time. With each payment, you'll keep your credit history current. If you have a line of credit, draw on it from time to time, as the need arises, and pay it off quickly. That'll keep it in good standing.

KEEPING A ROOF OVER YOUR HEAD

It's time to set the date for your mortgage-burning party. If you eliminate this single largest debt from your cash flow, you'll find yourself with a substantial increase in disposable income. But just getting rid of the debt isn't the only thing to consider. Since your income will likely be reduced during retirement, you'll need to do any fixing up that may be needed while you still have a strong income. Look at your house objectively. Does it need painting? A new roof? How's the furnace?

Look at the expenses associated with running your home, so you can get a clear picture of your fixed expenses during retirement. What does it cost to maintain your home? What are your costs for taxes, heating, and electricity? Think about the amount of space you'll be using when you retire. If your home is larger than you will need, consider converting the basement to a separate apartment to provide some additional income during retirement—or to provide a home for wayward children as they return to the once-empty nest.

If you plan to stay in the home for the long term, make sure that you take care of anything that will become difficult to manage as you age. Large lawns are tough to cut. Slippery floors, long driveways that have to be shovelled in the winter, and too many stairs can become real encumbrances, draining the pleasure from staying in your home. Think ahead to making your home accessible—install shower grips, modify door handles, lower curtain rods, and the like.

Also think about how much of what you'll be doing will be home-based, neighbourhood-based, or out of town. If you plan to spend lots of time at the cottage, do you really want to keep two houses going? If all your friends are in Florida in the winter, how will you feel? How many of your interests and activities take place close to your home? How close do you live to other family members?

YOUR PAY-YOURSELF-FIRST INVESTMENT PLAN

Your RRSP assets will likely be mainstays of your investment portfolio, so it's very important that you stay on top of them. Monitor the overall rate of return you're getting, and take a little time each year to evaluate your plan to ensure it's achieving your objectives. A small increase in annual return can mean a significant increase in your RRSP growth over the long term. Two percent may not sound like much, but it is. Over time, even a small difference in your rate of return can have a tremendous impact on the growth of your RRSPs. The following chart shows the difference in growth for $10,000 invested at various rates of return. As you can see, the differences are significant.

Years	2%	4%	7%	11%
5	$11,040	$12,161	$14,025	$16,851
10	$12,189	$14,802	$19,672	$28,394
15	$13,459	$18,009	$27,590	$47,846
20	$14,859	$21,911	$38,679	$80,623
25	$16,406	$26,658	$54,274	$135,855
30	$18,114	$32,434	$76,123	$228,923

Assuming you choose a portfolio of investments that gives you only a 2% higher rate of return, over 30 years, your investment would have earned an extra 78%.

If you think these differences are only applicable when you are building your assets, here's more good news. Once you retire and begin to make withdrawals, even a small difference in return can extend the life of your retirement portfolio. A portfolio of $100,000 invested at 7%, with an annual payout of $12,000, would last approximately 14 years, for a total payout of approximately $167,000. By increasing your return just 2%, the same portfolio would last over 17 years, for a total payout of approximately $205,000. With a return of 11%, the $100,000 portfolio would last almost 25 years, for a total payout of approximately $298,000.

There's no better way to get a big-picture perspective of your financial position than by completing a net-worth statement. Do this as part of your planning so that you can clearly see, in black and white, just where you stand financially.

Start by listing your assets. Be realistic about their value. Assets will include your cash on hand, in accounts, and on deposit. Check the value of investments such as stocks, bonds, and mutual funds in the financial section of the newspaper or with a broker. The cash-surrender value of your insurance should be stated in your policy. To estimate the value of cars, boats, and trailers, refer to comparables in the classifieds. And remember, while you paid the retail price for many of your possessions, you'll likely receive only the wholesale value if you decide to sell them. Now add up everything you owe. This will include your mortgage, outstanding balances on your line of credit and credit cards, and any loans you may have. It'll also include yet-to-be-paid bills (referred to as your "accounts payable"), as well as taxes owing. Subtract your total liabilities from your total assets, and you have your net worth.

Once you've completed your net-worth statement, take some time to look over your assets. Are you satisfied with their quality? Are they earning the return you expected? Are you satisfied with your total asset base? Perhaps you have a large amount of cash in a savings account. By moving that money to a term deposit or money market fund, you'll very likely earn a higher rate of return. Next, have a look at your liabilities. Are you paying the lowest possible interest? Can you renegotiate? How quickly can you eliminate these debts? Perhaps you have an investment that is not doing particularly well and that you could sell to eliminate all or a part of your debt. Even a small payment towards your mortgage principal will move you closer to being mortgage-free during retirement.

REVIEWING YOUR INSURANCE

If you don't have a preplanned funeral or a whack of cash set aside for your funeral expenses, at the very least, you should have enough insurance to cover the cost of planting you in the ground.

You may also need to have enough insurance to protect a dependant or two. With family structures changing, and children being born to people in their late 40s and early 50s, it's no longer fair to assume that all your dependants will be self-sufficient before you take leave of this world. Another important consideration that will have an impact on the amount of insurance you'll need is how your retirement income cash flow will change after the death of one partner. Let's say your spouse has a great pension, and after he dies, you'll receive 60% of the pension income. That's the typical survivor's benefit. Will that be enough? I know that you'll have fewer expenses with only one person to feed, clothe, and the like, but inflation will have done its dirty work in terms of reducing the purchasing power of your money. The question to ask is, "If my spouse dies 20 years after we retire, will there be sufficient cash flow from all sources to ensure I can live comfortably?" If the answer is no, speak to an insurance agent about getting extra life insurance coverage. At this point, the only thing you'll likely want to look at is term insurance. And prepare yourself for some pretty stiff premiums.

The alternative, of course, would be to put yourself on a savings plan—perhaps investing the amount you would have spent in premiums. Over the long term, you might end up ahead. You'll have to feel fairly secure in terms of how long you and your spouse will live. An unexpected death would cramp the plan.

TAX IMPLICATIONS

Your income-splitting strategies should be well-established at this point. But this is a good time to check how much retirement income you and your spouse will be receiving to make sure you're on the mark. If you find that one of you has significantly more projected pension income than the other, you can make all future contributions to a spousal RRSP to even the playing field. The trick is to pay the same amount of tax, so as a couple, you pay the lowest amount of tax possible.

One of the things many people are concerned about as they approach retirement is how their estate will be taxed. Most folks want to make sure that they pass as much of their remaining assets on to their kids as they can. Inevitably, the following question comes up: "Does it make more sense to use my registered assets first, leaving my unregistered assets to my children, or should I do it the other way around?" Good question. And not an easy one to answer.

Advisors often say you should leave your registered assets within the plan as long as possible, so they can continue to compound on a tax-deferred basis. However, as soon as you die, providing you do not have a spouse to whom to pass those assets, the full amount of the registered assets will be included in your income for the year of your death, and you'll likely pay a whopping amount of tax. The other option is to draw down on your registered assets first, so you're paying a lower rate of tax over a longer term, while leaving your unregistered (previously taxed) assets intact.

So what should you do? As with most things about money, it all depends. It depends on your specific circumstances: how much you have, how long you think you'll live, and what the mix is between your registered and unregistered assets. If the amount you draw from your registered assets moves you into the highest marginal tax rate, so you'll be paying the maximum tax anyway, it makes sense to leave the registered assets intact and have your estate pay the tax at the end when you no longer need the money. If you want to mitigate the loss to your beneficiaries, you can always use a portion of the money you pull each year from the registered pool to purchase a life insurance policy, which will help offset the loss to the Tax Man. For the average Canadian, however, life insurance at age 60 or 70 is very expensive, and the cost often outweighs the benefit. Or you can do what I plan to do: I see my retirement savings as my money, and I plan to spend it.

REVIEWING YOUR ESTATE PLAN

It's time to review and, perhaps, update your will, and get all the legal and financial information in order. If you haven't already done so, put your powers of attorney in place. If you're still hesitating about making a will, might I suggest a small shift in perspective. You're going to die. It's only a matter of time. And if you die without a will, you're going to make things very complicated for the people who have to clean up after you.

While estate planning is often seen as a discussion about death, it really isn't. It is a way to make the lives of the people you leave behind less stressful. It's also the only way to ensure your assets are distributed as you would want them to be.

Don't fall into the trap of thinking that your estate isn't big enough to warrant the time and money of bothering with an estate plan. And don't think that your lawyer, accountant, or financial planner will be able to step in and deal with the issues. Once you leave this beautiful Earth, money matters get put on hold until your estate is probated. If you die without a will, you just prolong the agony.

Immediately upon your death, the government will deem that your capital property has been disposed of. Any increase in value on a stock, bond, your cottage, or any other asset will be subject to tax at the current capital gains rate. There are some exceptions. You can transfer capital property to a spouse without paying tax. This defers the tax until your spouse dies. If you have U.S. assets, such as stocks, bonds, a business interest, or a condo in Florida, you might also have to pay estate tax on these assets. The problem that arises from this "deemed disposition" is that while tax may be payable, it may not be the best time to sell the asset. To sell would be to get less than fair value. Or perhaps you don't want to sell the asset at all. It may break your heart to think about your art collection, painstakingly acquired over the years, being sold off to pay the taxes on your family cottage. Whatever your feelings, your estate will have to deal with the legalities of your move from this world to the next.

If you don't have a will, you've effectively given up control over your hard-earned money to the government. You wouldn't do that in life, so why would you do it in death? I know you won't be here, but your spouse, children, and grandchildren will. Don't put them through that discomfort and aggravation. If you don't have a will, put down the book, go to the telephone, and call your lawyer. If you don't know whom to call, ask the law society in your area for a referral. It doesn't matter what it takes. *You need a will.* Get moving!

REVIEWING YOUR GOALS

Most of your goals will be focused on the near-term retirement date you've chosen. You'll want to have most, if not all, of your debt paid off. You'll want to make sure you're maximizing your RRSP contributions and growth, so you can accumulate as much as possible before you stop working. But those shouldn't be your only goals.

One of the biggest mistakes people make is thinking that at retirement, everything becomes fixed in time and space. There's a real sense that the accumulation of assets will end (what about investment income?) and that inflation will cease (what about the inflation that will erode your income throughout the 20 or 30 years that you are retired?). It's a mistake to see your retirement date as the end. It isn't. It's the beginning of a whole new stage of life. And it brings its ups and downs just as every other stage of life does.

Since retirement is a new beginning, think about how you will restyle your life. While a lot of people do little to prepare themselves mentally, this is one of the most important steps.

16

WHEN YOU RETIRE

Retirement means different things to different people, and it has its own series of stages, so you need to keep planning for the next stage.

Stage One, which I like to refer to as your Go-Go Phase, may include semi-retiring: working part-time, starting a new business, or working as a consultant. Or you may plan to stop working completely while you remain very active in other areas. Your active retirement might include extensive travel; activities such as golfing, skiing, or cycling; or active volunteering.

Stage Two—the Slow-Go Phase—would be your less-active years; the years when you plan to remain in your home, with or without help from others.

Stage Three—or your No-Go Stage—may be the years when you choose to move to a retirement home that provides you with the help you need in managing day-to-day activities and recieving specialized medical attention.

It's not enough to look at where you are now as you move into retirement; you must also look at the transitions you'll need to make as you move through the various stages of retirement.

YOUR SPENDING PLAN

Now's the time to tweak your spending plan. Look at what you're spending now, and then project your costs throughout your retirement. Costs will go up or down depending on what stage of retirement you're in. If you are still working part-time, or if you are travelling extensively, your expenses will be higher than they will be when you choose to sit at home on the porch watching the sunset.

You and your spouse should keep your figures separate, so that when you get into a discussion of how much either of you will have individually, you'll have a point of reference. You'll also need separate figures to calculate your income tax. Check with the Tax Man to see what the most current income tax brackets are for your province.

Use Your RRSPs to Your Advantage

If you benefit from a nice company pension plan, or if you'll be using your unregistered assets to provide an income stream, delay converting your RRSPs to keep the tax-deferred growth going for as long as possible. Converting before absolutely necessary means you may be forced to take income when you don't need it. If you don't need to draw on your RRSP savings at all, focus on minimizing the income you need to withdraw and, by extension, the tax you must pay. Using your younger spouse's age for the minimum annual payout calculation, or taking the income annually at the end of the year, will offset your tax liabilities. If you find that you do need to tap into your RRSPs to make ends meet, you can always make a withdrawal.

If you think your RRSP savings will be your primary source of retirement income, ensure the retirement income option you choose provides a steady stream of monthly income that will last at least as long as you do (and maybe as long as your spouse). RRIFs are usually my first recommendation—more about RRIFs shortly.

You must make a decision about what to do with your RRSP assets by the end of the year in which you turn 71. You could simply withdraw the money in cash. Careful though. What may seem like the easiest option can have negative tax ramifications. When you take cash from your RRSPs, that money is included in your income. This can push you into a higher tax bracket and result in your having to pay considerably more tax. The best way to minimize the tax implications is to convert your retirement savings to a regular stream of income using either an annuity or a RRIF.

Annuities

When you buy an annuity, you give an insurance company, bank, or trust company your money in exchange for a promise of a specific amount of income each month. There are two basic types of life annuities: a straight life annuity provides a regular income payout over your entire life; a joint and last survivor annuity provides income over your or your spouse's life. Sold only through life insurance companies, the amount you receive depends on several factors, including how much money you have, your life expectancy, your sex, and the interest rate in effect when you buy the annuity. Low interest rates mean low monthly incomes, which is one reason annuities tend to decline in popularity when interest rates are low.

There's a potential downside to an annuity: you'll be living on a fixed income, since the monthly payments always remain the same. What seems a princely sum at the outset may feel like a pauper's allowance in 20 years. Remember that surviving spouses will receive less income. The death of the first spouse usually means a 40% drop-off, so the survivor receives only 60% of the original income amount.

RRIFs
....

The retirement income alternative that has become very popular with Canadians is to convert their RRSP savings into a RRIF, which creates a flow of income during retirement. I like RRIFs because they provide the flexibility to design an income stream that meets your specific needs—in terms of amount and frequency—as well as the ability to increase or decrease your income as your needs change.

Your money is tax-sheltered as long as it remains in the plan, and you pay tax only on the money you take out each year. Basically, a RRIF is a continuation of your RRSP, so you can hold the same investments. You can open a RRIF at any age and roll over as much or as little of your RRSP dollars as you wish. You can choose from a variety of investment types, so you can use an investment strategy that will help you preserve your capital (to protect your future income) while maximizing your yield (to cover inflation).

There is a legislated minimum annual payout (MAP) that must be paid from the RRIF each year, with one exception: in the year in which the plan is set up, the MAP is zero.

The main advantage to a RRIF is flexibility. With a RRIF, you have not made a life-long decision. You've made a decision that can be changed at almost any time, depending on the underlying investments you're holding. You can change your asset mix, or you can take out more money than the minimum amount. And when you no longer want to be concerned with the management of your investments, you can buy an annuity using your RRIF assets.

So a RRIF gives you the flexibility to receive more income in years when you need it, and less in years that you don't. It gives you the flexibility to change your mind and change your investment strategy. And if you decide to take only the MAP each year, your RRIF is guaranteed to last a lifetime. Ultimately, it gives you more control over your money.

Remember, if you have no other source of pension income (which you need to claim the $1,000 pension income tax credit), then roll as much as you will need each year from your RRSPs into a RRIF (it'll be the $1,000, plus the applicable withholding taxes if the $1,000 is above your minimum annual payout amount), and take the full amount as a lump-sum withdrawal so you can receive this money tax-free.

Non-Registered Investments

Besides your RRSP investments, you may also have a port-folio of investments that are unregistered. Perhaps you have been buying bonds through a payroll deduction plan. Maybe you've been investing in mutual funds. Perhaps you've got some money socked away in a TFSA. Or maybe you have GICs, stocks, or a rental property or two, which can provide a regular income. Having established an investment portfolio to supplement your retirement income needs, you may now be looking for ways to manage the income from those invest-ments to supplement your cash flow in retirement.

If you are investing using GICs, stagger your maturities—instead of buying a single five-year GIC, split your money between one-, two-, three-, four-, and five-year investments. This will help protect against fluctuations in interest rates at renewal time. Also consider investing a portion of your nest egg in a redeemable GIC. This will provide you with the flex-ibility to get extra cash should you need it. While the interest rate on the redeemable GIC is a little lower, it's worth it to have access to cash—just in case.

If most of your investments have been in mutual funds, and you need some way of taking a steady income to supple-ment your other retirement income, ask about a systematic withdrawal plan. Each month you can redeem a specific dollar amount in mutual fund units, with the cash being deposited directly into your bank account. This strategy also allows you to use a dollar-cost averaging strategy, but instead of buying regularly, you'll be selling regularly. This will even out the ups and downs in the market, so you'll end up with an average selling price.

YOUR EMERGENCY FUND

By this time, you probably feel you no longer need an emergency fund. You may be right. It really depends on how often you receive your retirement income, how accessible your assets are, and how likely you are to hit an emergency at this point in your life. You know you won't be laid off. But what would happen if interest rates took a significant downturn for a few months, and you were forced to start dipping further into your capital to make ends meet? Or what if a sudden illness required you to lay out money for a nurse? How would you and your cash flow cope? As one person said to me as we sat together in a hospital, waiting for our children to be diagnosed, "Life is an emergency."

MANAGING YOUR MONEY

The key to keeping your cash flow working during retirement is to know when the money is coming in and when it has to go out. This is something of an adjustment for people who have been on the payroll for years and have received their salary every month on the second Friday, or on the 15th and the 30th. During retirement, this may take a little more planning.

You may receive income quarterly if you'll be earning dividends, or annually if you're earning interest. And depending how you structure your RRSP or RRIF payouts, your cash may flow in monthly, semi-annually, or annually. You need to know specifically when the money will come in and when the money will flow out. Some expenses, such as your tax bill, will come up quarterly. Others, such as insurance, may be annual. The whole idea of setting up a cash-flow chart is to know that you will have the income when you need it.

A cash-flow chart typically lists all your sources of income and expenses down the left side of the page. Each month has a column of its own going across the top. For each month, the sources of income and the expected expenses are written in, so that you know exactly when the money is arriving and when it is departing. It gives a clear picture of what you can expect, and it shows you where the potential holes may be, so you can adjust your income stream to meet your needs. If you know you'll have an insurance bill in December, you could arrange to take extra from your RRIF in November to cover the cost. Similarly, if you're concerned about meeting your quarterly tax payments, even if you're receiving a monthly income from your pension or annuity, you can arrange to have extra income—perhaps from dividends or interest from a GIC—paid to you to cover your tax bill.

KEEPING A HEALTHY CREDIT IDENTITY

The same rules that apply just prior to retirement carry through to retirement. Keeping a healthy credit identity is part of having a sound financial plan. Without it, you could find yourself in trouble. You may not ever need it, but if you do, it'll be there.

KEEPING A ROOF OVER YOUR HEAD

Where do you plan to live? In the same house or condo? Or are you planning to sell and move to a smaller home? The majority of most people's financial assets are tied up in their homes. Folks figure that when they retire, they'll sell, buy a smaller place, and have lots of money left over. But do you really want to move . . . away from your family . . . away from your neighbours . . . away from everything that's familiar? Most people don't, despite their well-laid plans.

For some people, the decision to move is easy. Perhaps they're attracted by warmer climes. For some, the lure of a small town or being part of a retirement community is very attractive. Or maybe the house is just too big or inappropriate for their needs. How much more income would you have if you sold your house, eliminated your maintenance and tax costs, and rented? Here's a calculation that may help:

Approximate value of home: $ _____

Less sales-related costs: $_____

Less any mortgage still owing: $ _____

Balance to invest: $ _____

Balance to invest: $ _____

Plus return expected at ____%: $ _____

Less tax payable on return: $_____

Net return: $ _____

Net return: $ _____

Plus savings on maintenance*: $_____

Less estimated cost of rental per year†: $ _____

Balance to invest/income: $_____

* When you sell your home, you'll likely eliminate many of your expenses, such as property taxes and expenses related to house maintenance, heating and cooling, hydro, snow removal, and gardening. Remember, unless your rent includes these costs, you'll still have to make provisions for some utility costs and, of course, things such as cable.

† Make sure you choose a home that you'll be happy to live in. Check the newspaper for the prices of rentals in areas in which you'd feel comfortable living. Investigate subsidized-housing alternatives. Don't underestimate your space requirements. Often people who move from houses to apartments feel "squeezed." Heed the words of a wise man: "Let there be space between your togetherness."

Reverse Mortgages

How would you like a way to live in your home while using the equity to finance your retirement? You can use a reverse mortgage to take a lump sum of cash out of the equity in your home. No interest or principal is due until the home is sold or the homeowner dies. If the appreciated value of the property is greater than the amount of the accrued reverse mortgage, the excess goes to the estate. If the value of the property is less than the amount owed, the financial institution that gave you the mortgage has to eat the difference. This is one reason financial institutions don't allow you to use the full value of your home for a reverse mortgage; they have to protect themselves from a decline in the value of your property.

It's important to understand that a reverse mortgage is a "rising debt" loan. This means that the total amount you owe grows over time. I have to admit to a bias against reverse mortgages, because I think you end up losing too much for what you get from the reverse-mortgage company. But you'll have to decide for yourself what's right for you.

Think about whether housing prices in your neighbourhood will likely appreciate or depreciate. Also consider interest rates and the various fees (legal, administrative, etc.) associated with the reverse mortgage, and how fast the debt on the mortgage will grow. Would selling your home and downsizing make more sense? Many lower-cost housing alternatives exist that you may wish to look into. Subsidized dwellings are not limited to public housing; non-profit housing and cooperative housing developments also offer alternatives geared to a retiree's income. You can get information on subsidized housing from non-profit and co-operative housing agencies.

If you decide your present home isn't suitable for retirement, you'll have to decide whether you will move within your community, divide your time between two communities (perhaps your cottage in the summer and autumn, and a warm climate in the winter and spring), or move to a whole new area. You'll have to think carefully about the implications of moving to a whole new community, or spending all or part of your time in another country.

YOUR PAY-YOURSELF-FIRST INVESTMENT PLAN

Even after you retire, you can continue to contribute to an RRSP, providing you or your spouse is under 71 and has a source of earned income, such as rental income or income from a part-time job.

As you move into retirement, you may be asking yourself, "Should I change my asset mix?" Rules of thumb abound in the financial world, and a common one is that your asset mix should be adjusted based on your age: Your equity portfolio should be equal to 100 minus your age. That would mean that at age 60, you'd hold 40% of your investments in equities.

Personally, I don't think any rule of thumb can be used for adjusting your basket of investments, since money personality is a huge factor in determining your comfort level. It's a difficult thing to explain, this idea of money personality, because feelings come into it. On the day you retire, if you have a good asset mix and it's been working for you, if you can sleep and your tummy says it's okay, stick with it. After all, every single person has her own comfort level or sleep factor. Some people are so cautious that they will only invest in term deposits and Canada Savings Bonds, and that's absolutely correct for them. They shouldn't be criticized for doing that. However, it is important that you regularly review your investment mix to ensure that as your life and priorities change, your asset allocation continues to satisfy your needs. If you find there are significant changes to your lifestyle, you may want to make changes to your financial picture.

REVIEWING YOUR INSURANCE

One reason for having insurance at this point in your life is to provide enough cash to meet the tax liability your estate will incur at your death. Economic conditions may make it an inopportune time to sell assets immediately after your death. And you may not want to liquidate some assets—such as the family cottage, which has a lot of sentimental value—so having a lump-sum benefit from an insurance policy would provide the cushion needed.

Let's take the example of a couple that has RRSP assets. When the first spouse dies, the assets can be transferred to the surviving spouse on a tax-deferred basis. In two words: No Tax. But when the second spouse dies, guess what? Tax—and bigtime! Let's say you and your spouse each have $100,000 in RRIF assets. Your spouse dies, and his $100,000 rolls into your plan. Now you have $200,000. Assuming you live on air and die with $200,000 remaining, your estate will have to pay a whack in tax to the government. Now let's say you had an insurance policy that covered those taxes owed, along with any other taxes calculated on your estate. You would be able to split the full value of your estate among your beneficiaries. The question to think about is this: how much estate protection will you need to cover your assets? If you feel you'll have sufficient cash to pay the taxes directly from the estate, that's cool. You won't need insurance. But if your estate will be eaten away by taxes, leaving far less than you imagined for your heirs, insurance could be the solution.

TAX IMPLICATIONS

Once you are 65, make sure you have enough pension income to take advantage of the $1,000 pension income tax credit. Convert a portion of your RRSPs to a RRIF, or buy an annuity (with registered or unregistered funds), to qualify for this tax-free income. People 65 and older also qualify for the age credit. If one spouse can't use this tax credit fully, the unused portion can be transferred to the other spouse's return.

Since the government has broadened the definition of disability, more people now qualify for the disability credit. If you think you might qualify, have your doctor complete the Disability Tax Credit Certificate (Form T2201). For more information, check the rules in the General Income Tax and Benefit Guide.

The pension income, age, and disability credits all qualify to be transferred. Since this can save you a lot on your taxes, don't overlook it.

Claim the HST tax credit. Since your income in retirement will very likely be less than when you were working, you may be eligible. Don't assume you won't get it; check it out.

Maximize your credit for medical expenses by having the lower-income spouse claim all medical costs. Private insurance premiums for coverage, both in and outside of Canada, qualify for this tax credit. The expenses you claim may be for any 12-month period ending in the tax year for which you're filing, so choose the time frame that gives you the largest claim. And since the credit is based on when expenses are paid (as opposed to when the service is rendered), it may make sense to prepay an upcoming expense to maximize your tax benefit.

$ **Gail's Tips:** If at any time in a year, you support a spouse or common-law partner whose net income is less than the specified amount for the year ($10,382 for 2010), you can claim a credit. This credit is reduced by your partner's income, and it disappears once he is making over the specified amount for the year.

••

If one spouse has dividend income but has little or no other income, and therefore cannot claim the dividend tax credit, the dividends can be reported on the other spouse's return. This transfer is particularly beneficial when it reduces the lower-income spouse's income enough so that the higher-income spouse can claim the spousal amount tax credit. Since partial claims are not allowed, whenever there is any opportunity to claim the spousal tax credit, all the lower-income spouse's dividend should be claimed.

Take advantage of the tax benefits of income-splitting by using a spousal RRSP and, if appropriate, splitting CPP benefits. If you have a high retirement income (even after income-splitting), manage your income to benefit from OAS at least once every two years by taking more income in one year (and saving some), so you can take less the following year and get your OAS.

If you have investment income, you can claim a number of expenses against it, including the expense of a safety deposit box and the interest on money borrowed for investment purposes.

Let one spouse claim all charitable donations. The Tax Man doesn't care who makes the claim. All he cares about is that you remit instalment payment on time. As a retiree, you're responsible for paying on time, and there can be heavy penalties for failing to follow the rules. Get the information you need to stay on the Tax Man's good side.

REVIEWING YOUR ESTATE PLAN

You can do a lot of estate planning outside a will to bypass the probate and executor fees. Assets that are not probatable can bypass your will and go directly to the joint-owner or beneficiary. This is of particular importance now that the costs of probating a will have risen. As well, assets passing through the estate are liable to the estate's creditors, but those that don't pass through the estate cannot be touched. Anything that can be held jointly, such as GICs and bank accounts, should be held in joint names.

Once you've decided what you want to do with your estate, update your will. Minimize the work for your executor by having complete documentation on where everything is, and minimize the stress on your family by planning your funeral. Make sure you have enough income to maintain your current lifestyle; then you can arrange your affairs to maximize the estate for your heirs and minimize work for your executor. If you have assets that you do not need to maintain your lifestyle, consider gifting them to children. As long as the person is over 18, there's no attribution. You can also make loans that are forgivable on death.

While the stages of life are reasonably predictable—some of us marry, some of us buy homes, some of us have children—the crap that can happen to us because of disability, divorce, widowhood, and myriad other changes is not. And that's what we'll deal with next.

PART FOUR

JUST
IN CASE

No matter how well you plan, life has a way of throwing punches that can knock you flat. If you want to survive, you've got to keep getting up. Life is about being resilient. This section deals with those knock-out punches. I wish we all could lay a plan and then peacefully follow through. That NEVER happens. No matter how it looks from the outside, every woman is dealing with something difficult in her life. There's no such thing as perfect. But there is a zone.

In the zone, you have things in perspective. In the zone, things are neither bigger nor smaller than they should be. It's a fairly quiet place. From time to time things intrude, but you find it relatively easy to rise above them. Changes don't bring panic. Uncertainty doesn't equate with sleeplessness. Life seems to flow around you with a certain symmetry and serenity. I've been in the zone, and I can tell you it is *wonderful*. Unfortunately, I can't tell you how to get there. You have to find your own way.

I can tell you that I found my way by being true to myself. I said what I thought, without being mean. I did what I wanted, without being irresponsible. I never said "yes" when I really meant "no." Perhaps, most importantly, I knew what I wanted and focused on that.

Now, this may seem odd coming from a woman writing about money but . . .

I got into the zone when money became less important to me. Once I realized that I had taken care of the details, I let go of the worry and started living every minute of the day. It came right in the middle of writing this book. Interestingly, all the research I did, all the lessons I learned about how money affects us emotionally, came home in a grand sweep, and I entered the zone. It wasn't always perfect. I'm not talking about perfect. I'm talking about happy. Some days, I still feel frustrated. Some days, I still feel bogged down. But most of the time, I feel alive, sunny, and able to share myself with others. I'm telling you, the zone is a great place to be.

Does this seem like an odd place to be talking about the zone? Well, I mention it here because I believe that being in the zone helps you to get through any of the next events with grace and a sense of completeness. And I'm not talking about how it looks from the outside. I'm talking about how it feels on the inside.

I have found through my life that those people farthest away from the zone are the ones most concerned about how things look to other people. They are secretive. Who cares what you make! Money doesn't define who you are. Who cares how much debt you have right now! Money is not a measurement of your worth. Who cares how much you've accumulated! A pile of money doesn't make you smarter. Remember, money is a tool that gets us what we need and want, so we can get on with our *lives*. Break the barriers of silence and secrecy, and move into the zone. Figure out what you want, and move into the zone. Be true to yourself, and move into the zone.

When I was a girl, my Aunty Angie told me something that has stayed with me my whole life. She quoted Shakespeare in my autograph book: "To thine own self be true, and it must follow, as the night the day, thou canst not then be false to any man." Will was right. Thanks Aunty Angie.

The categories we'll look at for each of the major life changes covered in this section are the same as in the previous two sections, so you'll be familiar with them now. The work you've done with them (or not) will determine the ease with which you adapt to the curveballs life throws at you.

17

JUST IN CASE YOU BECOME
THE SOLE BREADWINNER

Once upon a time, when my husband was laid off, I was faced with being the sole breadwinner. While I had taken care of myself all my life, the added responsibility of the family sent my face into spasms. I twitched. My husband said it was stress. I denied it. What stress? I could do this. I would just work harder, do more, spend less. But the overwhelming feeling of being the ONLY ONE on whom all the responsibility rested was almost too much to bear. I remember thinking to myself, "This is a turning point in my life. I have to look at things differently from now on." It's helped me to be more aware of men's burdens as they gracefully accept the role of primary breadwinner.

More and more women face the reality of being the sole breadwinner each year. Whether it is through divorce, widowhood, or because your partner is suddenly out of work, the stress can wreak havoc on your health, financial life, and relationships.

Barb has been the sole provider in her family since 1989, when her husband was laid off and he decided to stay home to look after the kids. "I am the sole provider," she says, "so I worry constantly. I worry about providing for the family. If I need credit, will I be able to get enough?" Funny coming from a vice-president of a bank, right?

Barb and I both agree that this is perhaps the most under-rated stressor that people carry when they are the sole bread-winners of their families. Traditionally, it has been the burden men have borne, and they haven't talked about the stress. They might get snippy, but they never say, "I am just so tired of being solely responsible for this." And since women haven't tradi-tionally been in the role of primary breadwinner, we haven't been aware of the weight of the burden. Now that we are find-ing ourselves in this role, we too are bearing up bravely, dying earlier of stress-related diseases, and sniping at our children.

Recognizing that the stress is there is the first step to dealing with it. You'll have to acknowledge the change in status. Talk about what the change in circumstances will mean to you as a couple, as a family, and as individuals. Continue to talk all the way through it. If you share your worry with your friend, the burden will immediately lighten. If your partner is not behav-ing like your friend, find a friend to share the worry with until your partner steadies.

If you've been living well within your means as a family, if you've got your emergency fund set up and a pretty clean credit situation, you're much more likely to make it through intact—home and all—than if you've been living way beyond your means and have run up thousands in credit card debt.

I can't remember where I first read the phrase "involuntary simplicity," but it applies to all those circumstances in which you are forced to simplify the way you live because of less money. There is a sweeping trend to simplification. The media is full of stories of how people are reducing their consumption and honouring frugality as a way of life. *Tightwad, cheapskate,* and *miser* used to have very negative connotations. These words are taking on new connotations as we move away from conspicuous consumption and towards simplification. In fact, stories abound about people who were forced into simplicity only to find that they loved it. They move to the country, grow their own food, and try to live on as little money as possible. They reuse and recycle. They share ideas, coupons, and resources. While they may be poor of pocketbook, they are rich of spirit. They build a community.

Now, this may all seem too much like a cloud-with-a-silver-lining scenario to you if your buddy has just been cast to the wolves by a former employer. But don't discount it completely. Yes, you'll have to survive over the next few days, weeks, and months managing the bruise to your pocketbook as well as the bruise to your partner's ego. But you will come through it. This is not the time to pick at each other's shortcomings. If you have children at home, this is not the time to scare them to death with threats of never again having two brass farthings. This is a time to take it slow, emotionally, while moving quickly, financially, to shore up your situation.

YOUR SPENDING PLAN

You'll need to keep your financial house in order so you don't add even more stress to your already-weighty burden. Reconciling yourself to living on less money is one of the hardest things to do—particularly when the decision is forced. Intellectually, you make all the compromises. Emotionally, you're way behind. Old habits die hard, especially the ones that let you have what you want, when you want. But die they must, because if you try to maintain the status quo, if you behave as though nothing has changed, you will drown in a quagmire of debt.

Time to reprioritize your spending plan. The rent or mortgage has to be paid. You need to put food on the table. But there may be several areas where you can cut back, cut down, or cut out to get by on a single income. People do it all the time and survive. The challenge is to do it and be happy. Take a copy of your spending plan and work through it to determine which costs will go down. Here are some things to consider:

- Can you eliminate child care costs for as long as you have only one income? If your partner is actively looking for work, shared daycare would be less expensive than the full-time daycare you used while you were both working.
- Have you reduced the budget for things like transportation, lunches, and ordering in dinner? Add it up, and you may find that the savings are substantial. As will be

the savings on work clothes, after-work entertainment, and income tax.

- Could part-time employment supplement the family income in the interim? Does your partner have skills that he could use to freelance or consult?
- Would a lifestyle change help? Do you still need the second car? Think of what you'll save on maintenance and insurance, never mind the boost to your savings, when you sell the car.

YOUR EMERGENCY FUND

Your current circumstances are the reason you need an emergency fund. If you have one, you're going to feel a lot safer moving through this trying time. As soon as you can, you'll need to start rebuilding it. It may take longer this time, but at least now you're convinced you need one.

MANAGING YOUR MONEY

While you may have had two or more accounts before you became a single-income family, having a single account will probably make more sense now, at least for the short term, especially if consolidating will reduce your costs. Look hard at the services you will be using. Some financial institutions offer no-charge chequing and ATM use, so hop around to see who has the best deal for you right now.

KEEPING A HEALTHY CREDIT IDENTITY

The easiest thing to do when you have a shortfall in your cash flow is to use your credit cards or personal line of credit to fill the gap. For those of you who intend to use your personal line of credit as your emergency fund, a word of caution: don't get complacent about the fact that you are accumulating debt that will eventually have to be repaid. If you plan to use your credit cards to get over the hump, make sure you're using the cheapest credit card you can find. If you add a 17% interest rate to your already-strapped cash flow, you're dooming yourself. Get a cheapie card, and if you're already carrying a balance on an expensive card, transfer your balance.

While I don't often advocate overdraft protection, because using it is such an easy habit to get into and such a hard habit to get out of, while you're adjusting to your new cash flow, overdraft protection may be a good idea. You won't need it if you are determined to stay within your means and are meticulous about your record-keeping. However, if your buddy tends to let things slide a bit, having overdraft protection to avoid NSF charges will keep your creditors happy, and you'll avoid the negative long-term implications of a rotten credit history.

KEEPING A ROOF OVER YOUR HEAD

Can you afford to continue living in your home on the income you are making? If so, for how long? How much debt will you be getting into if you attempt to maintain the status quo? How long will you likely have to do it on your own? Is there anything you can do to reduce your mortgage expenses, such as renegotiate your mortgage if rates have fallen, or rent a part of your home in the interim? There's no way you will have the answers to all these questions at your fingertips. So this is where your very important woman's intuition comes into play, along with some plain ol' common sense.

YOUR PAY-YOURSELF-FIRST INVESTMENT PLAN

Yeah, like you really think I'm going to be able to save ANYTHING while living on one income? Get real!

If your partner has just lost his job, you may put this on hold until you find your feet financially. If this is a life-choice decision, you may need time to adjust to your new lifestyle. In either case, if you don't get yourself back on track and start saving, you're asking for trouble. Everyone has to save. That doesn't mean you have to save your maximum RRSP contribution, or the amount your sister saves, or the amount the media advocates. But you do have to set something aside for the future. It's your responsibility.

REVIEWING YOUR INSURANCE

As the primary breadwinner, you are now solely responsible for your family's continued peace of mind. And for your own peace of mind, you better make sure you have enough insurance. If you had been counting on your spouse's work plan for life, disability, or health benefits, these need to be replaced. If you think that this isn't the time to make a cash-flow commitment to new expenses (like insurance, which nobody ever really uses anyway, right?), think again. What would your family do if you became disabled while you were the only one with a job? How would your spouse cope if you died? How will you cover those medical bills when they arrive? Insurance is not the place to skimp.

TAX IMPLICATIONS

Some good news: you will end up paying less tax as a family, and if your spouse has no income at all, you'll get a tax break there. Since you're now living on one income, you'll be claiming all the deductions and credits, so make sure you take advantage of everything you can to minimize your tax liability. If your partner has little or no income, remember to take advantage of the spousal tax credit.

While a tax refund may seem like a gift from the government, getting one means you aren't planning particularly well. The idea is to keep as much money as possible in your hands so *you* can put it to use, not to provide the government with an interest-free loan. Using the Tax Man as a forced savings plan may work for some, but the alternative makes more sense, financially.

REVIEWING YOUR ESTATE PLAN

You don't have a thing to do!

Sometimes it comes as a surprise when you find yourself the sole breadwinner in the family. Other times not. If you and your partner have decided that one of you should stay home to be with the children, and it makes more sense that you keep working, then you may have time to plan this change in lifestyle.

One of the best ways to see how it will work is to live on only one paycheque for the six months leading up to the change. You can use the other paycheque to actively pay down debt or to build a sturdy emergency fund for those unforeseen financial crises. Taking the money out of your cash flow will give you a good idea of what it will be like to live on a single income before it becomes reality.

Remember to check your insurance benefits to be sure you've got enough coverage for life, disability, and health. Redo your spending plan, and incorporate the changes you'll need to make to live on a single income. If you plan to eliminate your child care expenses, remember to leave some money in the plan for babysitting for things like doctors' appointments and "sanity time." Set some goals for eliminating or significantly reducing your debt before you make the switch to one income. Talk about the money/power shift that may take place and the warning signals you'll use to cue each other.

Becoming the primary breadwinner in your family, especially when it comes as a shock, is tough. Whether your partner has been downsized, or you have become the sole breadwinner because of widowhood or divorce, coming to terms with the fact that you are now the sole provider for your family, the shoulders upon which all rests, is a weight that can bow the strongest back. If you let the responsibility overwhelm you—as I almost did the first time this happened to me—you'll be no good to anybody. You need to take a deep breath, recognize that this is a learning experience, and move forward, one day at a time. You don't have to feel completely alone. You are only as alone as you choose to be. So ask for help. Whether it's coffee with a girlfriend to blow off steam, or a helping hand from family members who are willing to share their own bounty, don't let pride, embarrassment, or all the other dumb emotions get in the way. Remember, money is a tool. The fact that you're a hammer and a few screwdrivers short of a full tool set right now doesn't say anything about who you are.

18

JUST IN CASE YOU LOSE YOUR JOB

One of the life events that can shake a girl to her very foundations is losing her job. Not only do you have to consider the financial implications—how are you ever going to make the next rent or mortgage payment?—but significant social and psychological issues come into play. There's the loss of self-esteem associated with being terminated, regardless of the reason for termination. There's the sense of not knowing what to do next. And there's the loss of relationships; all those people with whom you worked will soon forget who you are as they move on with their lives and you with yours. It can seem pretty dismal, and you will wonder how you will ever live through it. But live through it you will. You've got to grit your teeth, believe you will be fine, and keep moving.

Before you can move ahead, you're going to have to deal with the personal anxiety of having joined the ranks of the unemployed. First comes the immediate sense of panic. How will you tell your partner? The kids? Your mother? While you may find it hard to believe right now, these very people whom you fear telling will provide you with enormous support so that you can deal with the trauma and get back on your feet.

If you're feeling a sense of guilt, or your self-esteem is lower than the belly of a snake, take a deep breath. There is no point in blaming yourself. You likely had little control over what happened. Today's economic reality is very different from the past, so we can't use the old rules and standards to make judgments about our worth and accountability. Shake loose the feelings that try to invade and focus on the future. Yes, you will get another job. No, you haven't let your family down. Yes, you will be fine, and so will they.

If you're furious at the world, know that this is a part of your response to the situation. You must get past this stage before you will be able to make a convincing show when you go knocking on doors. Don't deny the anger, since that will just delay your recovery. Do what you must to get past it. Meditate. Kick-box. Talk, talk, talk.

Perhaps the most important thing you will have to learn to do is ask for help. For many people, this is the most difficult thing of all. It shouldn't be. People love to help, just ask. And since you're far more likely to get another job because someone you know knows someone else than from the traditional route, tell everyone you know when you're ready to go back to work.

So often, the shock of the announcement throws people into a tailspin, and the last thing they feel like doing is sitting down to make a plan. But if you want to be successful in dealing with your unemployment, that's exactly what you'll need. First, you'll have to come to terms with your significantly reduced cash flow—forced simplicity, right? Then there's the prospect of going job-hunting. You'll need an up-to-date résumé, a good idea of the work you want to do next, and lots of contacts to get you that next job. Will you need to upgrade your skills? This would be the perfect time to do it. Ever considered self-employment? Don't rush into anything, but starting your own business may be the answer to your joblessness. Finally, there are the things you must do to keep yourself healthy as you deal with the stress of the termination and the job-hunt. Some women automatically turn to exercise routines. Others feed their emptiness with food. What will you use as your outlet?

YOUR SPENDING PLAN

Typically, when individuals are terminated due to economic factors rather than their performance, the dark cloud is often accompanied by a silver lining in the form of severance pay. One of your first questions will be: "How much do I get?"

Severance can be given as either a lump sum or as salary continuance. It's all a matter of whether you want to take the full amount in one fell swoop or use the salary continuance to provide a regular flow of income that would extend over a longer period.

If you decide to take your severance all at once, consider using your unused RRSP contribution room to shelter as much of it as possible from tax. Are you concerned about rolling money into an RRSP that you might very well need to live on while you look for a job? Don't be. As long as you choose an investment that leaves you the flexibility to pull money from your plan should you need it, you're set. A money market fund would be perfect. You can pull the amount you need to cover your living expenses on a monthly or quarterly basis while you are unemployed. You may have to pay a fee for withdrawals, so check with your financial institution before you decide how often to dip in. Once you get a job, you can use the money remaining to make more aggressive investment alternatives, if that suits your needs.

When you withdraw money from an RRSP, you'll pay withholding tax. Outside Quebec, the rate is 10% on the first $5,000, 20% on withdrawal amounts between $5,000 and $15,000, and 30% for amounts over $15,000. You'll have to include any amounts withdrawn in your income for the year withdrawn. Once you file your tax return, the true taxes owing based on your marginal tax rate will be calculated, so consider yourself warned: you may end up owing more tax.

While you may pay significantly less tax on RRSP withdrawals because your income while unemployed is considerably lower, try to make your withdrawals in denominations of $5,000 or less. You'll pay less withholding tax, and you won't end up with extra money outside the RRSP should the perfect job appear on the horizon.

Having figured out how much you'll receive from your employer, the next step is to take stock of what you have accumulated. If you have set up an emergency fund, and you have the required three to six months' worth of expenses covered, you now have proof that *telesis* works.

Make a list of all the assets you've accumulated: cash in the bank, money market funds, Canada Savings Bonds, GICs, term deposits, investments in mutual funds, stocks, or bonds, as well as any other sources of income you may have.

Unless you're one of the filthy rich (why does the language of money always sound as though it could use a good bath?), you're going to have to cut back. Review your spending plan to see which expenses can be reduced and which can be eliminated. Do you need to keep the kids in full-time daycare? Could you make arrangements with friends and family to spell you off when you need to go for an interview? This could save big bucks. What about your transportation and lunch costs? Those will go down. So, too, will your ordering-in and eating-out costs, since you'll have the time to make dinner at home now that you're not running in the door at 7:30 p.m.

$ **Gail's Tips:** Think about the kinds of things you could do freelance or part-time while you are looking for a full-time job. Would your employer consider using your services as a freelancer or consultant? What other employers might? Who have you met through your work that has expressed appreciation for or satisfaction with your efforts on their behalf? Offer to buy lunch, tell them what you want to do next, and ask them to help.

Finally, make a new spending plan incorporating both the reduced income and reduced expenses you've worked through. How much of a shortfall is there? How will you cover it? Hopefully, you have a nice, sturdy emergency plan that can fill the holes. If not, you may be forced to tap your other savings.

$ Gail's Tips: Regardless of whether you rolled your severance into your RRSP or you're just looking for a way to make ends meet, remember that money taken out of an RRSP can never be replaced, so it's gone for good. If the mortgage has to be paid and food put on the table, and the RRSP is the only resource you have, then the answer is self-evident. Remember that you'll pay tax on the money you withdraw at your marginal tax rate. Since the financial institution is only required to withhold 10%, 20%, or 30%, depending on the level of your withdrawal, come tax time you'll have to settle up with the Tax Man, who will want his fair share. Keep track of your withdrawals in the context of your entire income. The last thing you need is a tax bill you weren't prepared for.

If you were laid off late in the year, try to delay making the RRSP withdrawal until the calendar year following your layoff. Since you'll be taking that income in a year when you have yet to earn any other income, it may mean a lower marginal tax rate, depending on when you return to work. So think about the timing very carefully before you start pulling money out of your RRSPs.

YOUR EMERGENCY FUND

Since you were smart enough to set up an emergency fund, you're going to feel a lot safer moving through this trying time. Not so smart? Then you're going to have to cut back to the bare bones to make your Employment Insurance go as far as it can. And you better hurry up and get another job! And, by the way, now you know why you need an emergency fund.

MANAGING YOUR MONEY

You probably should consolidate all your money in one place for a couple of reasons. First, it will help you to see what you have. Second, it will likely cost less in service charges and fees. If you have a partner, talk about how you're going to handle the day-to-day money management. If you've always done it, and you're feeling a little overwhelmed, this might be the time to hand off to your partner, at least until you feel less shaky. If your partner has been in charge, now that you've got some extra time on your hands, maybe it's time for you to take a run at managing the spending plan. Whatever the outcome, the only way you're going to get through this crisis intact as a couple is to talk. Talk, talk, talk, talk, talk. If you're in the unhappy circumstances of not being able to talk to your partner, find a friend with whom you can bounce ideas around. It's important that you not stay bottled up. Some of the worst decisions are made when an issue is seen from only one perspective.

Now is not the time to make large expenditures. If you have committed to buying a new car, investing in your best friend's business, or going on a vacation, back out. If there is a penalty to pay, so be it. You are going to need every red cent you can lay your hands on to get you through the next little while.

By the way, don't be so proud that you forget to apply for Employment Insurance benefits, and when those run out, any other benefits to which you may be entitled. You've helped to support the system with your taxes. Now it is your turn to use the benefits. Taking care of yourself and your family means taking advantage of EVERY option available to stay afloat during the storm. Assuming you don't have an emergency fund, or it has run out and you are scrambling to come up with enough money to get by each month, here are some things to consider:

- Can you skip a mortgage payment? Some mortgage agreements allow you to skip a payment and have the amount added to your principal. While this increases your loan, it keeps your credit history from becoming tarnished.
- Are there assets you could sell to help make ends meet? This would be the time to sell assets that have appreciated, or to reap the benefits of long-term compounding of interest. What's the point of having assets if you can't bring yourself to sell them when you need the money?
- Can you borrow against your life insurance policy? If your life insurance has a cash value component, you may be able to borrow against it to supplement your cash flow in the short term.

KEEPING A HEALTHY CREDIT IDENTITY

So, should you tell your creditors you don't have a job, or should you hold back for fear they may revoke your only source of cash flow? Good question. Like almost everything else in life, it depends. Don't tell creditors who can call in a loan, because 10-to-1 odds are they will. This is one good reason that it makes sense not to have all your financial business in one place. (Everyone always talks about the benefits of consolidation. Here's a case where it may not be to your advantage.) If you have your mortgage at ABC Bank and your line of credit at XYZ Bank, you can call your mortgage company and negotiate a deal without running the risk that your personal line of credit will be revoked. If you're carrying credit card debt, for sure you should call and work out a payment plan. If you owe taxes, for sure you should call the Tax Man and work out a payment program.

Consider negotiating for a reduction of interest or for a reduction of the loan principal. In the first case, there's no point in the lender putting you into bankruptcy with astronomically high interest rates. In the second case, if you can pay off half of the entire balance, the lender may be willing to settle for that rather than losing the whole shebang to bankruptcy. Negotiate. Smile. Be very sweet. Since you are the fairer, more delicate sex, you might as well play it for all it's worth. This is not the time to be argumentative, authoritarian, or sly. You can be firm without sounding like a bully. You can negotiate without threats. Be upfront, honest, and sincere about wanting to work something out. Remember, it is your circumstances that have changed. Stay true to your character.

KEEPING A ROOF OVER YOUR HEAD

Okay, so you have no way of paying the mortgage and you're sure you'll end up losing the house. If you rent, you may already be looking for cheaper digs. Relax. Don't allow your emotions to make your decisions for you. As much as we insist on making money an emotional issue, it is really best dealt with logically. So before you stick that sign up on the lawn or pack your life's belongings to move, think about what you could do to cope. There are always alternatives.

Perhaps you could convert part of your home into an apartment and rent it to supplement your current cash flow. Whether you own or rent, a roommate may be one way of reducing your expenses. While the initial idea of having room-mates and borders may be offensive, vile, or intrusive, if it means you can stay where you are, if it means you can limit the disruption to your family's life, isn't it worth a thought or two?

After careful consideration, you might decide selling your home is the best option. It will really work to your advantage if you have built up considerable equity and can use that equity to get yourself re-established in more manageable digs. And it may be a necessity if you simply can't cope with the financial burden of staying where you are. Ask friends for advice, consult a trusted real estate agent, or check with your folks. Ultimately, you'll end up doing what feels right for you. But with enough input, you will have considered all the angles and can follow your instincts.

YOUR PAY-YOURSELF-FIRST INVESTMENT PLAN

No doubt this will go into suspended animation until you're working full-time again. It is very important that you re-establish your pay-yourself-first plan as soon as you can. The longer it takes you to get back into the savings saddle, the harder it will be, and the more you'll lose in terms of compounding return. This must be a top priority as soon as your cash flow has stabilized.

REVIEWING YOUR INSURANCE

While it may initially seem like a smart thing to do, reducing or eliminating your insurance to save on the premiums while you are unemployed can have long-term negative consequences. If you apply for new coverage later, you may need to have a medical checkup and your policy may preclude pre-existing conditions. Never mind the increased cost of premiums based on your new and improved age! Bottom line: don't cancel your insurance.

Check with your benefits co-ordinator at work to see if you can take on the premiums of your existing insurance benefits to continue being covered. If you've had difficulty qualifying for life insurance because of your age or health, converting your group policy to an individual policy is one way to start building your insurance portfolio.

Also keep in mind that Employment Insurance benefits may be clawed back if your net income exceeds a specific amount. The total amount clawed back will never exceed 30% of the benefits, but the remaining 70% will be taxable in the normal way. While Employment Insurance benefits may help with cash flow initially, if you've been a high-income earner, you may find that almost all your benefits are grabbed back when you file your next tax return. Just a warning so it doesn't come as a complete shock.

TAX IMPLICATIONS

Eventually you'll get another job. It may be right around the corner from where you now live or work, or it may be half-way across the country. There are tax benefits associated with relocating to take a new job, even if it is self-employment. If you move to a new home that is 40 kilometres closer to your new work location than your old home was—even if it is your own business—you can deduct substantial amounts for tax purposes. Once you become re-employed, if you're planning to move, see if you can arrange to meet the tests for deducting your moving expenses.

REVIEWING YOUR ESTATE PLAN

You don't have a thing to do!

$ Gail's Tips: Are there areas of your life that you've wanted to explore, but that you've never had time to delve into? Painting, writing, theatre . . . now you have time. But it won't last forever. If you really want to try something new, DO IT!

Is there a hobby or special interest you can parlay into a money-maker? Financial advisors often say that you should think carefully before you decide to go into business for yourself. That's true. But if you don't have a job anyway, and you have a good idea for employing yourself, why not go through the process of putting a plan together? What have you got to lose but time, and you've got plenty of that, right?

Make sure you don't get mired in your own misery and stop dreaming. If it's taking longer than you thought to get back into the swim, don't spend the time you have sitting on the couch watching One Life to Live. Remember, your one life is all you have to live, so don't waste it. Volunteer. Get involved with your local school, church, hospital, shelter, library, whatever. Stay busy. Meet people. Give of yourself. And keep telling people what you want. Believe, and you will get what you want.

19

JUST IN CASE YOU DIVORCE

Note: The provincial legislation referred to in this section is based on Ontario's Family Law Act. Please seek advice from a lawyer within your jurisdiction for the legislative ins and outs that apply to your situation.

I hate it when I hear a woman say something like, "Oh, my husband manages the money. He's much better at it than I am." It makes me cringe. I've raised my daughter to believe that she must be responsible for herself, including the management of her money. And I hope I've demonstrated to her that it is very important that she keep her hands on the reins of her financial life.

Did you know that after divorce, a woman's economic status generally falls by about 45%. All sorts of factors come into play: the oft-bewailed discrepancies in income between men and women; the fact that more women than men leave the workforce to look after family, resulting in a loss of skills and financial security; and women's naïveté in handling their separation and divorce. Women have been socialized to believe money is a man thing, and it's time for some new socialization. Women *must* learn how to handle money if they want to be sure they will have a secure future. And we must teach our daughters that, although marriage is a noble institution, they MUST be capable of doing all the things they need to be able to do to survive, take care of their babies, and get on with their lives.

But before we get into the money part of this, I'd like to talk a little about where your head goes when your love (or whatever it is that's been holding you together) walks out the door. As with just about everything else in life, it depends. It depends on whether you are the person leaving—whom I'll refer to as the "Leaver"—or the person being left—the "Leavee."

If you are the Leaver, you have time to plan. You can make an appointment with a lawyer, get advice, and ready yourself for the storm. You can learn the rules of the game and practise your moves and counter-moves ahead of the starter's gun. That's not to say that you'll be protected from the emotional upheaval and sadness that comes with a marriage breakdown. You will still grieve—dealing with divorce is not unlike dealing with death— but you'll do it at a different pace and time than the person you are leaving.

If you are the Leavee, you have no opportunity to prepare. The starter's gun is a shot to your gut. You are buffeted as your mind careens from one disastrous scenario to another. You are destroyed. A very close friend of mine describes her divorce as having shaken her foundation. "Suddenly, I felt all the societal taboos: a divorcee, ooh, a single mother, ugh. I felt I had lost my position in society. The security issues had to do with a lot more than just money. It was the emotional sense of myself that left. It took me a long time to accept and deal with that. There was a time when I was in public with my daughter, and I wore a fake wedding ring, because I couldn't deal with people thinking I was an unwed mother. You have crazy thoughts. Things come into your mind that would never occur to you if you were feeling safe and secure."

Where the Leaver has had time to prepare herself, the Leavee must make time—slow the whole thing down—so she can catch up emotionally. Where the Leaver has planned carefully, the Leavee must put together a plan. If you do it on the fly, it won't be your best plan. Since this divorce will affect you, and perhaps your children, for a long time to come, don't rush, or be rushed, into decisions. Time makes the difference. And the first thing you should do is see a very good lawyer.

You want a lawyer who has been specializing in family law. Interview her, just like you'd interview any employee that you are hiring. Don't waste your money on a lawyer who wants to spend lots of time chit-chatting or commiserating. Every minute she spends with you is a minute added to the bill. Ask how quickly you can expect her to respond to phone calls, letters, and motions, and if her strength is in mediation or in court. If you anticipate a custody battle that will end up in court, get yourself the very best lawyer money can buy. Anything less will cost you even more in the long run, and in ways you can't even imagine now.

One mistake that women make is that they have no knowledge of the family's financial affairs. If they are the Leavee, the panic isn't just "He's leaving." It's also, "I don't know anything. I don't have access to the bank accounts. I don't know what the mortgage payments are."

Take the case of Paula. Paula had a wonderful life. At 54, she drove a very nice car. Every year she went on a vacation. Her son was working and living at home, and her daughter was finishing her last year of university. Paula was well-educated, well turned out, and ill prepared for divorce. When the credit check was done on Paula's husband, the results were abysmal. Paula was guarantor on several of her husband's loans. "Oh, yes," she said, "I signed something, but I don't remember much about it." With his huge level of debt, Paula's husband fit the definition of bankrupt. His idea of negotiating was saying, "Look honey, if you're not prepared to accept what I'm going to give you, I'll just make an assignment and be done." And that would leave Paula holding an empty bag. Paula's lack of knowledge—and her seeming lack of interest—in anything financial left her vulnerable.

Margaret is at the other end of the scale. Hypersensitive to her mother's and father's messy divorce, Margaret always maintained control over her own money. She admitted to even being slightly secretive about her finances. "I don't think Mathew should know everything," she said. "It's just not his business. I don't expect him to tell me everything." Margaret was shocked to find out that while she had been very successful at wealth accumulation, Mathew hadn't been quite so prudent, but she still had to split the moola. "You mean I'm going to have to give him part of my assets? But he's the man. Why would I have to give him money?" she asked, astounded at the prospect. "I've been the responsible one. He's been the gadfly. Why should he get half?" That's equality, girls!

Danita is another case in point. Before marrying, she was an independent-minded career woman. After she had her second child, she decided to stay home, at least until the last baby was old enough to attend school full-time. Over time, her husband, Harry, encouraged her not to worry about the financial stuff, and she fell into the trap of losing touch with what was going on. Since Danita came from a traditional family, it seemed natural to give Harry the reins of their financial lives, while she concentrated on nurturing the children and making sure everything ran smoothly at home. Danita was stunned when Harry walked out. He came home one night, packed his bags, and left, saying, "You'll be hearing from my lawyer." With her fourth child still in diapers, she felt abandoned. The fact that Harry left for another woman didn't help Danita's self-image. She was furious and wanted revenge. And she'd use any tactic to make him pay.

Another mistake women make is to let emotion carry them away, as in Danita's case. Many situations can be resolved without the need for protracted litigation if cooler heads prevail. The parties can then walk out financially more intact.

YOUR SPENDING PLAN

If you've managed to get this far without a spending plan, you'll need one now. And if you're not familiar with how the money flows in and out of the family pocketbook, because the other guy's always taken care of it, it's time to become familiar.

Whether you are litigating or negotiating for your divorce settlement, you'll have to complete a financial statement. One section includes a budget with 69 different types of expenditures, which is meant to help you figure out your family's spending pattern and what that spending pattern will likely be in the future. Of course, if you've never had a spending plan, you probably have no idea what the numbers are. Go back to Part Two, where I explain what a spending plan is, how it works, and how to build one.

The budget section of the financial statement you prepare is, in large measure, what the judge looks at to determine your future needs for support. If you can't complete this properly— if you don't know what you're paying for taxes, entertainment, vacations, food, rent, medical expenses—you won't be able to paint a clear and complete picture for the judge. For example, people often don't know how much they spend on medical expenses. They don't know if there are any limitations on their family's medical plan or how long the plan lasts after divorce. They think that because they have a drug plan, they don't need a drug budget. But what about those items that aren't covered by the plan: headache, cold, and allergy medicine; antibiotic cream and Band-Aids; potions for diarrhea, stomach upset, and nausea? Anything purchased without a prescription is not covered, so everyone needs a drug budget.

People are usually so overwhelmed with their circumstances, they don't think about the minutiae. Without a guide to help you remember all the items that go under each section, you could very well forget important expenses. The result: you paint a less-realistic picture for the judge to use in making a decision. Since that financial statement is evidence, and the judge must work within the rules of the court, if you don't give complete evidence, it will be reflected in the judge's decision.

"If a woman comes to me before she's actually left her husband," says one divorce lawyer I interviewed, "I tell her that her mission is to go home and find every scrap of paper that she can and photocopy it. Unless there is physical abuse or serious verbal abuse, even if she has to stay with her spouse for another month, my view is she stays there because she has to prepare for this next step." That may include scouring the house for tax returns, investment information, and insurance details—everything that may be pertinent to a settlement.

If you're shaking your head saying to yourself that this feels scummy, that it's an invasion of his privacy, or that you're above such behaviour, give your head a shake. It is your right as a member of that family to know everything. If your spouse hasn't shared information with you, or if you haven't been paying attention, it's time to become informed. You must rectify your lack of knowledge to protect yourself, and perhaps your babies. And, quite frankly, you're saving yourself money on legal fees, because you won't have all the back-and-forth that comes with a lack of disclosure. The financial statement is supposed to be a complete disclosure. If your spouse has purposely or inadvertently left something out, and you know about it because you have informed yourself, then it's a relatively easy situation to fix. If you don't know what's going on, then you don't know when you're being had. It is healthy to be informed.

$ **Gail's Tips:** Don't forget to budget in your law-
yer's costs. The first thing you'll have to do is provide a
retainer. People often look suspiciously at lawyers when
they ask for a retainer, but the reality is that the exchange
of that money—even if it is only one dollar—is what estab-
lishes the client-lawyer relationship. Technically speaking,
for there to be solicitor-client privilege, you need money to
change hands.

To create a realistic budget for your divorce, ask what your
lawyer's hourly rate is at the office and in court, since they are
often different. If your lawyer uses a law clerk, find out how
that person's time is billed. And remember, everything costs
money. Your lawyer's time is the commodity you're paying for,
so expect to be billed for telephone calls and letters, as well
as face-to-face meetings. Remember that the more prepared
you are, the more cost-effective use of your lawyer's time you
can make. Keep a log of how much time you spend with the
lawyer and what was discussed. It's good to compare against
the bills and to gauge the progress you're making.

Also check on your lawyer's billing procedures. The last
thing you need is to go merrily along, fighting your ex-spouse,
only to find a $70,000 bill at the end of it all. Make sure you
get itemized bills at regular intervals, and have the lawyer
tell you once the retainer is used up. If you'll be counting on
a settlement to make good on your legal fees, gain your lawyer's agreement to a payment plan, and ascertain what the
interest rate will be on the outstanding balance.

As far as preparing for your visit to the lawyer, make a list
of all the real property you own and whose names every-

thing is in, so your lawyer will be able to register a "matrimonial home designation." It's a document that is registered on title, and it has no legal effect other than to flag to would-be-lenders that the property is a matrimonial home and spousal consent is required. This will protect you if your spouse tries to take out a mortgage without your knowledge.

. . . .

While you may end up with half the family assets as part of the divorce, you'll likely end up with less cash flow. Historically, women's standards of living drop substantially after divorce. Since women usually earn less than their male counterparts, moving from a dual income to living on a lower single-income stream means you may not be able to maintain your lifestyle. If you've been a stay-at-home wife who is now dependent on alimony and child support for income, you may find it difficult because you are not able to meet your previous expectations.

YOUR EMERGENCY FUND

Since there may be interruptions in your income as you go through the divorce, particularly if your husband is ticked off with the amount of spousal or child support granted to you, you better have a stash at the ready to fill the gaps. That may mean taking money from a joint account, pulling on a joint line of credit, or, in extreme circumstances, taking advances against a supplemental credit card to create a stash of cash you can count on.

Yes, I am advocating getting the money from whatever source is available to protect yourself. The road to divorce can be long and bumpy, and you may have to lay out a lot of cash along the way. Document where you've taken the money from, so you can provide the information to your lawyer (and to your ex's lawyer), identifying the fact that you know this will be flushed out in the accounting and final division of assets. If you're in the house with the kids, you can't risk missing mortgage payments. Nor can you miss tuition payments for school or other activities. If the furnace goes, the car dies, or some other unforeseen event occurs, you need a way to cope financially. Remember, you don't know what you're getting into in your separation or divorce. You'll still have to pay the lighting bill and the heating bill and the car loan. You can't afford to be left without money while your husband, the lawyers, and the courts try to decide how much it costs for you and your children to live.

Do you think this is extreme? It only seems so because you haven't yet had to live from week to week without money. I had a girlfriend who was left stranded by her ex when he left. For several months, she barely made ends meet while she continued to pay the mortgage (on an asset that was half his), buy the food (for herself and *their* daughter), and meet every other financial commitment. The stress was horrible, and she came within a straw of breaking. You must protect yourself. And that means having a healthy emergency fund *just in case!*

$ Gail's Tips: No matter what your husband promises as he exits stage left, take it with a grain of salt. Emotions and attitudes swing from one extreme to another during marriage breakdown, and today's guilt-induced promise can be easily rescinded tomorrow. Protect yourself. Get to work finding everything you can to take to the lawyer. Remove your name from all forms of credit. Fill up your emergency fund, and batten down the hatches.

MANAGING YOUR MONEY

As part of your new independent state of being, you'll have to set up a chequing account in your own name, if you have not already done so. If you've never managed money before, let me reassure you that it isn't hard, but it takes some practice.

Start by talking to a girlfriend or female family member who seems to be doing well on her own. Join a support group in your community, which can provide a wealth of information to help women make successful transitions and rebuild their lives. Ask at community centres, look in the Yellow Pages under "Divorce," ask friends and family, and seek out online communities.

Part of what you want to find out is how to best manage your money on a day-to-day basis. If you have a relationship with people at your bank, ask them for help. Since they are closest to the subject, they'll be the most expert. Don't worry about looking foolish. Nothing matters other than getting informed and learning how to take care of yourself.

Change your PIN number. Remember that Tuesday last year when you asked your ex to take some money out of the ATM for you? He has your PIN number. If you don't change it, you're allowing him the opportunity to mess with your accounts. Change them all. And don't change them to something obvious like your children's names. Use something obscure like the name of the first boy who nibbled your ear, or your great-aunt Lucy's birthday.

KEEPING A HEALTHY CREDIT IDENTITY

Do you have a credit card in your own name? Get one. (By the by, why isn't this ever an issue for men?) Remember, supplemental cards (the credit cards you use that are tied to your partner's cards) do jack squat to build you a credit history. It doesn't matter who pays the bill. If the card is in his name, then the reporting is in his name, and *you don't exist.*

What would you do if your husband cut off your supplemental card and you were in a department store buying your kids new boots when your card was declined? First, you would be mortified. Then you'd be angry. Save yourself the trouble. Get your own card, and get your name taken off his.

When Janet divorced several years ago, she discovered that all her credit cards were held jointly with her husband. While she had made payments consistently on the cards she had used, he had not been quite so punctual. The result: because all the cards where held jointly, her credit history was far less pristine than she imagined. Since Janet didn't write the credit card companies to have her name removed from the cards her ex was using, when he was lackadaisical about making payments during the months they were separated, he was also tarnishing her credit history. When she tried applying for her own credit, she found several banks unwilling to extend her credit because she was now living on substantially less income, and her credit bureau report showed a shoddy payment record. She was furious. Take a lesson from Janet's case. If you're holding cards on which you are jointly liable with your spouse, call and have those cards cancelled, and have new cards issued solely in your name. If you don't, and your better half decides to run those cards to the max, you'll be equally liable.

If you have a line of credit at the bank on which you are jointly signed with your partner, go and have your signature removed, if you can. If you can't, then write a letter, which you hand-deliver to the bank, that says, "As of today's date, no cheque can be drawn against this line of credit without both signatures." That way, no one is doing anything without the other's knowledge.

KEEPING A ROOF OVER YOUR HEAD

On separation, each party is equally entitled to live in a matrimonial home (that's possession, not ownership) until there's a court order saying one must get out, or there's a separation agreement where one party gives up the right. For strategic reasons, lawyers often warn people not to leave the home until they've seen a lawyer. Even if your husband tells you to get out, saying he owns the house because only his name is on the title, you don't have to leave. And if he comes home and tells you he's leaving you but not quite yet, you can't toss his stuff onto the lawn and lock him out, because changing the locks bars him from his right to possession. Remember, he has as much right to the matrimonial home as you do.

The matrimonial home is any residence in which either party has a legal interest (so that applies to the home you own or rent), and which is ordinarily occupied by the spouses as their family residence at separation or immediately before separation. If you have a city house that you ordinarily occupy, that's a matrimonial home. You don't need a document saying that. If you have a cottage that you ordinarily occupy a few weeks each year, that's a matrimonial home. You can have as many matrimonial homes as you live in. Investment properties don't count. You have to live in it at some point in the year.

"Living separate and apart" for the purposes of being "separated" does not mean you have to be living physically apart. There are situations where people cannot immediately get their own space. So living separate and apart can mean living in the same house. It can even mean sharing the same bed. The objective test for "living separate and apart" is this: would a third party looking in determine that these people are holding themselves out to the world as husband and wife? The judge looks for evidence to support the separation: not going out socially together, not doing the husband-and-wife things. Lots of people who grow apart simply carry on together as man and wife, while leading totally separate lives.

If you're dealing with a violent ex, while you're not allowed to change the locks, here's at least one good reason to have your ex charged for an assault: one of the terms of the bail order will be to restrict your ex from coming within a certain number of feet of your home. Then you can change the locks. While you would be technically violating the civil law (under which you are getting a divorce), most judges won't enforce that, since there's already a criminal order saying he can't go near the house anyway. You could also change the code on the alarm system, so that if he enters the house the police would be notified immediately. And you could change the frequency on your garage door, so he can't get in through the garage.

YOUR PAY-YOURSELF-FIRST INVESTMENT PLAN

Since you're completely dependent on yourself, if you're not taking care of your future, no one is. If you have earned income, you should be contributing to an RRSP. Get on a periodic investment plan. You can start with as little as $25 a month.

If you think you can't afford to be investing for your future because your present needs cost so much, ask yourself this question: if I don't save for my future, what will I live on when my future becomes my present? If you think you have plenty of time to catch up, ask yourself what you did with the last five years of your life, and how much you would have today if you had started back then. If you think the government is going to take care of your future, a gentle reminder: you thought your husband was going to do that too. You can't depend on anyone but yourself.

The other thing to think about when reviewing your investment strategy is how the divorce has affected your retirement plan. When RRSP assets are divided as part of a divorce settlement, this can significantly alter your retirement plans and colour how you will invest those dollars for the future. The most important question for many people is how to balance their risk tolerance with the need to grow their RRSP assets now that they are on their own. If you have stayed out of the work force to raise a family or you have a lower-paying job than your spouse, hold on to RRSP assets, particularly if your spouse will benefit from a company pension plan. With no RRSP room to catch up—because you went years without an income—you'll be starting from ground zero if you relinquish all your RRSP assets, particularly if you are in your late 40s or 50s and have less time to build a strong retirement asset base.

Often, women choose to keep the family home, giving up retirement assets in exchange. But this isn't always a smart move. With expensive upkeep and slow increases in real estate values, a home can become an albatross, inhibiting women from building the investment reserves they need to take care of themselves in later years.

Here are some other things to watch for:

- A 50–50 split of assets may seem fair, but if your spouse also has a company pension plan, that has to be taken into consideration.
- If you won't be entering the work force immediately, you'll need to negotiate extra income for investment

purposes, so you don't spend several years contributing zilch to your retirement plan.

- If your spouse has significant unused RRSP contribution room—if he could have made contributions but chose not to—those catch-up contributions aren't divisible after the settlement. Negotiate for a portion of those contributions to be made in your name (as a spousal contribution) prior to the division of assets, and ensure that the spousal RRSP will not be equalized. That way you'll have assets that can continue to grow on a tax-deferred basis.
- Keep in mind that once you are living separately, the RRSP rules for withdrawals from a spousal plan change. The money will be taxed in the hands of the plan holder—that's you—so don't go grabbing money out of your spousal plan thinking your old buddy will get stuck with the tax bill. You'll end up paying the piper.

REVIEWING YOUR INSURANCE

If you considered your partner to be your disability plan, it's time to get a new plan . . . no, not a new partner, a real disability plan; one that will be with you, regardless. You're the only one you can truly count on should you be unable to work. If you have kids, it's even more important. Do you really want to hear, "Well, since I'm supporting the children completely now, I think they should live with me and my new wife. After all, you have enough on your plate."

Life insurance is just as important. If your ex isn't in the picture a whole lot—some husbands do move away and start new lives, as if their previous lives and families never existed—then you must have life insurance to protect your children.

Another good use of life insurance is to protect the stream of child support payments you may be receiving from your ex. Any good lawyer will advise you to write into your separation agreement that your husband take out and pay for an insurance policy that will guarantee your children's support payments until a specific age. While the separation agreement and support order are binding on your ex-spouse's estate, if the estate doesn't have enough to fund the support, that's pretty well that. And if your ex agrees, you can insure his life, pay the premiums yourself, and have a party when he departs this Earth.

If your partner just can't get insurance, don't give up. Insist that you (if you are being paid spousal support) and your children be named as irrevocable beneficiaries on his RRSPs. While you won't be able to roll the money over on a tax-free basis, because you're no longer spouses, you can set up certain types of trusts to minimize the tax consequences. Every court order or separation agreement should contain some form of risk mitigation. Of course, there's absolutely no point in arguing for these types of provisions if you are not going to follow up to make sure they are in place. Each year, you should receive proof that the premiums are paid and that your interests and those of your children are protected.

Also keep in mind that if your spouse belongs to a group health plan, your joint dependent children should still be covered under that plan. If you just can't get on with your ex, but you want to ensure that submitting claims doesn't turn into a power trip, make sure that your separation agreement includes the specifics for when you'll receive payment for submitted claims. And since you probably won't be covered under his medical plan, make sure you get one of your own.

TAX IMPLICATIONS

Even if you're the person initiating the separation, there are some things that aren't top of mind: the Tax Man, for instance. But he should be. After all, how you structure the financial side of your divorce will affect your money management for years to come.

Divorce gives you a rare opportunity to fiddle with your RRSPs or registered pension plan without tax consequence. If company pension benefits or RRSP assets are being split between spouses, the rollover from one spouse's plan to the other's can take place tax-free. Remember, though, once you are living separately, the RRSP rules for withdrawals from a spousal plan also change. The money will be taxed in the hands of the plan holder, so don't take money out of your spousal plan thinking your ex will get stuck with the tax bill. You'll end up paying the tax. If you have no spouse, you can claim the equivalent-to-spousal credit for any qualifying dependant, including a child or parent.

Do you or your spouse have any unused RRSP contribution room you could catch up prior to your split of matrimonial assets? Any contributions made can be split, but contributions not yet made means there are fewer assets to split. To minimize the tax implications of transferring non-registered assets from one spouse to another, those assets might be liquidated to catch up unused contribution room, which can then be rolled over between spouses tax-free.

And then we have the small issue of contingent liabilities. Most people don't even know what "contingent liabilities" are, let alone take them into account when figuring out how to split their assets. A perfect example of this is a case where registered and non-registered assets are being equalized separately—let's say one person's taking the RRSPs and the other is taking the house. There has to be some recognition that the party holding the RRSPs will be taxed when those funds are withdrawn, so the RRSP holder should negotiate for those assets to be discounted for the tax that will be paid on them. The same kind of negotiation would protect the spouse who took the house as settlement if, a short while down the road, that house had to be sold. Factoring in the reduction in the asset for legal fees, real estate commission, HST, and incidental expenses evens the playing field in terms of income after taxes and expenses. You can choose not to have capital gains income attribution rules apply to you by formally filing an election at the next tax filing after the split of assets. Let's say Jane takes over an asset, such as a painting that is subject to capital gains tax. If the painting goes up in value and it's sold within the next year, the Tax Man would want to tax her ex-husband, John. By filing the election, the asset would be taxed in Jane's hands.

Of course, most decisions are about more than just the money involved. Many people have a stronger emotional attachment to their homes than to their partner's RRSPs. And other issues, such as not wanting to uproot children, come into play.

Once you're divorced and filing your tax return, take full advantage of all credits and deductions. As a single parent with children, claim the equivalent-to-married amount. Which parent gets to claim? The custodial parent. And a parent required to make support payments is not entitled to claim. If both parents have joint custody, and no money is changing hands, only one can claim this deduction. And if you can't come to an agreement as to who should claim, you'll be cutting off your nose, so to speak, since the Tax Man will simply rule that no one gets the deduction.

Don't overlook the HST and child tax credits. Since they are based on family income, you may not have qualified as a family unit. However, if you are a single income earner supporting a child, or you are thinking of skipping filing because you don't have much income, think again. The only way to qualify for these credits is to file, so sharpen your pencil.

Claim all your child care expenses. You'll need receipts that include the caregiver's social insurance number or daycare address, but you don't have to file them. Hang on to them in case your return is questioned.

Legal fees may be tax deductible if incurred to enforce a support order. So if you have a separation agreement or support order, and you had to incur legal fees to get those payments, you can deduct your legal fees. If you had to sue your spouse to get a court order for support payments, you can deduct those expenses too.

Divorce is never easy, but a little planning can make it less painful financially, especially when it comes to paying tax. Working together to resolve many of these issues may be the farthest thing from your mind, so get yourself a good lawyer and tax accountant, and let them do the job for you. The last person you should want to make money from your divorce is the Tax Man.

REVIEWING YOUR ESTATE PLAN

When you divorce, the law provides that any benefit to your former spouse in your will is revoked. However, that automatic revocation does not apply to designations made with respect to your spouse. So if your spouse has been named beneficiary of an insurance policy or of your RRSPs, you have to take steps to remove them as designated beneficiaries.

If you've executed powers of attorney in which you've named your ex to act on your behalf, remember to have them revoked immediately. There's no way I'd leave the decision on whether or not to pull the plug in my ex's hands. Would you? The same holds true for a financial power of attorney. This applies to brokerage accounts where your husband may have been making most of the calls, and you executed a power of attorney to give him the right to trade on your behalf.

If you've been married for a looong time to a really, really nice guy and have signed lots and lots of paperwork that you have not kept copies of, you have to get to work to collect it all back. A final word on keeping the paperwork: When I was divorcing my second husband, I had to come up with the Decree Absolute (my final divorce papers) from my first marriage. One would think that once divorced and remarried, there would be no need to hold on to the evidence of your prior bad judgment. But marriages, like wrinkles, can only be denied, not abolished. And so, since I had gleefully tossed all my pre-husband-number-two stuff when I was post-husband-number-two, my lawyer had to get another copy of my Decree Absolute—at a cost, of course.

For as many people as there are going through a divorce, there are as many different ways divorce can be done. Each player brings a unique set of goals, neuroses, and complications to the divorce. And every divorce must be played out according to its own script. That's clear when you read the tales of women who have already been where you are about to go.

For some, the divorce decision was pushed on them. For others, the decision was a moment of triumph. For most, living through the ending of one life and the beginning of another took incredible bravery. For no one was it simple. It meant disconnecting their lives from another and facing the future alone. It necessitated coping with all the detritus of those married years. It required picking up, dusting off, and starting all over again.

The underlying thread through all divorce stories is that you are the only person who can set the game plan to get you to the other end in one piece. There's no question that your journey will be a hard one. Whether you've initiated the divorce, or it has been thrust upon you, you'll likely experience (or have experienced) a period of significant unhappiness as you've struggled with the idea of separation. You will watch as your children suffer through their parents' conflict. But you will come through, as will your children. You will adapt. And you'll develop new routines, perhaps more quickly than you can believe right now. And if you feel you have failed because your marriage is ending, at least you can count your blessings that you will not have spent your whole life failing.

If you focus solely on the loss created by your divorce, you'll be living in the past. To look to the future, you must be willing to hope and to be optimistic about the new possibilities that are opening up.

Regardless of how lost, negative, abandoned, or rudderless you are feeling right now, you will have goals towards which you can work sometime in the future. Or perhaps you're excited at the prospect of setting out on your own journey—one where you read your own map (and get a lot less lost). Whatever the case, *do not make any significant decisions for the first six to 12 months.* This likely isn't the right time to deal with the stress of a new job, start a business, buy a new house, change your investment portfolio significantly, or remarry. It is perfectly fine to dream. Dreaming is good. Imagine all the possibilities. Work through all the scenarios in your mind. Just don't DO anything. You need time to adjust emotionally as well as financially, and that means cutting yourself some slack. Don't listen to those who try to impose a time frame on you with words of advice like, "Just get on with it." This is a huge change in your life, and you have to take some time to get used to it.

If you have someone to whom you can turn for financial advice, great. But you should already either have a relationship with this person, or it should be someone who has come very highly recommended. Follow your instincts. You should feel this person is helping you to understand your options, not simply trying to get you to make a decision.

You shouldn't be in a hurry to make financial decisions that will affect you or your children for the long haul. Instead, take notes, get second opinions, and study up on what's what. Create your personal plan of action. Don't worry, if the stock market skyrockets while you're on the sidelines, you'll get another opportunity. What you'll lose by jumping in too soon is sleep. And right now, girl, whether you are the Leaver or the Leavee, you need all the rest you can get to recover from your wounds.

20

JUST IN CASE YOU ARE WIDOWED

It's not unusual for women to report huge gaps in time after the death of a spouse. All the key things seem to get done, but they have little recollection of how. As with the other life-changing loss—divorce—those who are widowed need time to cope. And yet, it is at this very point that we seem to have the least amount of time, because so much needs to be done in those early days. We must make the funeral arrangements, contact family and friends, call the lawyer, find the will, and keep the house running.

Coping with the financial aspects of widowhood requires that you wear two hats. First, you must close your partner's financial books and deal with what has been left. Second, you have to continue (or start) dealing with your own financial books as you move through the next stage of your life.

In the first instance, there are a number of financial items you must deal with:

You must find your partner's will, if one exists. Hopefully, you've both made wills and you are aware of the contents and location of your partner's will.

If you are not the sole executrix, you will have to notify the executor. You should also contact an experienced estate lawyer for legal help if the estate isn't absolutely straightforward.

You will need to make funeral arrangements. If your partner left specific instructions in his will, you'll probably want to follow those instructions, though you're not legally bound to do so. If there are no instructions, then you'll have to decide how to handle the ceremony and your partner's remains. This is technically the job of the executor; however, if you have not been named executor, the person who has been named will usually defer to your wishes, as long as the cost of the arrangements are reasonable.

Get at least eight copies of the death certificate from the funeral home. This will mean you won't have to apply for more when you learn you need copies for just about everything.

Make sure your immediate cash needs will be met. If you had a joint bank account, the assets immediately become yours. You should transfer the funds in that account to an account solely in your name. Wait a few days, in case there are payments to your spouse that will be received shortly, or automatic deposits in your partner's name that are owed. If your spouse had an account solely in his name into which his income was automatically deposited, you won't be able to get to the money until the estate is settled, since his account will be frozen. You can, however, access his account to pay for his funeral.

Contact your husband's employer to find out how much of a final payment (salary, bonuses, vacation pay) will be coming to you. Ask for a summary of his income for tax purposes. Find out which of his benefits you will be entitled to and for how long. In all likelihood, you will no longer be covered under his group benefits, which means you'll have to get your own. Since many companies have insurance in place that provides death benefits for widows of employees, check this out.

If your partner was receiving a pension at the time of his death, you may receive all, part, or none of it. If your sweetheart was not yet retired, you may receive a lump sum from the plan, which can be transferred tax-free to an RRSP in your name. The plan administrator can provide you with the information you'll need about your choices.

If you're not up-to-date with what your husband had and where, you'll need to start tracking down what might be out there. If your partner belonged to associations or clubs, check with them to see if there was any insurance in place. Ask the credit card company if the card balance was insured. If not, your partner's estate will have to settle up.

Most of the activities related to tying up your partner's estate will be handled by his executor. If you are the executrix, and you feel out of your depth handling the legalities, consider either renouncing this role and hiring a substitute—an estate lawyer or a trust company—or hiring help to get you through the details.

While your financial circumstances may necessitate making some important decisions about where and how you'll live, resist making any life-changing decisions during the first six to 12 months as much as possible. As with women who divorce, there are significant stages through which you will have to pass emotionally. Making big decisions during the first year can not only be tough on you in terms of coming to the decision, it can be tough on you and your family when you have to live with the consequences. You want to move as slowly as you can to maintain your own peace of mind and comfort level.

Please, oh please, give yourself the time to grieve. It's okay to feel sorry for yourself. Whether you've been married for five years or 50, you will feel lonely. Ask for help when you need it. Plan your days. Keep lists (a journal might also be a good idea), since you may find it hard to remember things. You are distracted by your pain, so compensate. Don't give yourself hell for being weak, wussy, or simpering. Be kind to yourself. And don't let someone else try to set the timeline for your "recovery." This is your grief, and you must work through it at your own pace and in your own way. Finally, don't let anyone push you into a decision with which you are not comfortable. Sadly, there are people who may try to take advantage of your distraction to satisfy their own ends. If you feel you are being pushed, push back. If you can't, tell a dear friend and let her do the pushing for you. If it is your dear friend giving the unsolicited advice, smile and nod, turn a deaf ear, and let the advice slip quietly past you.

Use your friends to get the nurturing you need during this difficult time. There are also support groups that can help you pick up the pieces. Meeting other women at various stages of the grieving process will help. So will having someone like a counsellor or spiritual advisor to listen as you babble on about your feelings, fears, and worries. You also need to be careful about your health and well-being. Make sure you eat. It's easy to forget, and you might think you could stand to go a few days without eating, but this isn't the time. You need all your physical strength to deal with your emotional hurt. If friends offer to make you a meal, accept. Don't say, "Oh, no, I don't want to be a bother." I hate that! They wouldn't offer to help if they didn't mean it, but they don't want to have to force themselves on you either. Let them help. Try to get some regular exercise, and find a way to release the tension that will build up as you cope. Walking while focusing on your breathing can be great, and you can do it at your own pace. Try to avoid too much alcohol, caffeine, sugar, and tobacco.

YOUR SPENDING PLAN

While the emotional part of widowhood is never easy, having plenty of money makes the financial part of widowhood a lot less scary. But few of us are so fortunate. We may end up with a home, with or without a mortgage, some investments, some debts, and perhaps, some insurance. But we will also likely end up with a significantly lower income. If you did not work outside the home, the death of a working partner could bring your regular income stream to a complete halt. If your spouse was retired, death could mean that the pension income you were both receiving will be cut back severely. Your cash-flow may be constrained, even if you are asset-rich.

The first thing you need to do is review your spending plan. With a reduced income stream, you may have to liquidate investments as a buffer to your reduced cash flow. Don't forget to apply for death benefits provided by government programs, such as CPP, OAS, and Workers' Compensation. You or your partner's executor should file the paperwork for CPP benefits as soon as possible after his death, since there is a one-year limit on the payment of retroactive benefits. It's your job to find out about everything that is due to you. Look everywhere for hints and clues. Talk to your partner's stockbroker, insurance agent, accountant, lawyer, and employer. Look at his old tax returns to see if capital gains were declared on investments that might now belong to you. Look in the safety deposit box, in his desk at work, in his computer files—everywhere.

On the expenses side, what can you cut? Typical things include cancelling subscriptions and memberships in clubs or organizations, and asking for a pro-rated rebate. Cancel disability and medical coverage you no longer need. Look at your bank statement. What's being automatically withdrawn that should be stopped? With less regular income coming in, you may have to make some other changes to accommodate your smaller cash flow. While there are some areas in which your expenses will likely go down—the remaining family members will likely spend less on food, clothing, healthcare, and other items—some costs just don't go away. It'll cost the same to heat, light, and maintain your home.

YOUR EMERGENCY FUND

If you always figured you didn't really need an emergency fund because you had your partner, it's time to build an emergency fund. Depending on whether you are working or retired, you will need more or less. If you are retired and have a regular flow of retirement income, the emergency fund will help if something untoward happens. If you are still working, you not only need to protect yourself from unusual expenses, you need to protect yourself from interruptions in your income (due to illness or termination), so you need a very healthy emergency fund. Failing that, make sure you have a line of credit.

MANAGING YOUR MONEY

Women who have never had to manage money before sometimes panic at the thought of all they have to do. I remember seeing Joan Rivers being interviewed after the death of her husband. She said she didn't even know the name of her bank. Imagine. She's no dumb bunny, yet she left so much to her husband that she didn't even know where to begin.

First thing: don't panic. It may take more time to figure everything out, but you'll do it. Take it one step at a time. Breathe deeply, and then go through every piece of paper on his desk, in his drawers, in his pockets. Piece the puzzle together so that you have the full picture.

What if you don't like the picture? The accounts are overdrawn. There are bills that haven't been paid in months. The life insurance policy lapsed because the premiums weren't paid. I'm so sorry if you have to live through this, but live through it you will. You must be brave. You must let your friends help if they can. You must come to terms with the fact that you are now in complete control of your destiny.

You have to start somewhere, and that somewhere is at the bank. If you have not already done so, you'll have to establish a financial identity for yourself. That means setting up a chequing account in your own name, applying for credit cards, and the like. Go in and speak with the bank manager with whom your partner was dealing. If you feel that relationship is in the dumpster because of how far in the hole your husband was, then it's time to search for a new friendly banker. Ask a friend for a referral and a personal introduction. The more sway your friend has, the more willing the new banker will be to accommodate your needs. Be honest. Tell them what's happened and what your plans are.

When Rhonda's husband died and left her high and dry with no way to meet her expenses (she had a job but didn't earn enough), Rhonda went to her banker. She described her predicament and explained that she would be selling her house within the next six months. Because she had a good relationship with her banker, she was approved for a loan to get her through the crunch. She made it through, sold the house, repaid the loan, and is now completely loyal to her banker.

If you have never written a cheque before, think a PIN is something you use to hold pants together, and can't imagine how you're going to get by, ask for help. Your banker can help. Your best friend can help. Even your children may be able to help. Don't be embarrassed. The fact that you don't know is nothing to be embarrassed about. You should only be embarrassed if you are unwilling to learn. It's time to move ahead. So ask for help.

If you think you may be faced with shortages in your cash flow, consider applying for overdraft protection as a way of avoiding NSF charges. Of course, you won't need overdraft protection if you spend only what you have available. Ha! In a perfect world. In reality, people find themselves in a cash-flow squeeze from time to time. You can use overdraft protection to ensure that squeeze won't have a long-term negative impact on your credit rating. Remember, however, overdrafts charge significantly higher rates of interest than other forms of credit.

KEEPING A HEALTHY CREDIT IDENTITY

If you've never had to manage money before, you need to establish a credit identity for yourself, and you must keep it healthy. Having a whole bunch of credit cards that you never use doesn't win you brownie points. The only way your credit identity will shine is if you use your credit and repay it on time. And if you use the right kind of credit—credit cards, for example—using credit and building a credit history doesn't have to cost you a cent.

Since banks only charge interest when your credit card balance has not been paid off in full, if you pay off your balance each month, you pay no interest. You will have used the bank's money for anywhere from 30 to 60 days—and it will have cost you absolutely nothing. What a deal!

If you don't have any credit history, it may not be easy to qualify for your first card. One way is to use a secured credit card. With a secured credit card, the issuer assumes no risk—which is why they're willing to give you the card—because you provide the credit card company with enough cash to cover your balance. Financial institutions typically want twice the amount of credit you're asking for. So if you want a credit card with a $500 balance, you must put up $1,000 in cash. After you've made regular payments for about a year or so, the financial institution will drop the security requirement and return your deposit. And once you've had one credit card and established a good credit rating, you will always be able to get another or have your limit raised.

KEEPING A ROOF OVER YOUR HEAD

You may have to sell your home if you find that the costs of carrying the home are too high. Unfortunately, many people die without sufficient insurance to cover their outstanding debts, forcing the sale of assets to settle the estate. While a home held jointly will immediately pass to you, if the mortgage is too high for you to manage on your own, and there's not enough in the estate to pay it down, you could wind up selling and moving to a more affordable home.

When? When is the right time to tell the children, put up the sign, and start looking for a new place? That depends. It depends on how long you can maintain the status quo without digging yourself a huge hole of debt. It depends on how long you've been in the home and how attached you and your children are to the home and your neighbourhood. It depends on how willing you are to try alternatives. Could you rent a part of the house to help carry the mortgage? Would you be willing to share with a friend in a similar position? What are your other options?

There's never an easy, black-and-white answer to any question that involves feelings and money. It's a matter of balancing the need to live within your spending plan against your feelings. What's important to remember is that your feelings will be in turmoil, so you should be asking someone who doesn't have a vested interest in the decision to help you work through the pros and cons. That's not necessarily your grown children, who would love it if you would move closer, or your sister, who would love it if you would let her live with you because she loves your cooking, or your best girlfriend, who is a real estate agent and knows she can get you a terrific price right now. This impartial, unbiased other party shouldn't have anything to gain from any decision you make. (That's what impartial and unbiased mean.)

YOUR PAY-YOURSELF-FIRST INVESTMENT PLAN

If you are widowed while you are still working and building that nest egg for the future, you may face one of three scenarios:

1. You may find everything taken care of financially by a smart, well-prepared partner, who was insured to the eyeteeth and had dotted all the *i*'s and crossed all the *t*'s.

2. You might find yourself with little or nothing, struggling just to make ends meet.
3. You may be somewhere in the middle.

If you are well taken care of, you'll still have to make some decisions about how to invest the money you've been left. If it's in a trust and there's no thinking involved, carry on! Chances are if you're an in-charge kind of person, you'll want even a modicum of say in how your money works for you. Get educated about investing, even as you take the advice of trusted lawyers, financial planners, accountants, and the like. Remember, this is *your* money we're talking about. Don't be passive about it.

If you are struggling to make ends meet, I'm sorry you have to be dealing with your grief and a financial nightmare at the same time. It's shouldn't happen that way, but it often does. It is important to do whatever is necessary to get yourself back on track, and then take care of the future.

If you're somewhere in the middle—you have no horrendous debts, but you'll have to continue working for a living—once you've dealt with the pain, anger, and despair of being left, you can get back on track. You, too, will need to take care of your future, one day at a time.

REVIEWING YOUR INSURANCE

If you have children, parents, or anyone else who is now dependent on your income, you may need life insurance. If you don't have dependants, in most cases, life insurance shouldn't be a consideration. However, if you receive a number of assets from your partner, on which no tax had to be paid but on which a whopping amount of tax may be owed at your death, life insurance could help offset the tax bite for your heirs. You'll have to weigh the cost of the insurance against the need to protect your children from the Tax Man.

If you were covered for health benefits under your spouse's plan, you will need to go shopping for coverage for yourself and your kids. You might also want to consider upping the amount of disability coverage you have, depending on your other financial resources.

Remember to change the beneficiary designations on your own insurance, RRSPs, RRIFs, or anything else on which your partner was your beneficiary. A financially dependent child or grandchild under the age of 18 can be named as the beneficiary of an RRSP or RRIF. To be "financially dependent," the child's income must be less than the basic personal exemption, and no one else can have claimed a tax credit on the child's behalf. The assets are then passed to the child and must be used to purchase an annuity for a fixed number of years, which cannot exceed 18 minus the minor's age at the time the annuity is purchased.

TAX IMPLICATIONS

As a widow, you will inherit your husband's assets without tax consequence. Usually, at death, a person is deemed for tax purposes to have disposed of all their assets at fair market price. So if someone owned 200 shares of a stock bought at

$20 a share, and at the time of death the stock was worth $40 a share, the estate would have to declare a capital gain of $20 a share and pay tax on that gain. However, since you, as the widow, may inherit the shares at their original cost, there is no capital gain, so no tax is payable until you sell the shares or die, whichever comes first.

Your spouse's RRSPs or RRIFs can also be rolled over to you on a tax-deferred basis. You won't have to pay any tax on the money, provided you roll the funds, referred to as a "refund of premiums," directly into your own RRSP or RRIF. Or you could use the funds to buy a life annuity or a fixed-term annuity to age 90.

In terms of benefits you may receive from government programs, while the CPP widow's benefit is taxable in your hands, the monthly orphan's benefit (paid for children under 25, as long as they are in school) is considered to be your child's income and is taxable in his or her hands. If you plan to invest that money for your child, take care to keep it separate and apart from other money, so that it is easy to identify as the child's money for tax purposes. Insurance proceeds are also tax-free.

REVIEWING YOUR ESTATE PLAN

You'll need to visit your estate lawyer to change your will, powers of attorney, and any other documents in which your spouse was named. As well, decreases or increases in assets resulting from the death of a spouse mean you should review your own estate plan thoroughly.

Regardless of whether your partner suffered a terminal illness, or his death came as a complete shock, the finality will be staggering. If you know you will be widowed—that your partner's passing is only a matter of time—then there are some things you can do to prepare. The obvious ones include things like making sure all your insurance is paid up, having cash readily available, so you aren't cash flow poor while the estate is being probated—this would be a good time to consider a joint account—and knowing where everything is, so you're not scrambling to come up with the documentation you may need. You should also have assumed some, if not all, of the responsibility for the financial side of your life, so you are well-equipped to continue on your own.

However, there are many less obvious things you may need to consider. In some cases, you may find yourself facing huge debt as you also come to terms with your aloneness. If there is no way around this—if it is a matter of care for your beloved— then get yourself emotionally ready for accepting this debt all on your own. Another less obvious issue: will you remain in your current home on your own? Will you feel secure? How will you cope with the memories? While it is never a good idea to make big decisions so close to an emotionally traumatic event, if you are given time to prepare, this could be one of the things you seriously think about.

Another thing you can do to prepare is get in touch with groups you may need to use as support. Widows' groups, groups dealing with grief and bereavement, and people who can help you through the process will make things easier. You may not feel you need them now, but that's okay. After all, friends are friends no matter where you meet them. Also consider that you may not want to meet new people as you initially work through your grief. By forming those alliances sooner rather than later, you eliminate the stress of meeting new people during an already-stressful time.

Finally, buy yourself a good book on grief and have a read. Elisabeth Kübler-Ross wrote *On Death and Dying* in 1969, and it is still considered the definitive guide to coping with grief.

21

JUST IN CASE YOU MUST CARE FOR YOUR AGING PARENTS

Studies have shown that children are reluctant to talk to parents about financial topics. One study showed that 35% of people agreed with the statement, "I avoid discussions about money matters with my family." When presented with the idea that adults may need to assist their aging parents in managing their financial affairs, 31% said they'd never discussed their parents' finances. Even though tackling this "what if" question with parents can be especially hard, you must.

There's real danger in not knowing about a parent's financial situation. If you don't know your parents' financial status, it's hard to know what type of care would be affordable if they have an accident or get ill. If you don't know how your parents would want matters handled if they couldn't do it themselves, you won't be able to take care of them in the way they would want. If you don't know where all the important stuff is—the money, investments, insurance, safety deposit box, will, and powers of attorney—you'll be scrambling to find these things just when you're scrambling to cope with a parent's illness, disability, or death.

There are some prevailing attitudes to watch for if you find yourself in the role of caregiver. First, there's the *I'll-do-all-the-thinking-around-here* approach that involves taking total control and negates your parents' dignity. If this sounds like you, who voted you boss? It's the question your mom or dad would ask if they felt up to it. And it's a good question. After all, just because your notion of what should be done is different from your parents' ideas, it doesn't mean you're right and they are wrong. If you find yourself being very bossy because you're worrying about every little thing, take a deep breath. If there is no evidence that a problem exists with either of your parents, relax. It may be your own anxiety and guilt that drives you to make decisions for your parents that they are fully capable of making for themselves.

And then there's the *It's-your-life-do-whatever-you-want* approach that leaves parents to cope on their own due to an adult child's sheer frustration or lack of concern. This is also sometimes a symptom of denial: children don't want to acknowledge their parents' mortality, so they discount their inability to cope as "just a part of getting old" when these are problems that could be mitigated with proper attention. To walk away from issues simply because dealing with them brings conflict or consternation is irresponsible. Ultimately, when you watch your parents flounder, you'll be heartbroken and wish that you had stepped in sooner.

And if they will not let you help, if they push you away to maintain their privacy, to protect you from their angst, or to keep their identities separate, that brings its own heartbreak too. The best you can do is be at the ready with information when it becomes apparent that you must step in.

The person you're caring for should always be given as much control and involvement in financial decisions as possible. If you must assume full responsibility for a relative's finances, continue to share information with other family members. Sharing financial decisions as they are made may reduce the possibility of later recriminations. You might even want to consider family meetings to discuss finances, just to keep everyone current on spending and income. It's also wise to keep good notes about significant discussions you have with family members and the actions you take as a result.

Consider sharing duties with family and friends. While some regular responsibilities, such as paying bills or making deposits, might be done most efficiently by one person, don't be bashful about asking family, neighbours, and old friends to step in. Those with legal, health care, or financial training can be particularly helpful with certain tasks.

As life expectancy has increased, so too have the responsibilities adult children must assume in caring for aging parents. In the old days, you were done taking care of your children by the time your parents needed attention in their final years. But couples are having children later, be they first-time marrieds who delayed starting their families while they focused on their careers, or second-time marrieds where babies are part of the new union. As a result, more people are being crushed by the responsibility of having to take care of both their parents and their children. Women spend 17 years caring for their children and 18 years helping an elderly parent. Chances are, if you're a baby boomer, you're also a member of the *sandwich generation*. This is Faith Popcorn's term for adults who are caught between caring for their children and caring for their parents. And it barely describes the sense of being *so overwhelmed* that accompanies trying to do it right, do it better, or do it all.

It's hard to give parents advice. Sometimes it's because parents see their offspring as the wee ones they cradled in their laps, and are unable to acknowledge their expertise and experience in dealing with life's issues. At other times, it is because the adult children have acquired so much new knowledge—unlike their parents—that it seems both are from different worlds. Personality clashes can also arise as the child attempts to become mother to the mother.

One way to approach a parent who's unwilling to reveal financial particulars is to present several options, and ask the parent which one they'd like to pursue. You might choose to use a friend's death as a place to start talking about the "what-ifs." Or the death of a celebrity may provide an opening. You might also use your own financial review to ask for parental advice and begin the discussion.

You need to know where to find personal and financial documents in the event of an emergency. Find out:

- where they bank
- where their investments are held

- who their accountants, lawyers, brokers, financial planners, insurance agents, etc., are
- where they keep their will and who their executor is
- where they keep other legal documents, such as powers of attorney.

You're not prying. You don't need to know what's in the will, just where it is. You don't need to know how much insurance your parent has, just where it's kept. You simply want to know what documents to look for and where to find them in an emergency. Being aware of your parent's or parents' financial situation may also help you ensure dividends and interest are received, insurance is paid on time, pensions are administered appropriately, and so on. Approach your parent practically and non-confrontationally in a non-intimidating environment. Having a family meeting in which several family members gang up on an aging parent won't make your mom, dad, auntie, or grandmother any more open to your suggestions. And be prepared to suggest a discussion several times, or take small steps towards a full disclosure. If your parents are reluctant to talk to you specifically, offer to help them find a professional advisor, assuring them you'll back out once they're in good hands.

You've read all those headlines about the trillion-dollar inheritance the baby boomers can look forward to. That must mean their folks are pretty well-heeled, right? The reality for many "wealthy seniors" is that while they quite often have a home and live mortgage-free, they need income for upkeep of the house, food, clothing, and the like. The majority of women living alone have incomes below designated low-income cutoffs.

For many people, a home is their primary investment. It can be frustrating to be house-rich and cash-flow poor. Parents may need extra cash to take care of health issues, make modifications to their home to make it more comfortable, or add a cushion to their cash flow. However, they may not want to sell their home just yet, choosing instead to remain in familiar surroundings. The answer to this conundrum may be a reverse mortgage.

. . . .

($) *Gail's Tips:* Beware the financial scam! Targeting the sick or elderly has become a way of life. Since many elderly people are often lonely, they may be willing to trust strangers who call on them. They become the ideal prospects for telemarketing fraud, trumped-up home repairs, and other cons. If you discover a problem, don't be critical. Try not to embarrass your parent. Yes, it can make you angry, but don't take it out on Mom. Yes, it can frustrate you, but don't take it out on Dad. Report the potential con artist to the authorities. At home, calmly explain that the friendly person supposedly offering great deals may be a crook.

. . . .

MANAGING THE MONEY

Once you've got your hands on the goods, you may find stuff you just weren't prepared for: unpaid bills, misplaced documents, unfiled tax returns. Don't panic. Begin by making a list of all the things that must be remedied, write to the people who have been offended, and start cleaning up the mess. There is no point in getting angry. Yes, you will be frustrated, but the job at hand is to fix the problems, and yelling at your folks won't fix them any faster.

The other thing to avoid is judging your parents' choices. So what if your mother has a million dollars sitting in a savings account earning 0.25% in interest? That's her choice. Remember, it's her money. You might make suggestions for changes, but the decision should still be hers, at least until you assume full financial responsibility for her. Remember, older people are often more concerned about keeping their money accessible than about earning a big return.

Whether your parents remain on their own, live with you, or are in some other care, the responsibility for managing the day-to-day financial issues may, at some point, become yours. It's important to know where everything is. Without this information, you could spend months tracking down even the simplest information.

Cash flow will become an issue for you when your parents can no longer handle the routine transactions themselves. And there are a whole bunch of concerns that you'll have to address, ranging from who will pay the bills to how long the money will last.

If you're worried about the little things falling through the cracks, but you want to see your parents remain independent, here are some small steps you can take:

- Arrange for the automatic payment of important, recurring bills, and arrange to be notified if your relative misses a payment.
- Set up direct deposit of pension and benefit checks, so there are no delays in getting funds deposited, no checks are lost in the mail or forgotten at home, and notices about each payment and deposit can be obtained.
- Consider setting up a joint account with Internet or telephone banking privileges, so you can do a quick check to make sure everything in the account is going smoothly (no overdrafts!) several times a month.

Caring for an elderly parent will add so many additional thoughts to your already overloaded circuits that you should look for ways to eliminate routine tasks.

TAX IMPLICATIONS

Forty percent of primary caregivers pay out-of-pocket caregiving expenses of between $100 and $300 a month. But caregiving doesn't just affect your budget in terms of how much you have to spend. It can really take a whack at your income. Twenty-five percent of caregivers say that caregiving responsibilities have affected their job performance. Another 25% have had to quit work, retire, or change jobs. While the government has acknowledged the impact on our wallets, it has only taken small steps to alleviate this.

As of 2004, workers with Employment Insurance who take time off to care for gravely ill family members are eligible for six weeks of compassionate care benefits, provided their relative faces a significant risk of death within 26 weeks (six months). You can get up to 55% of your average insured earnings, to a maximum amount per week, following a two-week waiting period. However, the benefit is taxable and deductions are taken off the top.

You can also claim the Caregiver Amount if you provide in-home care for parents or grandparents who are 65 before the end of the tax year and who live with you. The credit amount is reduced dollar for dollar when the dependant's net income exceeds a specific amount that changes annually. You can also claim the Caregiver Amount if you're caring for family members between the ages of 18 and 65 who are dependent due to mental or physical infirmity.

There are many health- and age-related expenses that are allowable medical expenses, ranging from a truss for a hernia to a stair lift, bath bench, dentures, and air or water filters or purifiers. You'll need the advice of a tax specialist when dealing with complex medical expense claims. The definition of medical practitioner is not limited to medical doctors, but includes dentists, naturopaths, and a whole slew of other practitioners. It's important that you check with your doctor or tax advisor before you purchase items for a dependent relative, since many items can be deducted on a tax return if prescribed by a medical practitioner. Without the prescription, you'll get zip, zilch, nada.

Be prepared for out-of-pocket expenses. Caregivers don't get paid, often don't get thanked, and frequently don't get reimbursed for long-distance phone calls, travel, groceries, medications, personal care items, or other purchases. A survey by the National Alliance for Caregiving and AARP (formerly the American Association of Retired Persons) found that families caring for an elderly relative spend an average of $171 of their own money each month. This doesn't include "hidden" costs, such as unpaid leave from work. Keep your receipts for everything. You may need to produce them at some point to prove a claim.

The portion of medical expenses that is covered by any medical plan may not be included in the medical expense claim. However, the health insurance premiums will qualify as medical expenses. You must file original receipts with your income tax return to support all medical expenses claimed.

There are also several tax credits a child may claim for a parent. The equivalent-to-spouse credit is available to a single child who supports a parent. The personal tax credit can be claimed for an infirm parent. The disability tax credit requires a medical doctor to complete a special form certifying that the parent is "disabled," and any portion of this credit not used by the parent may be transferred to the child. There are other rules and restrictions for claiming these credits.

A child may claim the medical expenses paid for a dependent parent. The Tax Man publishes interpretation bulletins that list in detail what types of expenses qualify as "medical expenses," and which of these items must be prescribed by a medical practitioner. This extensive list changes from time to time. Please consult the Tax Man or a tax specialist for more information. A medical expense claim for a dependent parent will be reduced if the parent had net income for tax purposes above the basic personal tax credit amount. This reduction may be greater than the value of the medical expenses of the parent, and it may even reduce the medical expenses that the child is claiming for herself.

If your dependant is in a nursing home, you can claim medical and attendant-care costs as part of their medical expenses. Attendant-care expenses can include the cost of a companion or health care aide. There are detailed rules concerning the deductibility of attendant-care expenses, including whether the care is part-time or full-time, the amount paid for an attendant, and whether the parent meets the government definition of someone with a "disability." However, medical and attendant care are the most expensive costs associated with a nursing home, so a well-supported claim can result in a significant tax credit. Most nursing homes identify the portion that is eligible for the credit on their bills.

REVIEWING THE ESTATE PLAN

It is very important that your parent execute a will and powers of attorney, if they have not already done so. Since even beginning this discussion means facing difficult issues, such as death or incapacitation, people are hugely resistant to talking openly about them. Some people may be superstitious and feel they are tempting fate. But they will face a very real danger if they do not complete these documents.

Parents who are suddenly incapacitated, and have not

executed powers of attorney, will have lost their ability to name a trusted representative to control their affairs. And since there's a time lag before an attorney is appointed by the public trustee, during that time, no one has control or authority over things like paying bills or the mortgage, filing tax returns, and the like. Even if you have joint ownership of a home with your parent, you won't be able to make changes until someone is appointed to represent your parent's interest. And if your father has always controlled the finances, and your mom has no independent means, should he become incapacitated, she would become totally dependent on your resources while the province appoints an attorney.

Parents who are reluctant to sign documents that they feel reduce their personal control over their finances, and even their lives, should consider naming two children (or a child and a lawyer or an accountant) to act on their behalf. The two parties named then act as a check on each other. And the power of attorney can be left with a third party with specific instructions as to its release. As well, it can be limited in terms of the specific time period or specific acts.

It's up to the lawyer to establish whether your parent is mentally competent by asking questions about her estate, her understanding of what assets she has, and why she's in the lawyer's office at this time. As long as an individual can answer these questions satisfactorily, she is usually deemed competent. If the lawyer has concerns about her competency, she will ask for a medical assessment. This can be tough for an aging client to hear, but it may be necessary to ensure the legal documentation is valid.

About six million Canadians depend on a family member or friend to help them make it from one day to the next. According to Statistics Canada, one in five Canadians 45 years and over provide care to a senior. While 62% of these primary caregivers have been providing care for at least three years, 20% have been providing it for more than 10 years.

Imagine your child coming to you to say, "Mom, Dad, I don't think you're doing such a hot job of taking care of yourself anymore." It'd be pretty tough to hear. Unimaginable, even. So when the time comes to tell aging relatives the bad news, expect some resistance. They may object to the idea of having strangers in their home. They may hate the thought of spending money they feel they should be saving for the future. Whatever the barrier they throw up, your first step will be to help them determine and prioritize their needs, and then find resources. Never mind the angry words and accusations your mom or dad may throw at you. That's part of their reaction to this major change in their lives. And be prepared for lots and lots of questions. They need to be able to express their wants and make some of their own choices to feel in control.

It's never too early—or too late—to begin to start talking to your parents now about what they want as they age. Talk to your siblings about how you plan to divide responsibility for your parents' well-being. Talk to your peers about how they are facing the challenges of eldercare, the problems they have encountered, and the solutions they have found.

Take an objective look at yourself. Are you prepared to be a caregiver? How will you accomplish this, alongside your other roles as a spouse, parent, or business professional? Before you leap into making promises, think. It's easy to say, "You can always live with us" or "I'll never put you in a home," but a lot harder to follow through on these promises. And as you watch for signs that you'll have to step in, don't focus on what your parents can't do; focus on maximizing what they can do.

Communicating openly is the best way to ensure you and your parents age gracefully together. By preparing yourself and your parents for what will happen next, you will be able to honestly say: "I have done the best that I could."

How will you know when it's time to step in? Here are some warning signs. Maybe your mom or dad:

- doesn't change her clothes or get dressed in the morning
- has noticeable body odour or is unkempt
- has lost five kilos or more, or you notice that his or her clothes seem too big
- has very dry hands, feet, arms, or cracked lips, which might indicate dehydration
- has little or spoilt food in the fridge
- complains of shortness of breath when walking up stairs or after bathing and dressing
- stumbles or falls, or needs help getting out of a chair
- forgets about taking medications
- doesn't answer the phone or doorbell, declines social invitations, or stops attending church or community activities

- misplaces valuables or complains that things are lost or "have been stolen"
- has unpaid bills or notices about services being shut off
- becomes lost on familiar routes.

CARING FOR THE CAREGIVER

According to the Health Canada Caregiver Profile, 70% of primary caregivers say that providing care has been stressful. Of those, 77% say caregiving has created emotional difficulties for them. If you feel that you can no longer cope or that your own health is deteriorating, you may be suffering from caregiver burnout.

Not knowing what's going on is a stressor. Get as much information about your care-recipient's condition as you can. Work to reduce your sense of isolation. Find people to talk to, such as friends, family, or a small group of other caregivers. Don't ignore the obvious like your family doctor. She not only needs to know what you're going through, she may be able to provide useful referrals to a variety of resources. Join a support group. Just being able to share your experiences and expertise will help. Internet chat groups work for people who can't get to meetings.

Ask for help and delegate. Respite is important to your health and emotional well-being. Caregivers get burned out if there's no relief. And you shouldn't let anyone tell you how to spell relief. Relief can only be defined by what you need. Hospital social workers can let you know what you're eligible for and connect you with resources in the community. And don't forget about family service centres, the public health nurse, your corporate human resources department, or an employee assistance program. Join a caregiver organization or support group. Create a team to care for your lovey.

And, finally, strive for balance. You can't do everything, and you shouldn't feel guilty about it. The person who is receiving the care needs to have realistic expectations. If you're having trouble setting boundaries, ask a professional or a friend to act as a mediator.

CREATING A CARE TEAM

You're not Superwoman, you know, so be willing to accept that creating a care team is the best way to manage caregiving responsibilities. Some of the members of your team will be caregiving professionals; others will be friends and family members. If you're organizing the team, think of yourself as the team leader. As such you are responsible for co-ordinating the efforts of:

- *A doctor.* Your parent's doctor is responsible for maintaining her health care records. If she is not well, he will investigate her symptoms and refer her to a specialist, such as a cardiologist or a neurologist. Your parent's doctor or your own family doctor can give you access to community services, such as dietitians, occupational therapists, or physical therapists.
- *A geriatrician.* Geriatricians are in short supply due to the growing number of senior citizens. These doctors

have the expertise to monitor your parent's medication, lifestyle, and diet. They can treat any nutritional deficiencies your parent may have as well as any problems relating to memory loss. If your parent is undergoing a personality change due to the onset of dementia, a geriatrician can prescribe antipsychotic medication. There are restrictions in the number of annual visits that will be funded, but even a few visits are helpful when someone needs complex care.

- *A pharmacist.* A vital part of a "monitoring system," pharmacists watch for drug interactions, side effects, and potential allergies related to your parents's medications. Ask them to prepare medications in a dose-by-dose blister pack to prevent medication-related errors and to act as a daily reminder for older people.

- *A geriatric care manager.* Often a nurse, this team member can monitor your loved one's health and report symptoms to you before they reach crisis proportions. She can also take your parent to medical appointments, co-ordinate visits to specialists, and help implement suggested treatments, as well as helping you with caregiving-related problems.

- *A home-care team.* Nursing, personal support, home-making, cleaning, and companionship services are available 24/7. Some services are covered by your provincial health plan. You will need to pay for others privately. Use a reputable home health care provider and check references.

- *An equipment provider.* Wheelchairs, walkers, stair-lifts, and other assistive devices are available for use in the home. Get an equipment prescription (for tax purposes) along with the referral to a reliable retailer.

Friends and family members will also form part of your team. They can help you:

- provide home health care, including giving medications to your parent, performing basic medical procedures, communicating with health care providers, and organizing home-care services
- provide personal care, like toileting, grooming, and meals
- keep up with housekeeping and daily activities
- give emotional support to your parent, including things like visiting, making regular phone calls, and reading to him
- arrange transportation if your parent has an appointment and find someone to serve as an escort; they can also help you run errands and arrange transportation for social outings, religious services, or emergency hospital visits.

When you are sharing the care of a loved one with others, use a daily journal to:

- document significant events in your loved one's life
- monitor the person's condition
- organize any activities

- help caregivers communicate with each other
- allow quick access to important information.

Assembling a caring team means you can ensure your parent receives the best care while reducing the impact on you. But remember, you aren't obliged to accept help from everyone who offers, even if the volunteer is a close relative. You may decline any volunteer for any reason, especially if your loved one is uncomfortable with that person.

22

JUST IN CASE YOU BECOME DISABLED

I know a woman named Heather who has the fortitude of a brigade. Heather has multiple sclerosis. As a strong, career-oriented woman, Heather refuses to give up. Once, when we met at a children's movie—our daughters are about the same age—she was in a walker and expressing frustration at her latest setback. That week she had awoken to find that she would no longer be able to drive. Her frustration? How was she going to get to work?

I have to admit that Heather takes my breath away. I can hardly imagine wanting to go to work having discovered that my body could no longer direct my car. Heather didn't just want to go. She went. Her husband now drives her to and from work each day. It's just one of the concessions they have had to make to her disease and the disability it has brought.

Heather's story isn't meant to set a standard to which we must all strive. Her story is a prime example of how we must all find our own way to make the journey worthwhile. Why didn't she just stay home and rest? She couldn't. That, more than the disease, would have killed her spirit. Each person facing trying circumstances must cope in her own way. We must each seek the road that suits our step. We must walk gingerly alongside all those other women who are trying their best to make life work. And, wherever we can, we must lend a hand to help.

YOUR SPENDING PLAN

Regardless of how well-insured you are, you will have to make adjustments to your cash flow. And if you have arrived at this spot with little or no disability insurance, how you manage what you do have will dictate so much of how you will live your life.

The first thing you need to do if you have a disability plan is to find out when the money will come. This may seem straightforward. It can be. It can also be a nightmare. A girlfriend of mine was without disability income for well over a year, because the company carrying the plan refused to accept that she was at least 60% disabled. Once her Employment Insurance benefits ran out, she ran out of money. She had to cash in her retirement savings just to keep the roof over her head. A few weeks, even a few days, of paperwork for the insurance company can mean the difference between meeting your financial commitments on time and struggling to put food on the table. In a state of general vulnerability, it's easy to let things slide. But you can't. You must follow up, insist, and push to get what you need. If you don't have the strength, get an advocate to work on your behalf.

Your insurance company may have very specific wording about how it wants your disability described and your inability to work proven. Before your doctor starts writing letters and making phone calls, find out everything you can to make your case as strong as possible the first time. Yes, there is usually an appeals process, and you can always add more information. But each delay, each change in your circumstances adds time to the approval process and leaves you without an income for even longer. If your doctor has had no experience dealing with insurance companies, or with claims like yours, ask for a referral to a specialist, who will be better able to create a convincing argument on your behalf.

If you think your disability insurance is your right once you make a claim, you're like most people. We figure that since we've paid our premiums on time for 5, 10, or 20 years, we're entitled to our disability payments should we need them. The insurance company sees things a little differently. Since the disability claim can be huge over the life of the disability, they want proof-positive that you're disabled. Medical science's progress in documenting and naming new diseases means insurance companies are being faced with claims they never imagined would exist when early policies were written. They are keeping a careful eye on what a claim is for and how that disease or injury can be documented in supporting the claim.

If you are not covered by a private disability plan or a plan through work, you will have to seek social assistance. If you think dealing with a private insurance company is tough, wait till you get a load of how the government operates. It'll be slow. It'll be tedious. But what's your option?

Insurance disability benefits usually kick in after a waiting period, so the next step is to review your spending plan:

- Are there expenses you could minimize or eliminate completely—things like transportation, lunches, and ordering in dinner? Shared daycare would be less expensive than full-time. Do you still need the second car?
- Are there areas in which your expenses will increase?
- If you had a medical plan at work, will it remain in effect while you are disabled? If not, how will you replace the coverage of those costs?
- Are there assets you could sell to help make ends meet? I don't include retirement savings in this. Resist the urge to attack your retirement plan, since you're going to need that money down the line. Most disability benefits end at age 65, so if you think you're living on a small income now, you may have even less in the future.

YOUR EMERGENCY FUND

You've already had to deal with one emergency, so you now know the value of having an emergency fund. If you're living on a much lower income, it's easy to say that you can't afford to rebuild the fund you exhausted. But with less cash flow available, now more than ever you can't afford to be without one. After all, on a restricted cash flow, even the smallest of emergencies can put a severe crimp in your spending plan. It may take longer to rebuild your emergency fund, but you've got to start. Five dollars this month, $10 next, each little step will take you closer to your goal. Without the emergency fund, you will have to constantly worry about the "what ifs." Skip it. Do what you can to protect yourself so you have the money available, *Just in case!*

MANAGING YOUR MONEY

Consolidate all your money in one place, so you can easily see what you have and minimize your service charges and fees. If you have a partner, talk about how you're going to handle the day-to-day money management. If you've always done it, you may need to shift this responsibility to your buddy until you're physically and mentally able to cope.

Collect every single benefit to which you may be entitled. If you don't feel capable of making the calls or writing the letters, ask friends and family to help. You're gonna need money. Don't let anything you might benefit from slide away because you simply couldn't come up with the energy to apply. You must take advantage of EVERY option available to you.

KEEPING A HEALTHY CREDIT IDENTITY

Living on a reduced income and trying to manage your credit effectively is a fine line to walk. It's all very well and good to have scads of credit available on cards, and to use that credit to make ends meet when you must, but if you have no hope of repayment, it's a fool's game.

There's no question that from time to time, emergencies arise that you feel force you to look to credit as the answer. The most important question to ask yourself before you decide to swipe the card is, "When will I pay this off?" If the answer is, "Later," then you may be setting yourself up for a future of juggling one card against the other until the bankruptcy police catch up with you. Not a pretty sight. And not something you need in terms of the stress in your life. If you don't know when you'll be able to pay off your credit card, don't charge it. Pay cash. If you don't have the cash, do without. If you can't do without, you'll have to find another way. But if you get into the habit of allowing your credit cards to fill the gaps in your cash flow, you'll wake up a very sad girl one morning when they come to repossess your daughter's bed.

Some forms of credit offer disability insurance in the event that you cannot work and, therefore, cannot pay your bills. I don't recommend this feature, since, for the most part, the insurance doesn't pay off your debt. It simply takes care of the interest portion, so the financial institution isn't out of pocket and trying to collect from a vulnerable client. It helps to keep them from looking bad. It would be better to apply for disability insurance and have personal coverage that pays you directly, so you can then direct the money in the way that will do you and your family the most good.

If you find that you've become disabled while carrying a significant debt load, it's time to get on the phone and make some calls. You're going to have to explain to your creditors that you may be unable to meet your commitments in the short term. Try to work out a payment plan that minimizes the crunch to your cash flow. Negotiate to make a reduced single payment in lieu of paying the whole thing off over the next 10 years. Ask them to waive the interest. Tell them that without help, bankruptcy may be your only alternative. If the person on the other end of the line can't help you, ask to speak to his supervisor. Don't rest until you get some concessions from your creditors.

When Alison became disabled, she had being flying full force through life, charging up a storm and wreaking havoc at the mall. Suddenly, she came to a full stop and found herself with a mountain of debt she could not handle. "I was doing fine," she said. "Then this thing with my hands started and now I can't work. I can't type or input data. Some days I can't hold a pencil or brush my daughter's hair." Alison still had a personal line of credit that was in good shape—she had only used $1,200 of her $5,000 in credit. But she was maxed out on her credit cards and department store cards, for a total of $7,500 in debt. And she owed tax from two previous years. "What a mess," she said, as she looked at the papers on the dining room table.

I suggested Alison call the department stores' credit divisions first, since those cards carried the heftiest interest rates. After several calls, a letter from her doctor, and proof of her reduced income, Alison managed to negotiate a deal where she would pay two-thirds of the outstanding balance all at once—and that would clear her bills. Using her line of credit, she paid $3,000 to clear away $5,000 in debt.

The next call was to the Tax Man. Alison explained her situation, and he listened sympathetically. Most people don't realize just how thoughtful the Tax Man can be when he believes that you are honestly in a tough bind, particularly when the circumstances are beyond your control. He agreed to waive all interest and penalties, and to a very gentle repayment plan of just $45 a month for the principal tax owed.

Finally, she came to the charge cards. More heavy negotiating. More indications that if forced to she would have to declare personal bankruptcy. Finally, Alison won their acceptance of a repayment plan that fit with her cash flow. The result: the amount of her monthly income that went to servicing her debt dropped from $750 a month to just $325. "I can do this," she sighed with relief. Of course she can!

KEEPING A ROOF OVER YOUR HEAD

For women with partners, the prospect of becoming homeless is less of a threat. For women who are dealing with their disability on their own, it can be a constant worry. And if a woman has children, the stress is even greater. Dealing with this situation requires you to get some unbiased advice. I'm referring to the kind of advice a good friend can give by asking you a bunch of questions you may not yet have thought to ask yourself. And it doesn't hurt if that friend knows how the financial world operates.

The decision to sell or not sell, move and rent elsewhere, or stay where you are is a purely black-and-white decision. Or, at least, it should be. We often let emotion get in the way of logic—for the sake of continuity, for the sake of the children—only to find that in the end, we have dug ourselves such a deep hole that we'll never get out. Or we react too quickly, not considering all the options, and let opportunities slip past. Here's an example of what I mean.

When Emma came to me asking for advice on whether or not to sell her home—she was disabled with a drastic reduction in her income, and she had a daughter to care for—I asked why she wanted to sell. "I can't afford this house any longer," she said as she wept into her hands. "I have my daughter to care for, and I've little or nothing to live on."

"Where will you go?" I asked.

"I don't know."

"What are you paying for your mortgage and upkeep right now?"

"Just under $900 a month for my mortgage, so I'd estimate about $1,200 a month with taxes, insurance, and the like."

"How much longer do you have on your mortgage term, and at what rate?"

"It was originally a five-year mortgage at 9%, and I've got a year and a half left on it."

"Have you considered renegotiating the mortgage?"

"I'd have to pay an interest penalty, and I have no money."

"Actually," I said, "there's a thing called a 'blend and extend' mortgage, which very few people know about or understand. With a blend and extend, in effect, you would continue to pay 9% for the next 18 months, and then the current rate of 6% for the remaining term—I'd suggest you go long at these rates. In reality, the two interest rates would be averaged out based on the terms applicable, so you would end up paying less than 9%

now, but more than 6% for the rest of the term. Get my drift?"

"I understand that, but how would it help?"

"Cash flow, girl. Let's say you end up with a 7.25% mortgage. Your payments would go from about $900 to about $700 a month. That knocks $200 a month off your housing costs."

"Okay, but that's still too expensive."

"Didn't you tell me earlier that your basement is rentable?"

"Yes, but the house is so small, and that's my daughter's playroom."

"Not if you have to move, it won't be. How much could you rent it for, reasonably?"

"About $400 a month."

"So your housing costs would drop another $400 a month, right?"

"Yeah," Emma's face brightened. "I see what you mean."

"Okay, so tomorrow, you call the bank and find out the figures for the blend and extend, and then you can make some decisions based on the real financial facts. And start putting feelers out for someone for that basement apartment."

Emma could see her way clear for the first time in a long time. And all it took was one conversation, a little application of pencil-to-paper math, and a sprinkle of wholesome problem-solving.

YOUR PAY-YOURSELF-FIRST INVESTMENT PLAN

Depending on the type of disability you are living with, this may be more or less important. Disability brought on by terminal illness may negate, in your mind and that of most others, your need to build assets for the future. And if you are struggling to make ends meet now, the argument is moot. However, if your disability is one that will not affect your life expectancy, then you will need to make plans for the long term. Even a little put away regularly will make a huge difference in terms of the amount of money you will have when you finally reach 65 and your disability benefits end. If you do not put something away for the future, you may very well find yourself in an awful place at some point down the road. It is important that you save and that you invest. If you are not taking care of you, who will?

REVIEWING YOUR INSURANCE

Hopefully you had a disability rider for your insurance, so that your policy remains in good standing, even though you're no longer able to pay the premiums. The only way to know is to read your policy or check with your broker.

TAX IMPLICATIONS

People who suffer from a severe and prolonged mental or physical impairment are often entitled to a disability tax credit, which is a non-refundable tax credit, so if you have a low or no income, you won't benefit. However, the credit is transferable, so your partner may qualify to transfer all or a portion of the disability tax credit to reduce his or her taxes.

The criteria for qualifying for the disability tax credit are not precise. In the simplest terms, your condition must exist for more than 12 months, and it must markedly affect one or more of the basic functions of life—walking, eating, speaking, and self-care—or require a significant time commitment to manage life-sustaining treatments. Your disability has to be certified by a qualified practitioner using Form T2201. There is a self-assessment questionnaire on the form, so you can have a look-see to determine if you might qualify. If you think you meet the criteria, apply. There's no harm done if you don't receive approval, but you could get your hands on some significant benefits if you do. Seek help from a tax professional who is well versed in claims for disability tax credits. Not all tax professionals are (and not all doctors are familiar with the form and how to fill it out "correctly"), so find bodies who can help you.

REVIEWING YOUR ESTATE PLAN

If you are terminally ill, you must review your estate plan. It is surprising just how long you can delay something that you feel may be an unpleasant experience. But it will continue to remain an unpleasant must-do for as long as it remains undone. So DO IT! *Yes, it will be difficult for you, and it will be difficult for the loved ones with whom you must consult. But to do nothing, to die without a will, can create even more confusion and heartache.*

If you are severely ill when you make your will, you must seek the best possible estate planning advice to ensure that your wishes are acted upon, and not discredited due to your illness, after your death. If there are people you wish to protect, individuals you feel a responsibility towards, such as friends, lovers, parents, or children you must care for, then you must have a will.

In terms of your wishes while you are alive, there may come a time when you cannot make decisions—whether they be financial or personal care decisions—on your own behalf. You must have a legally executed power of attorney, naming a trusted individual to act on your behalf, so you can be sure your wishes will be respected.

I don't know if you can ever be prepared for disability. That's probably one of the reasons I waited until D-Day to write this chapter. After all, just the idea of becoming disabled was stomach-wrenching enough. Watching a close friend deal with her own debilitating case of multiple sclerosis, watching her relationship disintegrate, and watching as she swung from the highs of being able to cope one day to the lows of despair about never being able to cope again, was very hard.

The best advice I can give about preparing for a disability—assuming you can prepare because your condition is progressive and you still have time—is to surround yourself with your friends and ask them for help. Get involved in an association that deals with your disease and start to connect with like-minded individuals who can help you understand where you're going.

My only other advice is this: try to spend at least part of each week "other-focused." By this, I mean helping someone else cope. Your disability and its impact on your life, and on the lives of your family members, can be all-consuming. But it is never healthy to be totally consumed with ourselves and our own woes. Ultimately, there is always someone who could use our help to get over her hurdles. If you can take just a moment from your life to help that person, your spirit will be enriched and your burden lightened, at least for that moment.

CONCLUSION

Good money management isn't magic. And it doesn't require you to be some sort of financial wizard. It's all about doing the right things consistently. It's about being deliberate in the steps you take to attain your goals. That means saving some money, learning to invest for your specific needs, and taking care of the "what-ifs." It also means understanding who you are with money, and why, so you can shed your emotional baggage. If you face the Money Demons that inhabit both your wallet and soul, you can move on from there.

Remember, telesis is about making progress. And no matter what comes along to throw you off track, you are the only person who can control what you do next. Sinking into a quagmire of misery and self-pity won't get you into that house, out of debt, or back to school to build new skills. I'm not saying there aren't some times when a nice thick blanket and a huge box of chocolates can't be your best friends. But if you stay in that place, you can't move forward.

Whether you're a little in debt or a lot, recently widowed or living through a divorce from hell, movin' on up or in a job that feels like same-old, same-old, you can change your life. You need a plan.

Today, pick one thing you'll do differently. You might choose to stash your credit cards behind the refrigerator and shop with cash. (If you have to dig through all that gunk under the fridge to get your cards out, you'll think twice about how much you actually need those new shoes.) Or perhaps you'll call your insurance agent and find out what it would cost to protect your family should you meet your Maker. Maybe you'll put yourself on a monthly investment plan. With as little as $25 a month, you can start forming a habit that will hold you in good stead forever.

If you believe you're too deeply in debt to ever get out, give yourself a good kick. If you think you just don't have a head for numbers, it's time for a facepalm. If you're desperately afraid of taking control, go stand in front of the mirror. You, and only you, have the power to make the life you want. You can take control. You can be financially at peace if you want to be. But only you can make it happen.

Now you know the rules of smart money management. So follow them! It's your money. Take control. It's your life. Make it everything you want it to be.

INDEX

job loss, 333–35
  credit identity and, 341–42
  emergency fund and, 339
  home ownership and, 342
  insurance and, 343–44
  money management during,
    339–40
  pay-yourself-first investment plan
    and, 343
  Registered Retirement Savings
    Plans (RRSPs), 335–37
  spending plan and, 335–37
  tax implications, 344
journal of spending. See Spending
  Journal

lawyer, family
  as executor of will, 226
lawyer costs in divorce, 354–55
leases, 118–19
life cycle financial planning, xiv–xvii
life insurance, 189–92. See also
  insurance
  calculating how much is needed,
    195–97
  divorce and, 363–64
  factors in deciding whether you
    need, 192–95
  increasing face value, 203
  increasing the cash value of your
    plan, 203
  partnership and, 253–54
  retirement and, 295
  universal, 197–99
  what type to buy, 197–204
  when to buy, 190–91
  widowhood and, 384–85
line of credit, 83
liquidity, level of, 164
lists, making, 14, 17–18, 20, 31–32
living wills. See will(s)
loan(s). See also borrowing deci-
    sions; mortgage(s)
  assessing your need of, 106–7

consolidation, 112–13
markup, 108
total cost, 108–9

market timing, 171–72
marriage, xix, 249–251. See also
    partnership; remarriage
  assets and, 245–46
  contracts, xix, 246
  co-signing credit applications
    and, 102
  credit history and, 395–96, 249
  disability insurance and, 178–79
  goal setting within, 259–61
  powers of attorney and, 257
  tax implications, 254
  weddings, 129
  wills and, 218–19, 222–24,
    256–57
maternity benefits, 267–68
maternity leave, 266–67
matrimonial home, 360
medical expenses, 397–99. See also
    parents, aging
merchandise. See buying things
minimum annual payout (MAP), 305
Misers, 12–14, 34
money
  feelings about, 9–12, 29, 34–35,
    332
  getting back in touch with, 44–45
  nature of, 8
  as power, 33–34
  tracking your, 90–91
money management, 423
  aging parents and, 395–96
  children and, 267–69
  disability and, 413
  divorce and, 356–57
  job loss and, 339–40
  partnership and, 247–49
  retirement and, 289–90, 307–8
  sole breadwinners and, 327
  widowhood and, 379–81